THE POLITICS OF IMAGINATION IN COLERIDGE'S CRITICAL THOUGHT

The Politics of Imagination in Coleridge's Critical Thought

Nigel Leask

St. Martin's Press   New York

Library of Congress Cataloging-in-Publication Data
Leask, Nigel, 1958–
The politics of imagination in Coleridge's
critical thought.
Bibliography: p.
Includes index.
1. Coleridge, Samuel Taylor, 1772–1834—
Knowledge—Literature.   2. Coleridge, Samuel Taylor,
1772–1824—Political and social views.   3. Imagination.
4. Criticism—England—History—19th century.   I. Title.
PR 4487.I6L4   1988   821'.7   88–3265
ISBN 0–312–02041–4

To My Parents

Contents

PART THREE: THE BINDING OF
PROMETHEUS: THE ROLE OF THE
MYSTERIES IN COLERIDGE'S THEORY OF
CULTURE AFTER 1817

Acknowledgements

I am grateful to the many people who have contributed, directly or indirectly, to the writing of this book. Special thanks are due to my Supervisor, John Barrell, without whose stimulus and encouragement this study of Coleridge could not have been written as a *Politics* of Imagination. Also to Stephen Clark and Eamon O'Flaherty for four years' support and discussion, and to Patrick Healey for help with Coleridge's Greek. I am very grateful to Roy Park for giving me so much of his time (and patience!) in criticizing the first section, and to Paul Hamilton, to whom I owe my interest in Coleridge, for providing orientation and support for the present study. Any current work on Coleridge must be indebted to the editors of the new *Collected Coleridge*; mine is no exception. Finally, thanks also to Marc Silver in Bologna and Bruce Fink in Paris for organizing and word-processing my manuscript.

N.J.L.

List of Abbreviations

Coleridge

AR   *Aids to Reflection in the Formation of a Manly Character, on the several grounds of Prudence, Morality, and Religion* (London: Taylor and Hessey, 1825).

BL   *Biographia Literaria*, eds James Engell and W. Jackson Bate, 2 vols (London and Princeton: Routledge & Kegan Paul and Princeton University Press, 1983): *The Collected Works of S. T. Coleridge VII.*

Bl sh   *Biographia Literaria*, ed. with his Aesthetical Essays by J. Shawcross, 2 vols (Oxford University Press, 1907).

CIS   *Confessions of an Inquiring Spirit* (1840), ed. with intro. H. St. J. Hart, rpt of 3rd edn 1853, intro. J. H. Green and note by Sara Coleridge (London: A. & C. Black, 1956).

CL   *The Collected Letters of S. T. Coleridge*, ed. E. L. Griggs, 6 vols (Oxford and New York: Oxford University Press, 1956–71).

CN   *The Notebooks of S. T. Coleridge*, ed. K. Coburn, 5 vols (New York, Princeton and London: Routledge & Kegan Paul, 1957–   ).

CS   *On the Constitution of the Church and State*, ed. J. Colmer (London and Princeton: Routledge & Kegan Paul and Princeton University Press, 1976): *The Collected Works of S. T. Coleridge X.*

EOT   *Essays on his Times*, ed. David Erdman, 3 vols (London and Princeton: Routledge & Kegan Paul and Princeton University Press, 1978): *The Collected Works of S. T. Coleridge III.*

Friend *The Friend*, ed. Barbara Rooke, 2 vols (London and Princeton University Press, 1969): *The Collected Works of S. T. Coleridge IV.*

LR   *The Literary Remains of S. T. Coleridge*, coll. and ed. H. N. Coleridge, 4 vols (London: W. Pickering, 1836–39).

LS   *Lay Sermons*, ed. R. J. White (London and Princeton: Routledge & Kegan Paul and Princeton University Press, 1972): *The Collected Works of S. T. Coleridge VI*.

Lects 1795   *Lectures 1795: On Politics and Religion*, eds Lewis Patton and Peter Mann (London and Princeton: Routledge & Kegan Paul and Princeton University Press, 1971): *The Collected Works of S. T. Coleridge I*.

M   *Marginalia*, ed. George Whalley, vol. 1, *Abbt to Byfield* (1980), Vol. 2, *Camden to Hutton* (1984), (London and Princeton: Routledge & Kegan Paul and Princeton University Press, 1980–): *The Collected Works of S. T. Coleridge XII*.

Notes and Lects   *Notes and Lectures on Shakespeare, and some of the Old Poets and Dramatists, with other Literary Remains of S. T. Coleridge*, ed. Mrs H. N. Coleridge, 2 vols (London: W. Pickering, 1849).

Om   *Omniana: or Horae Otiosiores*, by R. Southey and S. T. Coleridge, ed. Robert Gittings (Slough, Bucks.: Centaur Press, 1969).

Ph L   *Philosophical Lectures*, ed. with intro. by K. Coburn (London: Pilot Press, 1949).

PW   *The Complete Poetical Works of S. T. Coleridge*, ed. with textual & bibliographical notes E. H. Coleridge, 2 vols (Oxford: Clarendon Press, 1912).

SC   *Shakespeare Criticism*, ed. T. M. Raysor, 2 vols (London: Constable, 1930).

TT   *Specimens of the Table Talk of the late S. T. Coleridge*, 2 vols (London: John Murray, 1835).

W   *The Watchman*, ed. Lewis Patton (London and Princeton: Routledge & Kegan Paul and Princeton University Press, 1970): *The Collected works of S. T. Coleridge II*.

Wordsworth

WPW   *Poetical Works*, ed. with intro. and notes Thomas Hutchinson, new edn rev. E. De Selincourt (Oxford University Press, 1936).

Prelude 1805   *The Prelude, or Growth of a Poet's Mind*, text of 1805. ed. with intro. and notes E. De Selincourt, Corr. by Stephen Gill (Oxford University Press, 1970).

W Prose   *The Prose Works of William Wordsworth*, eds W. J. B.
           Owen and J. Worthington Smyser, 3 vols (Oxford:
           Clarendon Press, 1974).

EY   *The Letters of William and Dorothy Wordsworth: the Early
           Years 1787–1805*, ed. E. De Selincourt, 2nd edn, rev.
           Chester L. Shaver (Oxford: Clarendon Press, 1967).

Introduction

The purpose of this study of the politics of Imagination in Coleridge's critical thought is to demand of Imagination that it be returned to a position of accountability in the practical realm, a position from which it has long been absolved. My concern is with the historical and social provenance of a term which remains one of the most privileged in our canon of critical judgement. The totemic power of Imagination is closely associated with a common unwillingness, or inability, to question its meaning and origin. It is enough that Imagination is the essence of art and culture, and beyond that, represents a paramount quality of personality, the lack of which limits the subject to a negative and instrumental function in society. Imagination may still retain vestiges of a critical function, as an amulet against the dehumanizing tendencies of technocracy and mass society, but only in the direction of a *contemptus mundi* which has come to dismiss the viability of political critique. The slightest contact with a practical interest threatens to break the spell, dissipating the authority of the unconditioned voice.

From such a perspective, an enquiry into the *politics* of Imagination, an insistence upon the materiality of this noumenal quality, will doubtless appear to be a gratuitous and reductive exercise. It is to be hoped that my first section will disarm objections coming from this quarter by showing the progenitor of this current notion of Imagination to have been a thoroughly political animal. My second and third sections show how a radical critique of the commercial and capitalist order came to enter into a historical complicity with its former opponent; an uneasy but nevertheless enduring pact between a 'dehumanized' political realm and its *tragic* antagonist, Imagination. This entailed a differentiation of powers whereby politics (the social and economic realm, as well as the art of governing), were emptied of all but minimal cultural significance, at the historical moment when they became nominally 'democratic', as a complement to the depoliticization of literature and art. The high value which our culture places upon Imagination has been contingent upon its separation (or alienation, in a recent version of the *agon*), from

1

worldly interest, a separation inaugurated by apologists of the hegemonic order, but increasingly accepted by its critics. Hence the unwillingness, even amongst some Marxist writers, to consider the ideological burden carried by the notion of an unconditioned aesthetic realm.

So deeply ingrained in our thinking is this polarization of the social and cultural spheres, that an analytic or theoretical critique of Imagination runs the risk of simply repeating its terms. Those unhappy with 'literature' as they find it should turn to political science or economics. In recent years, the 'theory revolution' in literary studies has pursued a more interdisciplinary approach, providing a formidable technology of critical terms and a grammar of interpretations with which to destabilize the idealism of the discipline. But this has too often simply relocated the idealism of cultural objects on a new site (more than ever the exclusive domain of the specialist), without exercising the sort of critical self-consciousness which would comprehend the status and history of literature as a social practice.

The belief which informs the present study is that only by understanding the historical and social formation of the romantic idealization of Imagination can we be free of its determination. Only by an act of historical self-reflection can we be aware of that persuasive cultural mystification, in the inauguration of which Coleridge played such an important part. Coleridge is a particularly suitable focus for such a study, in so far as he began his intellectual career as an advocate of a *civic* definition of Imagination, exponent of what Jurgen Habermas has called the 'Public Sphere', 'a decentralized and uninhibited discursive formation of the public will',[1] and ended it by defining the terms of an authoritarian and hierarchical culture closely linked to the *religious* sphere. Although Imagination was a close kin to the bourgeois commercial order (in so far as it was connected with the social interests of a professional, dissenting intelligentsia), it began by challenging the economic norms and social philosophy of that order. The transformation of Imagination in Coleridge's thought, in connection with events of the years 1795–1832, is a function of the contradiction which Habermas has discerned in the relationship of the political ideals and economic goals of the new order:

On the one hand, the fiction of a discursive formation of the will that dissolves political rule was institutionalized for the first time within the political system of the bourgeois constitutional state; on the other hand, the incompatibility of the imperatives that rule the capitalist economic system with a democratic process for forming the public will has become manifest.[2]

This contradiction is constitutive of the mounting tension evident in Coleridge's writing between a theory of Imagination as an integrative agency dissolving and dissipating social divisions and hierarchies, and as an otherwordly *consolation* which removed the practice of virtue from a public to a private sphere. The totemic value which Imagination still holds for our own culture is a vestige of its role as exponent of civic virtue, and of the part it played in a whole process of social emancipation, before its institutionalization and removal from the social and political domain. Coleridge's doctrine of culture as *mystery* was thus a seminal moment in the liberal idealization of Imagination. As the nearest approach to public virtue in a privatized commercial society, it stood as an *alternative* to political ideologies critical of capitalism. In this position it remains today.

In the years of his closest intellectual and poetic collaboration with Wordsworth, Coleridge theorized Imagination as the agent of the 'One Life', expressing an integrated Unitarian idea of culture which attacked the established hierarchy of Church and State, and especially its separation of political and spiritual authority. The provenance of his 'romantic materialism' in the political thought and cosmology of a seventeenth-century 'Commonwealth' ideology, rather than in the 'abstract rights' of French Jacobinism, casts the development of Coleridge's writing in a new light. The poetry of both Coleridge and Wordsworth in the productive years 1797–1805 was a sophisticated, if somewhat socially-marginalized, attempt to promote the civic values of an egalitarian commonwealth, and not the product of a conservative reaction to the failure of French and English radicalism. Coleridge's increasing scruples regarding the 'One Life' theory, however, are strongly evident by the time of the *Biographia Literaria* (1815–17). Intervening in the social and ideological crisis of the post-war years, in the context of new demands for parliamentary democracy and the breakdown of traditional structures of aristocratic social patronage, the *Biographia* struggled to reconcile its projected aims with prevailing social conditions. Whilst seeking to sustain an integrative civic definition of Imagination (notably in the

'Schellingian' sections of the first volume), Coleridge was veering towards a 'noumenal' definition of culture in his revision of the poetry and criticism of Wordsworth.

Coleridge's revision of Wordsworth (and by implication, of his own former account of the 'One Life'), has structural affinities with the political argument of Edmund Burke in *Reflections on the Revolution in France*. Both works were to some extent generated by a sensitivity to accusations of political apostasy. Burke's interpretation of the 1688 Settlement, the inauguration of the Whig order, denied that the Williamite (or the Hanoverian) successions had been in any way legitimized by republican 'election', or that political sovereignty rested in the hands of the people. The new dynasty had rather been determined by the customary and presumptive authority of 'law, as it stood at their several accessions of Protestant descent and inheritance'.[3] In an analogous manner, Coleridge presented Wordsworth as a cultural heir invested with the authority of a rich cultural tradition, rather than as the champion and imitator of 'the real language of men'. In both cases, authority based upon contractual and representative criteria was replaced by a prescriptive and professionalized rhetoric, of constitutional expertise and hereditary succession in the first case, and of 'poetic genius' in the second.

It is ironic that Coleridge's most sophisticated (and yet ambivalent) account of the 'One Life' theory appeared at the very point in time when his increasingly authoritarian cultural politics rendered it inapplicable. The influence of German Idealism on his middle and later years has absorbed the attention of many of his commentators, to the exclusion not merely of his political thought, but also of the ideological context in which these ideas were developed. There has been a tendency to overlook the continuity between the radical science and theology of the 'One Life' theory and German Idealism and Naturphilosophie, a continuity which determined Coleridge's growing reluctance to make public his metaphysical interests. The theory of Imagination presented in the twelfth and thirteenth chapters of the *Biographia*, largely derived from Schelling (Imagination was quite central to the German's early philosophy), rests uneasily with the Wordsworth criticism in the second volume. By 1817, Coleridge felt that the moral and political idealism of the 'One Life' had been appropriated by class interests and a sectarian political rhetoric which threatened a central cultural authority. But Coleridge himself came to identify the latter with the Anglican establishment and the unreformed constitution. Imagination was transformed from a radical critique of social hierarchy and prerogative power, and of the divisive tendencies of the commercial order, into a means of legitimizing a traditional cultural élite.

But the abiding importance of Coleridge's cultural politics lies in the fact that he was not prepared, like Wordsworth, to stop there, as literary apologist for an evanescent Tory interest. He sought rather to preserve the central authority of the 'One Life' in an inviolable sphere of culture, defined now in opposition to the political world as such. This was of course a conservative strategy in so far as it withheld cultural authority, the 'discursive formation of the public will', from the various new social interests emerging in the period. But the efficacy (and historical durability) of what I term Coleridge's 'Promethean' theory of culture lay in its appeal to disinterestedness, its claim to political impotence and its transcendence of the realms of rhetoric and ideological coercion.

The third part of my study is accordingly concerned with unmasking the hegemonic strategy of Imagination in the later writings, interpreting the overtly political work in the light of Coleridge's scholarly investigations into the classical Mysteries after 1817. The trope of *Prometheus Bound* dominates his later thought and provides the key to his seminal account of the epistemological relations between Reason and Understanding, to the historical relations between Cultivation and Civilization, and to the hypothetical relations between the institution of knowledge and civil society, as expounded in *The Constitution of the Church and State*.

The Promethean idea, and the notion of Culture as Mystery have constituted our own critical attitudes and practices, to the extent, as I suggested above, that only by comprehending the historical and ideological formation of this complex can we be free of its determination. To this end, the *Politics of Imagination* must, by its method, cross the boundaries which have come to separate literature from society, in order to re-connect and problematize the two realms which Coleridge's later cultural politics did so much to drive apart.

Part One
Coleridge, Wordsworth and the 'One Life' Ideal

1

Republicanism, Retirement and the Ideological Context of the *Preface to Lyrical Ballads*

In the years between 1800 and 1815 Coleridge shifted from a participatory to an essentially authoritarian definition of culture, a shift which had far-reaching ramifications for subsequent thinking about the relation between literature and politics. To understand how and why this happened it is necessary to appreciate the challenge of the ideas presented by Coleridge and Wordsworth in the *Prefaces to Lyrical Ballads*, and indeed the social and historical context from which these ideas emerged. The purpose of the two poets in 1800 was to integrate poetry with a specific socio-economic ideal, and to employ this idea of the 'One Life' to criticize a dominant political order in which the spiritual and material realms were strictly divided.

For this reason the *Prefaces* were constitutive, in a negative way, of Coleridge's conservative apologetic in the *Biographia Literaria*: they were the ghost which Coleridge in 1815 had to lay to rest. To comprehend the ideological context of these spectral *Prefaces*, raised from their slumbers partly at the behest of the energetic post-war radicals who wished to draw attention to the political apostasy of Southey, Wordsworth and Coleridge, we must overcome a common prejudice which often determines their interpretation. The *Prefaces* are too often regarded as isolated or idiosyncratic documents (in relation to the political polemics in which their authors had been involved before 1798), advocating a return to the solicitude of nature from the self-thwarting domain of politics and public life. The currency of this view is itself a testimony of the remarkable success of Coleridge's revisionary reading of Wordsworth in the *Biographia*.

Both the Preface of 1800 and the post-1802 additions are replete with the influence of Hartley's philosophy, echoes of the eighteenth-century primitivists, and the theories of Scottish and English aesthetics from John Dennis through Kames and Hugh Blair to William Enfield.[1] I am less concerned here with discussing these influences in terms of a 'history of ideas', than with tracing the political ideology which, I will argue, underpins and above all else determines the significance of the *Preface's* poetics. The social orientation of aesthetic, almost as much as of scientific, ideas has been afforded only secondary consideration by critics, perhaps as a result of a tendency in major thinkers from Kant to Adorno and Althusser, to regard works of art as being exempt from either instrumentality or ideological content. The influence of this intellectual habit, together with the fact that Wordsworth and Coleridge abandoned radical lecturing and pamphleteering after 1796, producing their most significant poetry in an atmosphere of retirement, has tended to obscure the close continuity between their political and aesthetic endeavours, as well as the activist and reflective phases of their careers. By mapping out the social and political peer-group of the two poets in this period, and by considering the poetry in the context of the political and intellectual interests of the group, I hope to remedy the partiality of an orthodox view of Wordsworth and Coleridge which accepts uncritically their own subsequent revisions of the 1790s.

The radicalism of Wordsworth and Coleridge in this period, or at least the collaboration which followed their first meeting at Bristol in 1795, cannot easily be identified with the ideology of any of the better-known radical groups of the 1790s.[2] It fits neither the mould of the upper-class Whig Reform groups, nor the populist Jacobinism of Paine and the francophile Corresponding Societies. Neither can it be described as a brand of Godwinism, for Coleridge attacked Godwin's *Political Justice* in 1795 (W 196), as did Wordsworth, implicitly, in his Preface to *The Borderers* (1796–97) and the *Essay on Morals* (1798) (W Prose I 79; 103).

Nevertheless Wordsworth and Coleridge's political circle did manifest its own distinct, albeit marginalized, culture, pursuing its ideological goals in a Unitarianism which verged on radical deism, in a political polemic which drew more heavily on the ideas of the English 'Commonwealthmen' of the seventeenth century than upon the Jacobinism generated by the French revolution, and also in the fields of poetry and science. These interests were pursued in a climate of increasing repression, and more damagingly, unpopularity. An understanding of the identity of this group, so essential in forming the subsequent intellectual development of Wordsworth and Coleridge, is precluded by a common tendency to interpret English radicalism in the 1790s as a monolithic Jacobinism, largely inseparable from the fortunes of the French revolution.

The resistance shown by members of this circle to the atheism and materialism of many Jacobins (deriving in a tradition from Hobbes and his French interpreters), as well as to the Newtonian theory of inert matter championed by the intellectual establishment, shows that they occupied an ideological middleground. The readiness with which Coleridge (and other intellectuals connected with 'advanced dissent') embraced German Idealism, the subject of Part Two, shows the extent to which the 'One Life' ideal was dissatisfied with the dominant paradigms of English and French thought. Coleridge's dynamic philosophy postulated an *anima mundi* permeating both mind and matter, a theory shared by the other members of his circle, and not merely a personal aversion to the empiricist's view of the world as 'an immense heap of *little things*' (CL I 349).

Two recent works concerned with Wordsworth and Coleridge's radical milieu are E. P. Thompson's essay 'Disenchantment or Default? A Lay Sermon', and James Chandler's book *Wordsworth's Second Nature*.[3] Thompson does valuable work in attacking the patronizing attitude of some literary critics to the political ideas of the young poets.

> [It is] as if, as each area of Wordsworth's political beliefs suffered disenchantment, it became available to the poetic sensibility – very much as if his mind were a country occupied by an oppressive mechanical philosophy in which one province after another was liberated for 'maturity'.[4]

Yet Thompson's notion of 'disenchantment' perhaps owes more to his personal experience of the post-1956 English Left than to a consideration of the impulse which led Wordsworth to write in the *Prelude* of 1805, on the subject of his political beliefs in 1795:

> . . . not doubting at that time,
> Creed which ten shameful years have not annull'd,

> (Prelude 1805 x 177–8)

Wordsworth does not stick at 1790, the date of the establishment of a Constitutional Monarchy in France, nor even at 1792, the hopeful dawn of the Girondin republic, before the execution of the king and queen and the bloody suppression of the Vendée rising. These lines suggest that it was Wordsworth's *republicanism*, not his loyalty to church and king, which was affronted by events in France after 1795. Indeed a series of sonnets written in 1802 celebrating 'National Independence and Liberty' compare the French to the English revolutionaries of the preceding century, finding the former wanting; they also assert the poet's continuing support for the 'homely beauty of the good old cause' in the same period (it should be noted) as his amendments to the *Preface to Lyrical Ballads* (WPW p. 244, sonnet xiii, l. 12).

Thompson's 'Disenchantment' depends too much on an unsubstantiated account of the two poets as Jacobins, a common enough error probably based on Coleridge's close association with the Jacobin John Thelwall.[5] But 'Disenchantment' is too vague a term insofar as it overlooks the ideological (although not 'party-political') radicalism which continues, in somewhat variant forms, and in an increasingly abstract manner, in Coleridge's writings until as late as 1815. The danger of conflating a politically active Jacobinism, manifest in organizations like the Corresponding Societies, with the more reflective and intellectual strategies of 'advanced dissenters' and 'Commonwealth' republicans of Wordsworth and Coleridge's circle, is that retreat from the political theatre is equated with ideological and political abstention. Thus for Thompson the poetry is a reflex of disenchantment, the *rigor mortis* of political radicalism. He describes it as the energy of the alienated mind: 'a search for a synthesis at a moment of arrested dialectic; a coruscation of perceptions coming from this tension'.[6] The efficacy of poetry in precipitating revolutions of state may never have been remarkable, but as the authors of the *Preface to Lyrical Ballads* (or, for that matter, the author of *A Defence of Poetry*) well knew, its consummate power as a vehicle for ideological confirmation was surpassed only by the rhetoric of Christian belief.

The relationship between Coleridge's 'spiritualized republicanism' and 'mainstream' Jacobinism is summed by his remark to Thelwall in a letter of November 1796 that 'We run on the same ground, but we drive different Horses' (CL I 253). The awkward conventionality of Thelwall's *Poems, Written Chiefly in*

Retirement (1801) suggests that the great radical orator did indeed regard his abandonment of the political theatre as an ideological and imaginative defeat. The same point may be gathered from Coleridge's *Table Talk* anecdote of 27 July, 1830:

> John Thelwall had something very good about him. We were once sitting in a beautiful recess in the Quantocks, when I said to him, 'Citizen John, this is a fine place to talk treason in!' '— Nay! Citizen Samuel,' replied he, 'it is rather a place to make a man forget that there is any necessity for treason.'
>
> (TT I 190–1)

Given Coleridge's development of the retirement ethic in later years, Thelwall was undoubtedly right in supposing that it could be construed as an *alternative* to political engagement; the point here is, however, to suspend judgement in order to understand exactly what the posture of retirement meant to the poet's circle in the late 1790s. In the following pages it will be shown that in the long run, retirement entailed a failure to match political ideals to social realities in the writings of both Wordsworth and Coleridge. What began as a critical stance, the adoption and application of an integrated life-style and ideology in opposition to the contemporary order, became a tacit complicity with that order, an idealization of culture severed from history and society.

But that retirement was a complement, rather than an alternative, to political intervention in the 1790s, is evident in the following letter from Coleridge to Thelwall in December 1796:

> I am not *fit* for *public* life; yet the Light shall stream to a far distance from the taper in my cottage window. Meantime, do *you* uplift the *torch* dreadlessly, and shew to mankind the face of that Idol, which they have worshipped in Darkness!
>
> (CL I 277)

Undoubtedly the impulse to retirement did partake of an element of disillusionment connected with the 'failure' of the French revolution, as the armies of the Directory swept into the republican Swiss Cantons in January 1798, thereby transforming a war against absolutist oppression into one of aggressive expansionism. Coleridge's poems of 1798, *Fears in Solitude* and *France: an Ode*, express the complexity of his response to the now-threatening military presence of France.[7] Also the tendency of conservatives at home to include the 'advanced' or 'rational' dissenters under the aegis of French Jacobinism produced the kind of 'Church and King' mob violence which destroyed Joseph Priestley's Birmingham laboratory in 1791. This, added to the traditional unpopularity of the dissenters, must have added a practical motive, the fear of persecution, to the attractions of the retirement ethic.

Nevertheless the impact of the French revolution upon them should not be overestimated. The ideological tradition represented by Coleridge's circle in the 1790s had a history which long preceded the events in France. The middle-class radicals associated with it had been involved in campaigns against the Test Act and the war against the American colonies, years before the storming of the Bastille. Despite an increasing tendency to employ intellectual, aesthetic and religious vehicles to express their social object, struggle for civil parity (the result of increasing government repression and unpopularity), there was by no means a sudden abandonment of political radicalism after 1798. The following pages will demonstrate a positive continuity between the 'civic religion' of the Unitarians, the agrarian communism of the Bristol Pantisocrats, and the 'perfect Republic of Shepherds and Agriculturists' which Wordsworth identified in the Lake District after 1800 (W Prose II 206).

The strength of James Chandler's study *Wordsworth's Second Nature* is its willingness to consider the major poetry as itself the expression of an ideology, rather than the reflex of thwarted idealism. It is neither the product of what Thompson calls 'disenchantment', nor, according to M. H. Abram's influential account, 'a displacement of millenarian political expectations'.[8] Chandler makes the point, central to my own account of the 'politics of imagination', that 'discussion of the political dimension of Wordsworth's major poetry runs the risk of remaining peripheral if it cannot take some account of the "spots of time" and the meditative Wordsworthian mode they epitomize'.[9] Hence the importance of locating the political orientation of the 'ethic of retirement' and the 'One Life' theory.

Chandler argues to this end that the language of custom, habit and 'second nature' which permeates Wordsworth's writing from the *Essay on Morals* (1798), particularly in the *Preface* of 1800 and the *Prelude* of 1805, is proof of his covert acceptance of Burkean conservatism. According to Burke's 'presumptive' argument, the hubristric abstract rights of Paine or Godwin, a 'private stock of reason', is challenged by custom, 'the general bank and capital of nations and ages'.[10] But misled by an overschematic Paine/Burke axis, Chandler fails to consider that the political ideology of Coleridge and his circle in 1795 also used the language of custom and affection against Paine and Godwin's interpretation of reason, but towards radical ends profoundly opposed to the Burke of *Reflections*. This ideology was politically affiliated to the 'New' Whigs whom Burke attacked so bitterly in his *Appeal from the New to the Old Whigs* (1791), rather than to the more plebeian radicalism of the Paineites. Coleridge's 1796 periodical *The Watchman* aligned itself with the constitutionalist Whig Club, upholding the 'principles of the British Constitution as established at the Revolution' against the sort of parliamentary prerogative displayed by Pitt's Seditious Meetings and Treasonable Practices Bill of 1795 (W 385). Coleridge, later in life, would try very hard to suppress the evidence of such party-political affiliations.[11]

Wordsworth appears to have shifted his political faith from the Paineite position of his *Letter to the Bishop of Llandaff* (1793) in the years following his meeting with Coleridge in 1795, to the 'customary' ideology of the latter, which was by no means identical with that of Burke. The group of Bristol Pantisocrats whom Wordsworth encountered in 1795 afforded him relief from what he came to regard as the aridity of Godwin's system (Prelude 1805 X 888–940). The fact that in his disillusionment he 'yielded up moral questions in despair' (Prelude 1805 X 900) does not mean that Wordsworth then adopted a conservative and Burkean position, but rather that he came to reject the individualism of Godwin's system, with its bid to build 'social freedom' on the rational 'freedom of the individual mind', rather than upon the religious and political principles of the kind which we will see Coleridge advocating in his 1795 lectures and writings (Prelude 1805 X 824–6).

There are certainly points of language and ideology common to both Burke's conservatism and the politics of the 'spiritual republicanism' advocated by Wordsworth and Coleridge after 1795. Burke's claim to represent the 'ancient' tradition of the Whig revolution of 1688 was regarded with scorn by his radical and 'New Whig' opponents. His shift from a position supporting the American colonists in the *Speeches on Conciliation with the Colonies* in 1775, to his attack on the new French constitution in *Reflections* exemplifies what Caroline Robbins has called the 'Whig double-standard'. This is brought home by the fact that when Burke and Priestley first met, 'they seemed to have no differences in matters political except that Burke looked to the great Whig families to check the Crown, and Priestley to a more equal representation of the Commons'.[12] The fundamental differences in their respective interpretations of 1688 were lying latent, however, awaiting the ferment of events connected with the French Revolution to bring them to light. The 'Whig double-standard' often resulted in political opponents using identical ideological arguments against one another. In *The Watchman* Coleridge was full of admiration for Burke's rhetorical power, but lamented the political end to which it was put (W 30). Wordsworth's *Essay on Morals* also preferred rhetorical means of conviction (including poetry) to the cold systematic reason of Paley or Godwin. This contrasted with his earlier position in the *Letter to the Bishop of Llandaff* in which, echoing Paine, he voiced his suspicion of 'Burke's intoxicating bowl' (W Prose I 49). Burke's means were admired, his ends were not.

To the political group which he described as the 'New Whigs', Burke was that most despised of creatures, a political apostate, in the same mould as Richard Watson, bishop of Llandaff, or Pitt himself. As Coleridge succinctly put it in 1796:

> As the flames which rise from the altar of Freedom, he kindled that torch with which he since endeavored to set fire to her temple.
>
> (W 39)

In the footnotes to his *Sonnets on Eminent Characters*, Coleridge commemorated Burke's act of venality in crossing from the Whig to the Tory bench, and his acceptance of an annual state pension of £1200 (PW I 80–1). In 1809, Coleridge still had cause to censure Burke, although by 1818 he had become the paradigmatic 'man of method'.[13] Wordsworth expressed similar reservations concerning Burke's integrity in a rare early comment on the statesman in 1804 (EY 491), and even in the admiring account of Burke in the first of the *Two Addresses to the Freeholders of Westmoreland* (1818), he attributed to Burke's acceptance of the state-pension a common tendency to undervalue his political acuity and foresight (W Prose III 158).[14] The lines on Burke which Wordsworth added to book seven of the *Prelude* between 1820 and 1823 are a testimony to the unequivocal admiration which he, like Coleridge, felt for Burke in later years.

Perhaps the most outstanding evidence for Wordsworth's distrust of Burke in the early years, however, are the following lines from book ten of the *Prelude* of 1805, seeking an explanation of the poet's desperate espousal of Godwinism in 1794–95:

> Enough, no doubt, the advocates themselves
> Of ancient institutions had perform'd
> To bring disgrace upon their very names,
> Disgrace of which custom and written law
> And sundry moral sentiments as props
> And emanations of these institutes
> Too justly bore a part.

(Prelude 1805 x 849–55)

This clearly implicates Burke as one of the 'advocates . . . of ancient institutions' who precipitated Wordsworth's overreaction, causing him to embrace Godwinism. Burke is far from being seen as the source of the poet's redemption, as Chandler argues. Wordsworth was still involved with Godwin in 1795, for the philosopher's diary records five visits from the poet between February and August of that year: but it was in Coleridge's criticism of Godwin's 'Stoical Morality', with its subordination of customary affections and benevolence to a purely rational appraisal of worth, that he ultimately found deliverance from a system which had become increasingly uncongenial to him.[15]

In the third of the 1795 *Lectures on Revealed Religion*, Coleridge attached Godwin's rejection of politics proper, his lack of faith in the ameliorative potential of good government, in terms of great importance for an understanding of his own political creed. Godwin's *Political Justice*

> builds without a foundation, proposes an end without establishing the means, and discovers a total ignorance of that obvious Fact that in virtue and in knowledge we must be infants and be nourished with milk in order that we may be men and eat strong meat.

(Lects 1795 164)[16]

Extreme caution should therefore be taken in identifying the 'ethic of retirement' as a form of Burkean conservatism. The *Old Cumberland Beggar* may be a 'conservative' poem in so far as it opposed the brand of rational reform which sought to confine mendicants to the workhouse. But the values of the customary community which it championed were a rebuke to the values of the contemporary establishment upheld by Burke, which Wordsworth regarded as having succumbed to the evils of commerce, luxury, class-differentiation and imperialism. A participatory and active life of social intercourse alone had the power to transform individual proclivities to vice into civic virtue, the 'mild necessity of use compels / To acts of love' (WPW p. 444, ll. 99–100), a principle which Coleridge also sought to promulgate in his poem *Religious Musings* (1796) (PW I 108, ll. 198–224).

A tendency amongst modern critics to regard the nascent 'rights of man' radicalism of the urban artisan and working class as the exclusive forebear of nineteenth and twentieth century socialism has resulted in the designation of the ideology of custom, and the spiritual, rather than secular, orientation of Wordsworth and Coleridge in the late 1790s, as being already a form of conservatism. The next section will show that the 'One Life' ideal should be rather identified with an *older* form of radicalism partaking of many of the political, theological and cosmological ideas of the 'Commonwealth' tradition, which had its origins in the previous century, and which by the end of the eighteenth century was being modified, dispersed, or assimilated.[17]

2

Unitarians, Commonwealthmen and the 'One Life' Theory

The political ideology of Wordsworth and Coleridge in the second half of the 1790s stands at an equal distance from both Jacobean and Burkean conservatism, and is best approached by being considered in relation to the other intellectual interests with which it was associated. Only in terms of this wider connection will the continuity between the political ideas of 1795–96 and the *Preface to Lyrical Ballads* become evident, for the latter work carefully disguises its political ideal.

The discursive practice of Coleridge's thought in the 1790s assembled republican political theory, Unitarian theology, natural and chemical sciences and poetry in its field of enquiry, a grouping which might seem to be an odd assortment and yet which is clearly represented in the 1795 *Lectures on Revealed Religion*. The first of these lectures used electricity and magnetism to advance its 'argument from design' against both Atheists and Anglican theologians (Lects 1795 112), and a liberal interpretation of Newton's theory of matter was presented as a support for Christian evidence (Lects 1795 96–103). Lectures Two and Three described a form of christian communism based on the seventeenth-century English republican James Harrington's *Commonwealth of Oceana*. Lectures Four and Five defended revealed religion by internal and external evidences denying the divinity of Christ and suggesting that early Christianity was Unitarianism corrupted by priests, mystagogues and Gnostics. The intellectual 'package' presented in these lectures was indebted to the thought of Joseph Priestley, although Coleridge is considerably more politically extreme than Priestley in his advocacy of agrarian communism and his attacks on commerce (Lects 1795 lxiv). The editors Lewis Patton and Peter Mann perhaps unjustly suggest that Priestley's 1777 *Disquisitions Relating to Matter and Spirit* was the target of a

19

remark in Lecture Three attacking the 'materialism' of the Stoic idea of Deity as an emanation from the universe (Lects 1795 156). Priestley carefully argues in that work that matter is the offspring of the 'creating mind' of God and that He is the *'incomprehensible . . . the object of our most profound reverence and awful adoration'.*[1] The 'Unitarian materialism' of both Priestley and Coleridge is more accurately described as a form of pantheism, in which God is at once an inherent force in matter and yet retains a certain transcendence. As more than the sum of the world, He is quite different from the endless chain of causes proposed by atheistical materialists writing in the tradition of Hobbes.[2] Priestley's attempt in the *Disquisitions* to discover an intelligible connection between motion and thought, body and mind, is the most probable source for Coleridge's denial of dualism and the Newtonian doctrine of inert matter in his celebrated December 1794 letter to Southey 'I go farther than Hartley and believe the corporeality of *thought* – namely, that it is motion – (CL I 137). The next section shows how Priestley's theory of matter links Coleridge with the German Naturphilosophers, notably Schelling. Priestley was influenced by the 'illustrious' Roger Boscovitch (the epithet is Coleridge's in 1809 (Friend II 11)) whose 'physical point' theory of matter was also an important influence on the seminal work of Naturphilosophie, Kant's *Metaphysische Anfangsgründe der Naturwissenschaft* (1786).[3]

Many of Coleridge's friends and intellectual associates in the 1795–1800 period were Unitarians or 'rational dissenters' associated with Unitarian circles: William Frend, a mathematics tutor at Cambridge; J. P. Estlin, who published an attack on the atheism of Paine and the French sceptics Volney and Dupuis;[4] Benjamin Flower, Joshua Toulmin, George Dyer, the Rev. John Edwards and Thomas and Josiah Wedgwood. To give some idea of the comprehensive scope of this group in different areas of public life, we should consider three other eminent affiliates. The moderate Richard Price, who never made the full doctrinal leap form Arianism to Unitarianism, was, like his friend Priestley, the author of an influential work of political theory as well as of scientific and theological works, and of course the target of Burke's fulmination in the *Reflections*.[5] Gilbert Wakefield, classical scholar and divine, whose anti-war *Spirit of Christianity* (1794) was the major source for Coleridge's *Religious Musing*, was imprisoned for sedition.[6] The veteran reformer and Unitarian Major Cartwright was active in all three of the principal reform movements of the period, the

Wilkesite lobby, the 1790s and the post-war Hampden clubs which sought to unify the various strains of English radicalism. Like Coleridge, Estlin and others, Cartwright attacked Paine, arguing in 'constitutionalist' terms that political change should be achieved 'under the shadow of the old forms'.[7]

Coleridge's immediate associates in Bristol and Nether Stowey tended to share his own intellectual interests: the most important members of his circle were Robert Southey, poet and fellow-Pantisocrat; Thomas Beddoes, a radical physician, naturalist and chemist, whom he first met at a 1795 rally against Pitt's 'gagging bills'; Humphry Davy, Beddoes' colleague at the philanthropic 'Pneumatical Institute', and Tom Poole, a tanner and agriculturalist, with Coleridge a co-member of the republican 'Tepidarian Club'. Poole's agricultural expertise was a crucial element in Coleridge's plan to realize his dream of an agrarian commune at Stowey. Dorothy and William Wordsworth complete this list of Bristol acquaintances, emphasizing the variegated intellectual milieu from which the famous literary collaboration emerged.[8] An interchange of intellectual interests is evident; Coleridge, Wordsworth and Southey were interested in science, Beddoes had published in 1792 an epic poem, *Alexander's Expedition*, attacking British imperialism, and Humphry Davy modestly claimed that if he had not been the greatest scientist of his age, he would have been its greatest poet.[9] Coleridge's fellow-Pantisocrat Robert Lovell, his friend George Dyer and Stowey co-resident Charles Lloyd (son of the Quaker banker) were all publishing poets. Nearly all the names mentioned in this group can be considered under the aegis of the 'ethic of retirement' which should be distinguished from the Godwinian and Paineite circles. Coleridge's and Thelwall's comments upon each other are instructive in establishing the parameters of these respective radical groups. In a 1798 letter to Dr Crompton, Thelwall bemusedly describes Coleridge's principal concern in politics as 'the republic of God's own makings', adding that the divine patronage does not prevent the scheme from 'levelling sedition and constructive treason',[10] Coleridge, on the other hand, described Thelwall in a 1797 letter to Wade as

> the only *acting* Democrat, that *is* honest for the *Patriots* are ragged cattle . . . boastful of the strength of reason, because they have never tried it enough to know its *weakness*.
>
> (CL I 339)

The intellectual concerns which Coleridge shared with the other members of this circle, notably poetry, theology and Bible criticism, science and republican political theory, will be traced from the 1795 *Lectures*, through the 1800 *Preface* to the *Biographia Literaria* and the later thought. Although Coleridge's ideas changed, his field of intellectual interests did not, even when it was transmuted into a German idiom after about 1802. The hypothesis of such a continuous tradition in a state of transformation between 1796 and 1817 will shed new light on the interrelationship between the early and later texts. It will also take us beyond the notion of an 'epistemological break' in Coleridge's thought, in which a 'radical' native empiricism based on Lockean and Newtonian epistemology was replaced by German Transcendentalism, conservative in tone, and more-or-less favourable to the theorization, if not the practice of, the 'creative imagination'. The first task in determining the internal coherence of the odd assortment of interests described above is to establish whether they were linked by any common themes and purposes; the scientific and aesthetic fields, for example, have traditionally been treated as discrete by historians of ideas as well as literary critics. If a common purpose unites these diverse fields, it can then be linked with the social and political aims of the group.

Coleridge's lines in his poem *The Eolian Harp* (1795) provide a suitable starting point, although their context in a poem which ends by questioning their hubristic (and rhetorical) power should be borne in mind:

> And what if all of animated nature,
> Be but organic Harps diversely fram'd,
> That tremble into thought, as o'er them sweeps
> Plastic and vast, one intellectual breeze,
> At once the Soul of each, and God of all?

> (PW I 102, ll. 44–8)

In a December 1796 letter to Thelwall, Coleridge specifies this pantheistic theory of the 'One Life' (the term added to the poem in 1817) as being based upon the 'plastic immaterial nature' which he associates with the theories of the Scottish physiologist Alexander Monro (CL I 294).[11] The 'plastic power' of Nature, the *anima mundi*, had a seventeenth-century provenance, entering the language of natural philosophy via the Neoplatonic 'Spiritus', the mediator between matter and spirit. The term was commonly used in the 1790s, but Coleridge probably derived it from Ralph Cudworth's *True Intellectual System of the Universe* (1678) which he borrowed from the Bristol library in May 1795.[12] He could also have found it in James Harrington's hermetic work *The Mechanics of Nature*, included in Toland's edition of the latter's *Works*, also read by Coleridge in this period.[13] Coleridge's letter to Thelwall then runs through a series of other arguments concerning the perennial eighteenth-century matter/spirit debate, concluding that he does not 'know what to think about it', although inclining to the immaterialist line which regards Life as 'I myself I', a 'naked spirit', which, he jokes, is 'a mighty clear account of it' (CL I 295). Coleridge's poetic expression of this philosophical and scientific question, his emotional and experiential awareness of a doctrine explicitly associated with medical theory is highly significant here. Indeed it can be compared with his ambition for nature poetry expressed in the preface to the 1796 *Sonnets from Various Authors*. Coleridge hoped for a poetry which will 'create a sweet and indissoluble union between the intellectual and material world' (PW II 1139), an effect which W. K. Wimsatt had defined as a characteristic of romantic nature imagery.[14]

The 'plastic power' which defies the dualism between matter and spirit, and which Coleridge invokes here is of course identical to the power which comes to be theorized as *Imagination* in later years, that 'sublime faculty, by which a great mind becomes that which it meditates on' (CN III 3290). The quest for a 'something *one & indivisible*' underlying and animating the world is perhaps above all others the unifying principle of Coleridge's multifarious writings, although it will be seen how his statement of the 'One Life' is persistently checked and qualified, from the 'mild reproof' in the last lines of the 1796 *Eolian Harp* to the cautionary 'letter from a friend' which interrupts the transcendental deduction of imagination in chapter thirteen of the *Biographia* nearly twenty years later. The present attempt to associate the unifying power of imagination with the ideological goals of a somewhat marginalized social group will offer an explanation for the fact that this principle for Coleridge in 1815, seemed to subvert the established hierarchy of church and state.

Given the importance of the scientist's theory of matter for the genesis of Coleridgean imagination, the relations between

Priestley's discussion in his *Disquisitions* and Coleridge's 'sweet and indissoluble union' must be considered in more detail. Anticipating Coleridge's 'clear account' of 'naked spirit' in the December 1796 letter to Thelwall, Priestley had denied the solidity and inertness of matter. Rather than being solid and impenetrable, matter is really a product of spirits, the indifference of the constitutive powers of attraction and repulsion.

> Matter is not that *inert* substance that it has been supposed to be: that *powers of attraction* or *repulsion* are necessary to its very being, and that no part of it appears to be *impenetrable* to other parts. I therefore define it to be a substance possessed of the property of *extension*, and of *powers of attraction and repulsion*. And since it has never yet been asserted that the powers of *sensation* and *thought* are incompatible with these (*solidity*, or *impenetrability*, and consequently a *vis inertiae*, only, having been thought to be repugnant to them); I therefore maintain that we have no reason to suppose that there are in man two substances so distinct from each other, as have been represented.[15]

Priestley used a modified version of Hartley's associationist theory of mind to show how thought and matter interpenetrate and give rise to each other, anticipating Coleridge's discovery of the 'corporeality of *thought* – namely that it is motion' (CL I 137).[16] This manner of overcoming the dualism between body and soul should not be confused with the 'mechanical' materialism which simply did away with both the soul and final cause, a doctrine which Coleridge in the *Biographia* likened to a chain of blind men in which 'infinite blindness supplies the place of sight' (BL I 266). Both Coleridge and Priestley sought to spiritualize matter rather than to effect a universal reduction to the conditions of materiality. This is an important point to bear in mind when considering the 'romantic materialism' underlying Coleridge's theory of Imagination; the term is easily misleading given the predominance of 'mechanistic' materialism, but it should be emphasised that as long as dualism is denied, the terms 'spiritualist' and 'materialist' mean the same thing.

It is this denial of dualism which is the common intellectual goal of Wordsworth, Coleridge and their circle in the years after 1795, unifying their various discursive endeavours. On the scientific front, Coleridge's friend Humphry Davy assumed Priestley's mantle, and in his 1799 *Essay on Heat, Light and the Combination of Light* he 'attributed powers of attraction and repulsion to matter, and denied the existence of substantial caloric'.[17] In the poems Davy was writing at the same time such as *Spinozism* (1800–1) (with its apotheosis of the 'One Intelligence'), or the *Untitled Verses*

> Here in my Kindling Spirit learn'd to trace
> The mystic laws from whose high energy
> The moving atoms, in eternal change,
> Still rise to animation.'[18]

Davy pursued the 'integrative ideal' which sought the laws of matter in the laws of mind. Davy doubtlessly recognized a kindred purpose in Wordsworth's *Lyrical Ballads*, the proofs of the second edition of which he corrected in early 1801. Roger Sharrock has argued that Wordsworth's awareness of Davy's arguments in his *Introductory Discourse* to a series of lectures on chemistry at the Royal Institution in January 1801, was manifest in the comparison between the poet and scientist which he added to the revised 1802 *Preface* (W Prose I 140–1).[19] Davy would certainly have recognized his own preoccupations in the following lines from the 1805 *Prelude*:

> . . . my mind hath look'd
> Upon the speaking face of earth and heaven
> As her prime Teacher, intercourse with man
> Establish'd by the sovereign Intellect,
> Who through that bodily Image hath diffus'd,
> A soul divine which we participate,
> A deathless spirit.

> (Prelude 1805 v ll. 11–17)

It has been convincingly argued that Priestley's theory of matter was closely integrated with his theology and 'rational dissent',[20] and the same point should be made in relation to the natural philosophy, and the political and religious thought of Wordsworth and Coleridge in the 1790s. In the next section we will see Coleridge struggling to suppress such a connection in the years after 1817. Priestley, like the other rational dissenters, regarded science as a radical weapon, exemplified by his famous remark that the corrupt establishment 'has equal reason to tremble even at an air pump or an electrical machine'.[21]

In the *Disquisitions* Priestley overtly used his matter theory for the purpose of theological polemic, denying the divinity of Christ, who, although a great teacher and moralist, should no more be worshipped as a god than any other man or woman. Priestley denied that the notion of a soul distinct from body was anywhere present in Scripture; it was rather a heathen superstition propagated by Egyptian and Greek priestcraft to mystify the rational and self-evident truths of religion for its own ends. The introduction of the doctrine of the Trinity into Christianity by the Gnostics signalled the corruption of the Unitarian early church by mystagogues of the Roman hierarchy, a usurpation continued to the present day by the Anglican establishment.[22] Coleridge closely followed Priestley's argument in his 1795 *Lectures on Revealed Religion*, concerning the appropriation of the spiritual egalitarianism of the early church by the civil hierarchies. The goal of this Unitarian argument was to undermine the hegemonic power of Anglicanism and expose the 'mystery' of the Trinity to the light of reason, a mystery which was shown to derive ultimately from the pagan superstition of a division between body and soul. Coleridge described the doctrine of the Trinity as "a mysterious way of telling a plain truth" (Lects 1795 208). My final section will show how he came to revise his opinion about the role of the Mysteries in religion, a subject in which he took a keen interest in later years.

Wordsworth's attack on the 'motley masquerade of tricks, quaintnesses, hieroglyphics, and enigmas' in the 1802 *Preface* (W Prose I 162), the qualities which characterize 'poetic diction', drew heavily on the Unitarian argument. The Unitarian (in contrast to the Anglican) preacher speaks the 'real language of men'; like the Wordsworthian poet, he is 'a man speaking to men', rejecting a mystificatory rhetorical authority over the civic community (W Prose I 138). The political order which Thelwall referred to as Coleridge's 'republic of God's own making' aimed to interpenetrate the spiritual and the secular, the religious and political realms, thereby entailing a community based upon egalitarian principles, rather than a hierarchy based on divine sanction. The integration of matter and spirit sought by the scientists was here carried over into the religious and political fields, a point emphasized by Coleridge in the lectures. He regarded the tendency to entertain 'so mean an opinion of matter' and to hold the body in contempt, as having led to the denial of the humanity of Christ by the Gnostics; the account of matter as *vis inertia* held by the contemporary Newtonian establishment should be considered as his real target here (Lects 1795 197–8). The Gnostics regarded Christ as a spiritual emanation from the supreme being, a doctrinal error which had had severe repercussions for the true or 'material' Christians. The worship of Christ led to his canonization and to the mysteries of the roman hierarchy, a mystery 'darkening the understanding (which) depraved the Heart, and introduced Sensuality' amongst Christians. This led to the demise of their communistic societies, to accumulation and 'the lawfulness of unequal Property'. The political result of Trinitarianism was the corruption of the church and the oppression of its members; 'honorary Distinctions became the universal Creed' (Lects 1795 202).

Clearly the 'politics of imagination' were in the 1790s an overt and radical attack on both religious and political establishments, and especially a political tyranny endorsed by Anglicanism, the priests of which Coleridge exemplified in 1796 by the image of 'a man holding the scourge of power in his right hand and a bible (translated by authority) in his left' (PW I 117n). The poetic, religious and scientific manifestations of the 'One Life' ideal are clearly linked to the social and political goals of the group loosely termed 'rational dissenters'. The 1689 Toleration Act still withheld from Catholics and Unitarians the limited degree of Toleration offered to Presbyterians, Congregationalists and other more moderate dissenting groups, cutting them off from all civil power. Not surprisingly their animus was levelled at the established church which blocked their progress in civil society, and the doctrine of which was based upon the Trinitarian 'division of powers'. The Unitarian denial of dualism must be regarded in the context of this ideological struggle, historically connected with the 11-year Commonwealth of the preceding century, when the power of the Monarchy, the Lords and the Bishops had been briefly levelled by the dissenter's Puritan forebears. Unitarianism was the ideological expression of an independent middle class which, in the words of Harold Perkin, 'could afford the luxury of dissent from the Landlord's religion': as such he sees it as 'the sublimated form taken by class antagonisms in the old society.[23] Caroline Robbins has shown the connection between the rational dissenters and the tradition of the eighteenth-century 'commonwealthmen' who sought (to a greater or lesser extent), to propagate a republican interpretation of the 1688 settlement, in order to minimize the losses which their social interests had suffered as a result of the restored, albeit limited, power of the Crown and the Anglican establishment.[24]

The principal intellectual components of the *Lectures on Revealed Religion* are certainly consistent with the religious, political and scientific manifestations of this older tradition of commonwealth thought. These are, namely, a Socinian attack on *both* Atheism and Trinitarianism, a scientific criticism of 'hylozoic' materialism (the doctrine of 'thinking matter') as well as of inert, lifeless matter, a criticism claiming a privileged interpretation of Newton; and the advocacy of an egalitarian and predominately agrarian commonwealth.[25] The same concerns had been at the centre of the work of John Toland, one of the most celebrated and enigmatic of the 'commonwealthmen', almost a century before Coleridge's lectures. Toland, a figure much discussed of late by historians of scientific and political thought, was an Irish Catholic who had converted to Presbyterianism and thence to Socinianism. His religion is more properly described as pantheist, a term which he himself probably coined, and his politics republican. Thomas MacFarland has described Toland as 'a near-professional heretic', and his reputation may well have determined the silence maintained by many Unitarians with regard to the source of many of their more challenging ideas.[26]

Coleridge's attack on the Mysteries in 1795 was within the tradition of Toland's *Christianity not Mysterious* (1696) and *Letters to Serena* (1704), as mediated through the writings of Priestley and other 'rational dissenters'. Another significant link is evident between Toland and Coleridge (and indeed the German Naturphilosophers) when we consider the influence upon Toland's *Letters to Serena* of Giordano Bruno, hermeticist, Copernican and last of the Renaissance Magi, whose importance has recently been resurrected by Frances Yates.[27] Bruno's pantheistic and Unitarian heterodoxy led to his being burnt to death in 1600 by the Catholic hierarchy. Coleridge quoted a long passage from Bruno in *The Friend* and announced a projected biography of the Nolan heretic

(Friend I 117–18; CL IV 656). In the *Biographia* he was hailed as the founder of the 'Dynamic System' of philosophy, of which the German Schelling was the most successful improver, a system which sought to substitute 'life and progressive power for the contradictory *inert force*' of matter (BL I 162–3). Bruno's 'One Life' theory also influenced Schelling, who published in 1802 a philosophical dialogue entitled *Giordano Bruno; oder über das göttliche und natürliche Princip der Dinge*. Bruno's pantheism was only one of the interests shared by the rational dissenters in England and the German Idealists.

Toland's Socinian argument in *Letters to Serena*, like Priestley's and Coleridge's, was supported by a theory of matter as being imbued with motion, aimed at the Latitudinarian Anglican establishment, which championed Newton's dualistic *vis inertia*, the doctrine of lifeless matter. Toland's pantheism sought to prove the interpenetration of spirit and matter, without losing the notion of an independent Deity as final cause. Toland attacked the brand of hylozic atheism which did away with the final cause; it was a fault which he discerned in Spinozism.[28] This anticipated Coleridge's attack on atheism in the first of the *Lectures on Revealed Religion*, a position which he distinguished from the 'spiritualized pantheism' he would later describe as his creed in the early eighteen-hundreds. He summed it up in the formula 'God was = the World, the World was not = to God.'[29] Coleridge mentioned Toland in passing in *The Watchman*, although the passage which he cited is a misattribution (W 35 n2). Toland's commonwealth interests would have been familiar to Coleridge from his edition of Milton's *Collected Historical, Political and Miscellaneous Works* (1698), from which he quoted in *The Watchman*, and from his edition of *The Oceana and other Works* of James Harrington (1700).[30] The agrarian republicanism of Coleridge's second *Lecture on Revealed Religion* is pure Harrington, as transmitted through the medium of Moses Lowman's popular *Dissertation on the Civil Government of the Hebrews* (1740). Coleridge shared his interest in the 'real Whig' commonwealthmen with John Thelwall, who in 1796 republished Walter Moyle's *Essay on the Constitution and Government of the Roman State* (1699), a work which analysed the Roman agrarian laws in the terms of Harrington's political thought.[31] Through Toland, his close association of scientific and political ideas is again made evident here, of considerable importance in tracing the development of the 'politics of imagination' in the years *after* Coleridge's abandonment of an overtly radical and Unitarian stance.

J. G. A. Pocock has argued that Toland's political thought, articulated at a time of shifting affiliations amongst the various power-groups of post-1688 England, was 'replete with the ambiguities of the emerging alliance between Old Whig theorists and a Country which would soon be a Tory, party'.[32] Margaret Jacob has succeeded in applying this 'contextualist' approach to Toland's thought in the more difficult case of scientific ideas. A brief consideration of her argument will cast some light on the social and political history of Coleridge's 'One Life' theory. Jacob is concerned with the institutionalization of Newtonian ideas by the Latitudinarian Anglican clergy in the period following the English Revolution. The Boyle Lecturers Clarke, Stillingfleet, Tillotson and Bentley were associated, as liberal clergymen, with the social and economic interests of the bourgeois commercial order which had been served in the institution of the new dynasty. They were opposed, in an order of descending priority, to the power of freelance entrepreneurs and commercial freebooters, to the landed gentry, and to the power and prerogative of the court. Jacob describes how these social motives influenced the natural philosophy of the Boyle Lectures:

> Only a natural philosophy such as Newton's that embodied non-mechanical assumptions about Nature was compatible with the social philosophy of the Latitudinarians. Matter has to be dead and lifeless – passive – for only then could providence be said to operate and spiritual forces be made dominant in the natural order and in the affairs of men. If matter moved by its own inherent force, God would be rendered useless and men would pursue their interests unimpeded.[33]

Although this particular argument was aimed at the 'mechanicism' of a rival commerical ideology, based on Hobbesian moral oportunism and economic materialism,[34] the hegemony of the Latitudinarians was also threatened by another social group, namely the commonwealth or Country party, represented by men like John Toland, Walter Moyle, Anthony Collins and the Third Earl of Shaftesbury. In *The Friend* Coleridge described these men (in many respects the ideological ancestors of the rational dissenters of the 1790s) as 'pious Deists'.[35] He had himself inherited their interest in the political thought of Harrington, Milton and Algernon Sidney, as well as a pantheistic natural philosophy dated back to the cosmology of seventeenth-century radical sectaries like Gerard Winstanley.[36] Both Winstanley and Harrington had argued that matter possessed inherent life and motion, a belief transmitted to Toland and Shaftesbury (it is at the heart of Shaftesbury's rhapsodic dialogue *The Moralists*), as well as to the German poets and Naturphilosophers so keenly interested in the English Deists.[37] This transmission provides us with the genealogy of the 'One Life' theory so central to the thought of Priestley, Wordsworth and Coleridge.

In addition to being partisans of a country ideology opposed to the influence of urban commercial groups (be they radical Hobbists or establishment Latitudinarians), the commonwealthmen

> actively sought to strip the church of its political and social power and to enhance the power of parliament at the expense of King and Court. The Freethinking movement of the early eighteenth century represented in one sense a revival and continuation of traditional country opposition to the Court.[38]

The following pages will show that both Coleridge's idea of Pantisocracy and Wordsworth's 'perfect Republic of Shepherds and Agriculturists' (W Prose II 206) drew heavily on what might be termed a 'fundamentalist' interpretation of the commonwealth tradition, notably in terms of its agrarianism and pantheistic natural philosophy. The political vision of both writers in this period was considerably more extreme than the moderate, 'laissez-faire' principles which Priestley advocated in his essay on *The First Principles of Government* (1768). It should be remembered however, that Priestley's politics became more radical in response to the ferment of events in the 1790s.[39]

In his *Lectures on Revealed Religion* Coleridge opposed a version of the Harringtonian agrarian commonwealth to the corrupt and belligerent commercial order represented by Pitt's administration. He identified this 'republic of God's own making' with the millennial Kingdom of Christ on earth, the visionary goal of the 'One Life' ideal. Using the Mosaic theocracy and the communistic orders of the early churches as his models, Coleridge sought to adapt the seventeenth-century commonwealth ideology to the limited powers and marginalized social situation of a small group of 'saints'. The 'elect' groups which he celebrated in his poem of 1796, *Religious Musings* (PW I 111) would form the nucleus of such an agrarian commune, based on the moral teachings of Christ and propagating its pure republican manners through polemic, poetry and science. Such also was the ethic which Wordsworth and Coleridge advocated in the *Preface to Lyrical Ballads*, representing (with new literalism) a whole way of life in which the traditionally transcendent values of the *Civitas Dei* were integrated with the secularity of the *aeternitas mundi*.

The 'politics of imagination' can now be seen to have invoked the old European republican tradition, the eighteenth-century survival and dispersal of which has been so elegantly described by Franco Venturi in his *Utopia and Reform in the Enlightenment*.[40] Appealing to a virtuous economy and polity surviving at the heart of the modern state and the modern sensibility, it took as its model the 'real language of men in a state of vivid sensation' (W Prose I 118), of the shepherds and freeholders who 'hourly communicate with the best objects from which the best part of language is originally derived' (W Prose I 124). This heartland of virtue is neither a remote province nor an ahistorical utopia, however, but a reality sustained by the permanent and elementary forms underlying the 'quaint tricks', the 'vicious refinements' of modernity. There is here no sense that modern civil, economic or moral arrangements have progressed beyond those of Wordsworth's 'chosen vale' with its spartan manners. Underlying the hieroglyphics of 'poetic diction' or the mystificatory incantations of Anglican priestcraft are disclosed the stately spoken words of Wordsworth's 'grave Livers' (WPW 156 97), just as at the heart of the sprawling empire still lies the sustaining virtue of the mountain republic.

The fate of this civic ideal in the subsequent writing of Wordsworth, as well as Coleridge, was to be transposed from a political and moral challenge to a spiritual *consolation*. Coleridge, like many other more 'liberal' commentators came to regard the literal advocacy of pastoral and agricultural republicanism as a form of bigotry, an obdurate and primitivist inclination to an ideal of culture which was quite inadequate to the complexities of modernity. Whether his revised version of the civic ideal presented in the guise of the theory of Imagination in the *Biographia* did any better, will be the main issue at stake in part two below. At least until 1815, however, a vestigial respect for the participatory civic ideal prevented Coleridge from travelling the same road as Montesquieu or Kant, in inscribing the political and moral virtue of the republic in a noumenal realm which was permitted to give the rule to conduct only by proxy. The evanescence of this classical doctrine of politics is perhaps nowhere better represented than in Rousseau's *Discourse on the Origin of Inequality*, in which the violent contrast between the civil and the savage states is reproached, but only in an impotent and oblique manner, by the dedicatory panegyric to the ancient virtue of the Genevan republic. Coleridge's bid to save the 'One Life' vision from dispersal would succeed only at the cost of a concession which vitiated the continuing political efficacy of the civic tradition.

3

Agrarian Communism, Pantisocracy and the *Preface to Lyrical Ballads*

The source for Coleridge's second and third *Lectures on Revealed Religion*, Moses Lowman's *Dissertation on the Civil Government of the Hebrews* (1740), had been recommended by Joseph Priestley as an exemplary argument for the 'evidences' of Christianity, and was a work, as the editors note, 'much approved in orthodox as well as Dissenting circles' (Lects 1795 122). The presentation of contentious political argument under the aegis of Christian apologetics is a strategy which Coleridge repeated in these lectures, the radical force of agrarian communism being disguised as an attack on the atheistic opponents of revealed religion. Although it is significant that Coleridge actually denies the practicability of the Agrarian Law (a law commanding the 'levelling' or equalization of property) at the end of the sixth lecture, citing the 'render unto Caesar' text beloved of Christian quietists, it is clear both from the tone of his presentation of this 'Admirable Division of Property' among the Jews (Lects 1795 119) and from his advocacy of the Agrarian Law in *Religious Musings* (PW I p. 122, ll. 339–46) and in private correspondence, that he was exercising caution in the public expression of the ideal. In the years between 1795 and 1801 Coleridge persistently attempted to put his dream of Pantisocracy and agrarian communism into a practical form.

Citing Lowman's *Civil Government of the Hebrews* as 'an astonishing example of the vitality of Harringtonian ideas', Caroline Robbins suggests that its author had confused Harrington's *Oceana* with the theocratic republic of the ancient Jews.[1] In fact Lowman's work is closely based on another of Harrington's treatises republished in the Toland edition, the second book of the *Art of Lawgiving* (1659), which located the ideal of Oceana within the narrative of Christian eschatology.[2] Thus the basic principle of Coleridge's second lecture – that human proclivities to vice and self-interest can be tempered and ameliorated by equalizing property and providing a genuinely equable and respresentative government – reiterates a major theme of the *Art of Lawgiving*. Coleridge's political principles here are quite distinct from those of other contemporary radicals: from those of Rousseau, who regarded the civil state as essentially corrupt, the reflex of human imperfection; from Godwin's, who sought to build political upon individual liberty and who was opposed to all systems of political representation; and from those of many, like the followers of Brissot, of Thomas Paine or of Thelwall, who argued for the equalization of rights, but not property, perceiving the impracticability of the Agrarian Law in predominantly commercial societies.[3]

Harrington had endowed the eighteenth-century Commonwealthmen with a spiritualized politics verging on the heretical earthly paradise when he wrote 'the highest earthly felicity . . . is an equal and well-ordered Commonwealth'.[4] The Agrarian Law, instituted by God himself in the division-by-lot of the lands of the Canaanites, provided the key to an immutable republic based on inalienable tenure and entailment.[5] The institution of a fifty-year jubilee prevented accumulation, as did a total ban on commerce and usury.[6] The Mosaic constitution ensured a perfect balance between power (equal property rights), and authority (a genuinely representative government). The Congress or Assembly of 24 000 men was composed of a rotated militia representing the entire Jewish nation, balanced by an 'upper house' or Senate of 70 wise men (the Sanhedrin), who could deliberate and propose laws but not enact them; the Assembly would accept or reject these on the strength of a balloted vote.[7] This theoretically infallible model of political perpetuity stood in radical contrast to the traditional Polybian cycle in which governments by monarchy, oligarchy and democracy succeeded each other inexorably, as each form came to the end of its 'natural' life. Self-rule by the people in Assembly and Senate excluded monarchy and the 'jure divino' claims of priesthood, representing a perfect combination of religion and civil authority: the only authority worshipped by the citizens was God, the embodiment of the 'good orders of commonwealth' according to the law of nature.[8] In 1795, Coleridge considered the Levites to be a body of teachers who had no claims to superogatory authority over their fellow-citizens; although part three below will show the different interpretation to which they were susceptible in the 1829 *Constitution of the Church and State*. When the Jews committed the foulest crime of which human nature is capable, namely demanding a human monarch, it was the usurping authority of the priesthood which was to blame for inciting the people to idolatory; the Levites had been all along the weak link in an otherwise perfect and well-ordered commonwealth (Lects 1795, 133).

Christ's mission, according to Harrington, Lowman and Coleridge, was the returning of the Jews, and now also the Gentiles, to the pristine purity of the Mosaic republic. Or rather, to return them to a *purer* state by abolishing the flaw of priesthood which had vitiated its otherwise perfect constitution. Christ's twelve apostles figured the twelve tribes of Israel, his seventy disciples the seventy elders who composed the Sanhedrin. Here is Harrington's account of the perfection of the early church:

> So thus far the government of the church instituted by Christ was according unto the form instituted by Moses. But Christ in this form was king and priest, not after the institution of Moses, who separated the Levites unto the priesthood, but as before Moses, when the royal and priestly function was not separated, and after the order or manner of Melchizedeck.[9]

In his second lecture, Coleridge explains that Melchizedeck was an elected rather than a hereditary lawgiver, a priest of 'peace and love', in contrast to the warmongering Anglican clergy (Lects 1795 138). Only his title is misleading: in a theocracy there are strictly speaking no priests because all men are priests, according to the ideal of a perfect proportioning of power to authority. The point is analogous to the 'spiritualized' materialism of the 'One Life' theory; there is no spirit separate from matter, because matter is itself imbued with the power of spirit. Coleridge explained the political ramifications of this essential doctrine of authority:

> the very name (Priest) is no where applied to Christians in the new Testament except in one Text – and there it is said, Ye shall be all Priests – in the same sense as it is elsewhere – Ye shall be all Kings, and, I suppose, if we were all Priests and all Kings, it would be all one as if there were no Priest and no King. (Lects 1795 137–8)

To question the trenchancy of Coleridge's radicalism on the grounds that he was a 'Christian' rather than a 'Jacobin' is to miss the point of his endeavour to integrate the meaning of the words 'religion' and 'politics', meanings sundered by priestly hierophants and hirelings in order to mystify their usurped authority by 'jure divino' sanctions. In contrast to this 'differentiation of powers', the godliness of the 'republic of God's own making' was the result of its repudiation of all forms of ecclesiastical authority.[10] In *Religious Musings*, Coleridge linked this spiritualized agrarian common-wealth with Christ's millennial kingdom on earth:

> Return pure Faith! return meek Piety!
> The kingdoms of the world are your's: each heart
> Self-governed, the vast family of Love
> Raised from the common earth by common toil
> Enjoy the equal produce. Such delights
> As float to earth, permitted visitants!
> When in some hour of solemn jubilee
> The massy gates of Paradise are thrown
> Wide open, . . .

> > (PW I 122, ll. 339–46)

The tradition of eighteenth-century 'commonwealth' thought which derives from Harrington is clearly a major ingredient of this curious combination of Christian spirituality and 'levelling' radicalism, a tradition which Thelwall, commenting on the *Watchman*, found to be laden with 'the furious prejudices of the conventicle' and the 'outrageous violence' of 'the old sect in politics and morals' (CL I 212). If Divinity is embodied in a 'well-ordered commonwealth', as a soul in a body, then clearly the problem of human vice can be remedied by good orders of government which spiritualize and desensualize individuals. As Harrington expressed it in *A System of Politics* 'good orders make evil men good, and bad orders make good men evil'.[11] Coleridge preserves faith in the power of civil organization to tame errant passions in a manner that is not possible according to Godwin's system of rational appeal, which fails to allow for the greater forcefulness of passion over reason. Coleridge finds an economic and political explanation for human vice which offers an economic and political solution: 'The real source of inconstancy, depravity, and prostitution, is *Property*, which mixes with and poisons everything good – & is beyond doubt the Origin of all Evil' (CL I 214). But Property also offers the possibility of improvement, Coleridge announced in a November 1796 letter to Thelwall 'The origin of Property & the *mode of removing* it's evils – from the last Chapter of my Answer to Godwin, which will appear now in a few weeks – ' (CL I 253). The physical objects of the passions, property and its pandar imagination, are also the instruments of amelioration; the agrarian system of property advocated by the Pantisocrats will 'asphetarize' and extirpate the evils attendant on acquisition. In his *Monody on the Death of Chatterton*, Coleridge likened the well-ordered commonwealth to a dance:

> O'er the ocean swell
> Sublime of Hope I seek the cottag'd dell
> Where Virtue calm with careless step may stray;
> And, dancing to the moon-light roundelay,
> The wizard Passions weave an holy spell!

> (PW I 130, ll. 143–7)

Both Wordsworth and Coleridge considered that poetry itself partook of this order as the rhetorical equivalent of 'aspheterized' property, a strict economy of the passions. This was the advantage which Wordsworth discerned (in the 1798 *Essay on Morals*) in imaginative literature, that 'picture of human life' which has 'sufficient power to melt into our affections . . . to incorporate itself with the blood & vital juices of our minds', in contrast to 'publications in which we formally and systematically lay down rules for the actions of Men' (W Prose I 103). Poetry, like 'aspheterized' property, is a sensuous means of desensualizing the mind, directing its appeal to man as he *is*, a creature of passion and habit, rather than as he *ought* to be, according to Godwin, always exercising perfect rational preferences and receptive to rational dicta.[12] In *Religious Musings*, Coleridge emphasizes this equation between the aesthetic and the economic agents of amelioration, both in a sense offspring of Imagination:

> So Property began, twy-streaming fount,
> Whence Vice and Virtue flow, honey and gall.
> Hence the soft couch, and many-coloured robe,

The timbrel, and arched dome and costly feast,
With all the inventive arts, that nursed the soul
To forms of beauty, and by sensual wants
Unsensualized the mind, which in the means
Learnt to forget the grossness of the end,
Best pleasured with its own activity.

(PW I 116–17, ll. 204–12)

The declamatory, bombastic *Religious Musings* had still to learn 'manners truly republican' from its master, Milton, namely that poetry should be 'simple, sensuous and passionate'. But the integrative vision of the *Conversation Poems* and *Lyrical Ballads* would body forth a moment or synthesis between the aesthetic and civic ideals, a harmony between the poet and his community. The synthesis was momentary, for it would bifurcate into the sublimated aestheticism of *Biographia* volume two, and the Tory partisanship and poetic parochialism of the later Wordsworth.

The connection we have traced between the 'ethic of retirement' and a tradition of commonwealth radicalism should challenge a commonly-held notion that the 'private and domestic tone' of the *Conversation Poems* and *Lyrical Ballads* represented a Burkean 'shift from a public to a private focus' imbued with loyalist political significance.[13] This retreat from the political theatre was in part a response to censorship and ideological repression; but it should also be remembered that retirement had long been a rhetorical tactic, in the Horatian and Juvenalian idiom, of the literary opponents of the court and the commercial order in the eighteenth century. Agrarian republicanism and the poetry with which it was associated may be viewed as a fundamental and literal version of the 'Patriot' ideology (in the tradition of Pope's *Imitations of Horace* or Johnson's *London*), emerging from an oppositional 'country party' polemic pitting its impeccable moral vision against the exigencies of modernity and the burgeoning commercial empire.[14] Coleridge's *Morning Post* articles on the French Constitution in 1799–1800 show for the first time a cynical acceptance of the fact that the 'feudalistic' property relations and 'gothic balance' of the unreformed constitution might be taken, for pragmatic reasons, as an approximation of Harrington's agrarian balance (EOT I 48). But his letters before this date show a recurring desire from 'aspheterization' and the formation of an agrarian commune. The original scheme to found a Pantisocracy on the banks of the Susquehanna river was in part based upon Brissot de Warville's idealization of the American frontiersmen, on whom 'nature, education and habit had engraved the equality of rights'.[15]

This scheme was replaced in 1795 by the less ambitious project of founding a communal farm in Wales (CL I 150). By the time that Coleridge moved to Nether Stowey in late 1796, the ideal was centred on the person of Tom Poole, whose character was the inspiration for Wordsworth's 'Michael' (EY 322).[16] Poole would teach Coleridge the arts of husbandry whilst he continued to preach and write from the moral fortress of his 'cottage economy'. A combination of agriculture, domesticity and radical Christianity is the keynote of the project in this period, as is clear from a November 1796 letter to Charles Lloyd Snr.: 'Shall I not be an Agriculturist, an Husband, a Father, and a *Priest* after the order of *Peace*? an *hireless* Priest' (CL I 255). Even after the 'escape' to Germany, which Kelvin Everest regards as the culmination of Coleridge's effort to 'live in a manner that asserted his highest values',[17] Coleridge was planning a 'little colony' in Italy or the south of France, based no doubt upon the Spinozistic principles which absorbed him in late 1799 and 1800; the colony would be composed of Tobin, Humphry Davy, William and Dorothy Wordsworth, Southey and his own family (CL I 553–6). The move to Keswick in July 1800 should be seen as part of the same quest, and Coleridge was jealous of Wordsworth's discovery of the agrarian ideal in his own 'roots' amongst the freeholders of Westmoreland and Cumberland. 'His habits are more assimilated with the Inhabitants there', Coleridge wrote in March 1800, 'there he and his Sister are exceedingly beloved, enthusiastically' (CL I 582).

Coleridge, who unlike Wordsworth had spent his childhood 'In the great city, pent "mid cloisters dim"'' (PW I 242, l. 52), was unable to find the redemptive agency in his personal past; undeterred, he worked hard to compensate on the level of theory. Whilst in Germany he sketched an 'Essay on the Bauers', a history of slavery and serfdom, in a 1799 letter to Josiah Wedgwood (CL I 464–70). In December 1799 he recommended that Southey should write a 'History of Levellers and the Levelling Principle' with special application to Sparta, Crete and the Roman Agrarian Laws, in which, as was mentioned above, Thelwall had awakened public interest by his 1796 republication of Moyle's

Essay on the Roman State. Coleridge offered to write a 'philosophical introduction' to a work which he hoped would 'enlighten without offending' (CL I 544). This is an important point of comparison with the 'disguised' politics of the 1800 *Preface to Lyrical Ballads*: historical subject matter and judicious presentation of this 'History of Levelling' would hide the work's radicalism, so that 'Boys & Youths would read it with far different Impressions from their Fathers and Godfathers – and yet the latter find nothing alarming in the nature of the Work, it being purely Historical' (CL I 554).

The connection between such projects as these and the political ideology of the *Preface* is reinforced by Wordsworth and Coleridge's 1801 letter to Charles James Fox. The customary virtue of the Lakeland 'Statemen' (the local name for a freeholder) is associated with 'their little tract of land (which) serves as a kind of permanent rallying point for their domestic feelings'. Their civic virtue is manifest at the personal and linguistic, as well as the political levels, for the freehold ensures an inalienable self-possession inscribed as 'objects of memory in a thousand instances when, they would otherwise be forgotten' (EY 314–15). The effect of such a civic arrangement upon language is essential to the poetic theory and practice of the Lyrical Ballads, as has been shown by Frances Ferguson:

> What Wordsworth describes in rustic language is not a specific diction or syntactic ordonnance of words. Rather, rustic language is presented as a pattern of language which is self-enclosed – not in its limitation but in its self-circling processes. The nearly obsessive return to particular words, places and images in the poems of *Lyrical Ballads* is to be seen less as poverty than as an intensity which explores all aspects of the individual words and objects.[18]

The 'perfect Republic of Shepherds and Agriculturists' which Wordsworth found and celebrated as poet and 'hireless Priest' was imbued with the spirituality of the Harringtonian and Coleridgean models, rather than the secular rationalism of more recent republican experiments in France, for 'an equal and well-ordered commonwealth' was, in the case of the Israelites, 'the reign of God!'[19] All citizens are monarchs, priest or poets in such a commonwealth, a fact which is still evident in Wordsworth's 1810 account of the Lakeland clergymen, 'in clothing or in manner of life in no respect differing . . . except on the Sabbath-day' from other members of the community (W Prose II 200–1).

The 'chosen vale' upon which the poet looks down at the opening of the eighth book of the *Prelude* is implicitly distinguished from the 'false paradises' of literature (the Miltonic 'Tartarian Dynasties'), its inhabitants from the rustics of 'Arcadian Fastnesses' and the clowns of *The Winter's Tale* (Prelude 1805 viii, ll. 119–221). Although Wordsworth here alludes to the lines in book four of *Paradise Lost* where Milton favourably compares Eden to the 'false paradises', it seems that the mountain republic does not echo the untried perfection of pre-lapsarian Eden so much as the millennial perfection of Christ's reign on earth.[20] The subjects of this 'paradise' are subservient to none but 'God and Nature's single sovereignty' (Prelude 1805 ix 238), free from the modern blights of concentration in cities and division of labour:

> The heart of Man, a district on all sides
> The fragrance breathing of humanity,
> Man free, man working for himself, with choice
> of time, and place, and object;

> (Prelude 1805 viii, ll. 150–3)

In a fallen world this paradisical existence is contingent upon spartan manners and economy, the severity and industry of *Michael*, for example, whose son Luke goes to the bad as soon as he moves to the city.[21] But the consolation won by thus shouldering the burden of labour is the incarnation of a divine order, as Wordsworth makes clear in his literalizing of the image of the 'good shepherd'. The shepherd's 'heavenliness' is equated with his lonely and arduous work high in the mountains:

> . . . him have I described in distant sky,
> A solitary object and sublime,
> Above all height! like an aerial Cross,
> As it is station'd on some spiry Rock
> Of the Chartreuse, for worship. Thus was Man
> Ennobled outwardly before mine eyes . . .

> (Prelude 1805 viii, ll. 406–11)

Wordsworth transforms the priestly hieroglyphics, for which, in Coleridge's words, Christ had never been 'a physical body, but a phantom', into a vision of earthly redemption (Lects 1795 198). A similar troping of celestial language from a heavenly to an earthly sphere is evident in the above mentioned poem *Michael*. The spartan manners, incessant but self-fulfilling industry and habits of egalitarian respect which eighteenth-century travellers alike Dr Brown and Thomas Gray had admired in Grasmere and Keswick, are emblematized in this poem by the guiding light which shines from the window of Michael's cottage.[22] The light is a token of the family's 'easy industry', spinning, carding wool and repairing implements until well into the night:

> And from this constant light, so regular,
> And so far seen, the House itself, by all
> Who dwelt within the limits of the vale,
> Both old and young, was named THE EVENING STAR.

> (WPW 105–6, ll. 136–9)

The heavenly locus of the star has been translated to earth, although its light is no less 'heavenly' for that; and it is significant that the poem's metaphor for sublimity, the star, is discovered by the poet as a native growth of the valley. 'Poeticization' and the bestowing of 'religious' epithets is a collective responsibility, the 'secret ministry' of the community rather than an invention of the poet's, a point which recurs again and again in Wordsworth's receptivity to the language spoken by the lakelanders.

But the motif of the 'evening star' has a wider significance in Wordsworth's poetry of this period.[23] It returns the religious impulse to its civic origins in a tradition deriving ultimately, perhaps through the heterodoxy of a writer like Toland, from Cicero and Pliny, for whom the gods had been civic heroes deified amongst the stars or the forms of nature:

> Antiquity, being sure that Nature's Force,
> Would Brass and Marble Monuments consume,
> Did wisely its own History transmit
> To future Times by Heav'ns eternal Fires.[24]

The project of returning the gods to earth had been undertaken by these 'mythic' critics of religion, who feared their power becoming literally 'unearthly'. The Ciceronian 'naming of places' underlies the aim of Wordsworth's poetry, which dramatizes the act of naming, the bestowal of celestial titles, and emphasizes the emanation of such names from earthly virtue alone. In his own particular way Wordsworth shows in *Lyrical Ballads* the necessary interpenetration of spirit and matter, the 'One Life' of Coleridge or Beddoes or Davy. Poetic language sundered from its provenance in earthly passions and earthly orders is but 'a counter-spirit, unremittingly and noiselessly at work to derange, to subvert, to lay waste, to vitiate and to dissolve' (W Prose II 85).

Wordsworth's 'evening star', which Shelley in 1814 feared has set for ever[25] is replete with political and historical connotations which may only be briefly considered here. The evening star which, according to the *Prelude*, had presided over 'dances of liberty' in Calais in 1790, is seen twelve years later to rest only 'on England's bosom' (Prelude 1805 vi, ll. 380–1; WPW p. 241 Sonnet I). The patriotic significance of the star of liberty 'Thou, I think, should'st be my Country's emblem' (ibid. ll. 6–7) is qualified in the subsequent sonnets 'dedicated to National Independence and Liberty'. 'What we had then' is not what we have now, as sonnet xiii makes clear:

> Plain living and high thinking are no more:
> The homely beauty of the good old cause
> Is gone;
>
> (WPW p. 244, sonnet xiii, ll. 11–12)

The light which shines now only from Michael's secluded mountain cottage had its rising in the 'manners, virtue, freedom, power' of the John Milton whose 'soul was like a star, and dwelt apart' (WPW 244, sonnet xiv, l. 8) and the seventeenth-century commonwealthmen:

> The later Sidney, Marvel, Harrington,
> Young Vane, and others who called Milton friend.
> These moralists could act and comprehend: . . .
> Taught us how rightfully a nation shone
> In splendour: what strength was, that would not bend
> But in magnanimous meekness. France, 'tis strange,
> Hath brought forth no such souls as we had then.
>
> (WPW p. 244, sonnet xv, ll. 3–6, 8–10)

Perhaps the pathos evident in Wordsworth's treatment of the evening star is due to its rising and setting in another age: for all its moral and rhetorical power as a rebuke to courts and to cities, and its distrust of the social relations of the cash nexus, the political ideology which supported it was inadequate to the analysis of the new forces of industrial capitalism. If forced to make a choice between a 'corrupt' constitution, the power of which was at least apportioned to real property, and the new democratic structures of political authority based on the enfranchisement of the bourgeoisie and, ultimately, the urban proletariat, it would, and did, choose the former, thereby betraying its noblest reformist goals. As Coleridge cynically put it in late 1799 'the more delicate superstition of ancestry' might still counteract the 'grosser superstition of wealth' (EOT I 55). We know the negative connotations of the word 'superstition' for him in this period: but nevertheless the qualified acceptance of the former expedient paved the way for a feudalistic and hierarchical interpretation of agrarian republicanism. Both Zera Fink and J. B. A. Pocock have shown the importance of this qualification in the ideology of eighteenth-century classical republicanism: Milton, Harrington and Algernon Sidney were seen as idealists whose vision had largely been realized in the 'gothic balance' and 'ancient virtue' of the 1688 constitution. As the authority of the great Whig Oligarchs (whom E. P. Thompson has called 'those great constitutional brigands')[26] was challenged by the growth of a democratic consciousness, the critical and reformist vision of the 'One Life' became either, as in the later work of Wordsworth, a noble mask superimposed upon the wizened features of the Tory landed interest, or, in Coleridge, the redemptive agency of 'cultivation', increasingly defined in opposition to, even in defiance of, the civic and political realm.

4

The *Preface to Lyrical Ballads* and Coleridge's Interpretation in *Biographia Literaria*

Despite the lengths it goes to disguise the fact, the *Preface* which Wordsworth and Coleridge collaborated on in 1800 should be read in the context of agrarian republicanism which we have traced above. After all, the 'Essay on the Elements of Poetry' projected by Coleridge in October 1800 'would in reality be a *disguised* System of Morals and Politics' (CL I 632). Whatever objections Coleridge would raise after the publication of Wordsworth's 1802 amendments, indicative of an important shift in his own thinking about culture and politics, the 1800 version at least seems to represent a coalition between the thought of the two men. The *Biographia* explains how Coleridge and Wordsworth approached the Lyrical Ballads from different directions, but their respective roles as 'naturalist' and 'supernaturalist' poets should be read as symptomatic of their effort to integrate rather than divide the natural and spiritual realms, in accordance with the 'One Life' ambitions of their republican/unitarian milieu (BL II 6–7). The subsequent rift between an 'aesthetic' Coleridge and a 'parochial' Wordsworth should not blind us to the fact that until late 1800 *both* men regarded the poet as a 'man speaking to men', and one whose rhetoric was based on the 'real language of men in a state of vivid sensation'. We will examine the significance of the 1802 amendments below, but first of all will consider the *Preface* as it stood in 1800.

The *Preface's* fundamental radicalism, and one which survived Coleridge's 1815 recuperation, was its criticism of 'Poetic Diction'. Neoclassical poetic machinery, rhetorical bravura and sentimental set-pieces seemed to subject experience to an arbitrary and appropriative order, the literary equivalent of the 'Lorraine glasses'

46

which allowed connoisseurs of the Picturesque to view the fluxile landscape bathed in the light of Lorraine's paintings.[1]

In his discussion of the difference between the acceptable effect of enhancement produced by metre, and the unacceptable coercion exercised on the reader by 'poetic diction', Wordsworth uses an explicitly political language. Metre is based on a contractual agreement, 'certain laws, to which the Poet and Reader both willingly submit', whilst poetic diction is 'unrepresentative' insofar as it betokens the poet's having usurped an authority to which he has no rights: 'the reader is utterly at the mercy of the Poet respecting what imagery or diction he may choose to connect with the passion' (W Prose I 144). Poetic diction is the symptom of 'a whole multitude of causes' which have both engendered it and conditioned its acceptance; the political language is no fortuitous metaphor. Urbanization; division of labour and its corollary, uniformity of occupation; the moral enervation caused by 'rapid communication of intelligence'; all are familiar targets of an oppositional jeremiad against courts, cities and commerce (W Prose I 128). 'Savage torpor' is the consequence of abandoning participatory virtue as the political subject becomes transformed into the *object* of arbitrary power. The alternative proposal of the *Preface* seeks to invest rhetorical authority in a more 'representative' language, expression of the affective and economic habits of 'low and rustic life' (W Prose I 124). Wordsworth is throughout vague about the nature of the 'civil arrangement' determining the Lakelanders as paradigms of his 'common language'. It is significant that the word 'republican' is omitted, a term which the *Guide to the Lakes* (1810) uses with moral aplomb, although now in a severely qualified fashion (W Prose II 206). Perhaps the *Preface*'s lack of specificity permitted the sort of willful misinterpretation exemplified by Coleridge's 1810 comment recorded by Crabb Robinson:

> Wishing to avoid an undue regard to the high and genteel in society, Wordsworth had unreasonably attached himself to the low, so that he himself erred at least. He should have recollected that verse being the language of passion, and passion dictating energetic expressions, it became him to make his subjects and style accord.[2]

In this anticipation of his argument in volume two of the *Biographia*, Coleridge ignores the fact that the Agrarian commonwealth of the Lakes excludes both social and linguistic, as well as economic, hierarchies; he effectively reinscribes Wordsworth's ideal within a traditional social and rhetorical structure. 'Social vanity' plays no part in the expression of the Lakelanders; from the 'sameness and narrow circle of their intercourse . . . they convey their feelings and notions in simple and unelaborated expression' (W Prose I 124). The language which Wordsworth seeks to emulate arises 'from repeated experience and regular feelings' and is 'a more permanent and a far more philosophical language than that which is frequently substituted for it by Poets' (W Prose I 124). Coleridge would take special exception to this pointed and subversive use of the authority of 'philosophical' in the *Biographia*.

The language of the Lakelanders is 'philosophical' because such men 'hourly communicate with the best objects from which the best part of language is originally derived' (W Prose I 124). Such objects are not just sticks and stones, or even mountains, as those who see Wordsworth as a perpetrator of the Cratyllic fallacy have tended to argue.[3] The redemptive objects and the passions with which they are inextricably involved are rather connected to the culture of agrarian freeholders, sharply distinguishing the habits and language of such men from those of farm labourers or mill workers. The notion of equally proportioned and entailed property freehold, the 'little tract of land' as a bulwark against accumulation, corruption and arbitrary authority emerged from the Commonwealth tradition, which Harrington had defined as a state in which 'the whole people be landlords, or hold the lands so divided amongst them, that no one man, or number of men, within the compass of the few, or aristocracy, overbalance them'.[4] Many of the poems in *Lyrical Ballads* are psychological studies of the Harringtonian dictum that 'good orders make evil men good, bad orders make good men evil'. If it be objected that many of Wordsworth's poems describe solitary, a-social individuals, vagrants, mad mothers and leech-gatherers, and *not* virtuous and industrious freeholders like *Michael*, then it might be stressed that this is a case of the exceptions proving the rule. The exceptions show the efficacy of 'good orders' in action by dramatizing their redemptive, healing quality. For example, the almost threatening indifference of *The Old Cumberland Beggar*, his utter dependence and uselessness to the society in which he lives, have been metamorphosed by time and custom into a kind of 'secret ministry' quite invisible to the 'bourgeois democratic' social reformer who would clamp him in the workhouse and make him earn his bread. The beggar's role is thus analogous to that of 'the little tract of land':

> . . . The villagers in him
> Behold a record which together binds
> Past deeds and offices of charity,
> Else unremembered, and so keeps alive
> The kindly mood in hearts which lapse of years.

> (WPW 444, ll. 88–92)

Charity itself, like the husbandry of the stony tracts of land, embodies the agency of 'good orders': 'the mild necessity of use compels/To acts of love' (ibid., ll. 99–100). Independence is a gift of an equable and homeostatic commonwealth, of a mutual *dependence* determined by the balance of power with authority. Inalienable tenure ensures the transmission of this ideal authority-structure in time, a point which Wordsworth emphasized in his *Guide to the Lakes*:

> Neither high-born nobleman, knight or esquire, was here; but many of these humble sons of the hills had a consciousness that the land, which they walked over and tilled, had for more than five hundred years been possessed by men of their name and blood.   (W Prose II 206)

Often Wordsworth pitched his account of the 'good orders' of the mountain republic in the past perfect, however, and in the stories of characters like Margaret in *The Ruined Cottage* or the Ewebanks in *The Brothers*, there is an elegaic note attesting to the attenuation of the ideal by the encroachments of the commercial order. Coleridge also acknowledged this in his second *Lay Sermon*, which will be discussed below. It is a work which sounds the death-knell of his former idealization of landed property as the balance of dominion, now abandoned to the perception that market forces have undercut real property, dictating the fluctuating value of rents. The Wordsworth of the *Two Addresses to the Freeholders of Westmoreland* (1818) would cling obdurately to the landed interest, but a more interesting development was evident in the work of his early and middle years. Seeking to internalize the inalienable tenure of the freehold, he psychologized the traditional forms of transmission and continuity examined above into an order of memory, which in the form of the *Prelude*'s 'Spots of Time' became the agent of redemption. The internalization of a civic order into an ideal of personal 'cultivation' standing apart from the social domain is an important element in Coleridge's developing cultural theory, a theme which will constitute much of parts two and three below.

Subsequent developments notwithstanding, the Freeholder rather than the poet was still the 'hero' of the 1800 *Preface*; his language, based on regular contact with 'the best objects from which the best part of language originally derives' is still the more philosophical of the two. This is a political and not a hypostatized aesthetic language which considers men with reference to 'those points in which they resemble each other rather than manifestly differ'. The poet's communication with such men, and indeed his participation in their civic arrangements (Wordsworth's cottage and plot of land at Grasmere are significant in this connection) will produce 'a class of Poetry . . . well adapted to interest mankind permanently, and not unimportant in the multiplicity and in the quality of its moral relations' (W Prose I 120).

This emphasis is beginning to shift, probably at Coleridge's behest, in the 1802 amendments to the *Preface*, as well as subsequent alterations up to 1850, notably in terms of Wordsworth's new stress on the role of the poet and the 'purpose' of the poems. Poems which in 1800 had sought to 'enlighten', to 'exalt' the taste and 'ameliorate' the affections of the reader, by the time of the 1838 alterations were aimed rather at 'strengthening' and 'purifying' (W Prose I 126–7). The legacy of the 'good orders of commonwealth' is now no longer a challenge, a rebuke, to the urbane establishment but rather a *confirmation* of its authority as it stands and as it must continue to stand against the meddling of reformers and rationalizers. Radical and conservative positions dovetail in this period as the moral force of contrast because a covert complicity between the agrarian ideal and Tory ideology. The transition is captured perfectly in a passage from the *Guide to the Lakes* where the 'feudal' proprietor is theorized as the link between the agrarian ideal, now reduced virtually to the status of fiction, and the conditions of political modernity:

Venerable was the transition, when a curious traveller, descending from the heart of the mountains, had come to some ancient manorial residence in the more open parts of the Vales, which, through the rights attached to its proprietor, connected the almost visionary mountain republic he had been contemplating with the substantial frame of society as existing in the laws and constitution of a mighty empire.

(W Prose II 206–7)

In the 1802 amendments to the *Preface*, however, the political shift is as yet unhinted at, for the predominant influence upon it is Coleridge's bid to transform the paradigm of 'common language' from a political to an aesthetic locus, to ask the question 'What is a Poet?'

Coleridge's attempt to redefine the 1800 *Preface*'s definition of philosophical language has too often been read according to the unhistorical terms of an aesthetic 'correction' of a mistaken mimetic theory by an 'expressive' poetic characteristic of the properly romantic view of art.[5] Coleridge's attempt to discover, in his formulation of the poetic imagination, a transcendental locus for the 'common language' was chronologically related to the period when he began a series study of German Transcendentalism and aesthetics.[6] Kant's account of the autonomy of the art-work in his *Critique of Judgement* and Schiller's distinction between the *naive* and *sentimental* in poetry undoubtedly played an important part in his effort to extrapolate an autonomous 'poetic passion', a property of the poet in the act of creation, from the 'philosophical' language of the farmers and shepherds to whom Wordsworth was connected by an accident of birthplace. Coleridge found in Schiller a concern with defining the aesthetic condition as one which sublimated political determinations:

Poetic genius ought to have strength enough to rise with a free and innate activity above all the *accidental* hindrances which are inseparable from every confined condition, to arrive at a representation of humanity in the absolute plentitude of its powers.[7]

Coleridge's attempt to define poetic imagination as a centralized and 'common' language was a response to a trait in the 1800 *Preface* and in Wordsworth's shorter poems, which, he feared, 'he wrote at times too much with a sectarian Spirit, in a sort of Bravado' (CN I 1546). 'Sectarianism' in the context of what I have described as 'the Whig double standard' could mean more than one political position; Wordsworth's poems might be appropriated by the Tory landed interest for their opposition to the commercial order, or by the post-war radicals for their egalitarian and republican principles. But behind Coleridge's argument in the *Biographia* was doubtless the fear that the *Preface* and the *Lyrical Ballads* might play into the hands of the radicals, a fear very nearly confirmed by the republication of Southey's *Wat Tyler* in 1817, an incident discussed elsewhere.

The ideological significance of the *Preface* in the early nineteenth century is a complicated matter; both liberal and Tory commentators seemed confused as to the bearing of the work, as the relevant *Edinburgh* or *Quarterly* Reviews show.[8] The liberal Francis Jeffrey, for instance, stressed that Wordsworth's ideal of a 'philosophical' language was an eccentric attempt to preserve a defunct idiom, or a subversive bid to imitate the language of a subordinate class; like Coleridge in the remark recorded by Crabb Robinson (note 82 above) he considered Wordsworth's 'uniformitarian' idea of community as a failure to comprehend the fact of class differentiation in modern society:

> His composition, in short, will be like that of a person who is attempting to speak in an obsolete or provincial dialect; he will betray himself by expressions of occasional purity and elegance, and exert himself to efface that impression by passages of unnatural meanness or absurdity.[9]

William Hazlitt also criticized Wordsworth's idiosyncratic and egregarious egotism, which he associated with Rousseauesque primitivism. Based on the democratic principles of the French Revolution, Wordsworth's 'levelling muse' would steamroller the eminence and distinction of all but its author: 'a thorough adept in this school of poetry and philanthropy . . . does not even like to share his reputation with his subject; for he would have it all proceed with his own power and originality of mind'.[10] For Hazlitt, only an urbane language would do to express the 'common sense' of an increasingly urbanized and metropolitan culture, so that Wordsworth's championing of the virtues of a primitive rustic community was really no more than a mask for his egotistical refusal to submit to common values. People took no interest in Wordsworth because he took so little interest in them.[11] Another, more sympathetic, critical reading which may have influenced Coleridge was that of John Stoddart in the *British Critic*; like his fellow-Scot Adam Ferguson, he was aware of the value of the Lakeland community as a 'common scene of occupation' but feared that it had been attentuated to a point beyond the possibility of regeneration:

> Mr Wordsworth seems to be peculiarily well situated for the subjects of such a study. The vicinity of the Lakes in Cumberland and Westmoreland (the scene of most of his poems) is chiefly inhabited by an order of men nearly extinct in other parts of England.[12]

All these views really demanded a return to 'correct' standards of poetic language, associated with an educated and polished class; as Adam Smith put it whilst criticizing the homely style of the Scots vernacular poet Allan Ramsay the elder, 'it is the duty of a poet to write like a gentleman', a remark copied by Coleridge into his notebook in August 1801.[13] It will be argued below that Coleridge was not much happier with the 'common sense' standards defined by either Hazlitt or any of the Scots reviewers than he was with Wordsworth's 'real language of men', but nevertheless his objections in the *Biographia* should be considered in the light of a shared perception of the evanescence and eccentricity of the language of the Freeholders.

As early as July 1802, Coleridge had resolved to act as 'arbitrator between the old School and the New School' in matters poetical (CL II 830); this in principle involved showing that 'philosophical language' was the language of the poet and not his subjects. Wordsworth's 1802 amendments show an amusing tug-of-war between the views of the two men. When he defines the poet as 'a man speaking to men', for instance, he is led into a string of qualifications, in effect a Coleridgean special pleading for the authority of the poet. But when Wordsworth defines poetic passion as 'far from being the same as [those] produced by real events', he finds that the language of specifically poetic passion 'falls short of that which is uttered by men in real life' (W Prose I 138). Language evolved from the poet's 'fancy or imagination' is inferior to that which is 'the emanation of reality and truth' (W Prose

I 139); and 'dramatic poets of composition are defective, in proportion as they deviate from the real language of nature, and are coloured by a diction of the Poet's own, either peculiar to him as an individual Poet or belonging simply to Poets in general' (W Prose I 142). Given the 1800 *Preface*'s equation of poetic diction with a form of arbitrary power, it is clearly not easy for Wordsworth to implement Coleridge's suggestions. 'Emotion recollected in tranquillity' has been as far as Wordsworth will take the agency of an 'autonomous' poetic passion, and even this falls far short of Coleridge's account of the poet's relations to his subject, in the case of Shakespeare.

> [The Poet] himself meanwhile unparticipating in the passions, and actuated only by that pleasurable excitement, which had resulted from the energetic fervor of his own spirit in so vividly exhibiting, what it had so accurately and profoundly contemplated.
>
> (BL II 21)

Little wonder that Coleridge was so dissatisfied with Wordsworth's 1802 amendments. Writing to Sotheby that July, Coleridge sketched what would become the theory of metre expounded in the *Biographia*: 'Poetry justifies, as *Poetry* independent of any other Passion, some new combinations of Language, and *commands* the omission of many others allowable in other compositions' (CL II 812). Coleridge replaces Wordsworth's pastoral sketch with a 'portrait of the artist'; however much he might protest in the *Preface* against 'poetic diction', the fact remains that he is a poet writing poems. The most salient reminder of this, Coleridge points out, is the fact that the 'selected' and metrical form of Wordsworth's poetic language is as sharply distinguished from everyday speech as the poet's education and self-consciousness is distinguished from the manners of the Lakelanders amongst whom he has sought to disguise himself.

Coleridge's subsequent influence upon the Wordsworthian definition of community can be traced from the 1802 letter to John Wilson, with its account of the poet's necessary eminence (EY 352–8), to the *Essays on Epitaphs* written initially for Coleridge's 1809 *Friend* (W Prose II 45–119). The move here from the 'little tract of land' to the churchyard is significant, replacing the 'real language of men in a state of vivid sensation' with 'the general language of humanity as connected with the subject of death'! (W Prose II 57). A Unitarian sensibility has given way to the traditional Anglican 'separation of powers', for Wordsworth's epitaphs harmonize with the Coleridgean idealization of the country church as a 'germ of civilization' and his account, in chapter eleven of the *Biographia*, of the exemplary trusteeship afforded by ecclesiastical, as opposed to lay, property (BL I 227). A similar paradigm underlies the resigned and religiose pronouncements of the Pedlar and Parson in the 1814 *Excursion*'s lengthy panegyric of the 'churchyard amongst the mountains' (Bks 5 and 6). As Kenneth MacLean has pointed out, Wordsworth fluctuated between a 'Coleridgean' ecclesiastical ideal and a Tory prediliction for the feudal order: Wordsworth slips from property to the Church in the 1814 *Excursion*. The only mention of property as a basis for the affections in the *Excursion* is the Wanderer's birthplace, a small farm. But the *Pass of Kirkstone* (1817) and the *Freeholders of Westmoreland* (1818) restore the principle.[14] Wordsworth's feudalistic interpretation of the constitution in 1818 is significant as a 'Neo-Harrington' reorientation of the ideal of agrarian communism underlying the 1800 *Preface*. In a sense the epitaph symbolizes the values of the ancient feudal family which Wordsworth now found conveniently to hand in the genealogy of Lord Lowther, the Tory member for Westmoreland: the language of epitaphs is a point of communion between the living and the dead, permanent, traditional, representative and above all, sincere.

Coleridge's dissatisfaction with Wordsworth's otiose brand of Anglicanism and its close connection with the Tory landed interest, which he regarded as having abandoned its paternalist social obligations, will emerge in the following pages, especially in part three. The historical complacency of this alliance would be challenged to some extent by the liberal 'Broad Church Movement' and the Christian Socialists, both indebted to Coleridge's thought.[15] The vapid traditionalism of the position to which Wordsworth had moved from his marginalized radical stance is summed up in the aridity which determines his idea of community in 1810: 'to be born and to die are the two points in which all men feel themselves to be in absolute coincidence' (W Prose II 57).

5

Wordsworth in the
Biographia Literaria

Coleridge's critical 'tour de force' in the second volume of the
Biographia had the intention and the effect of imbuing with
respectability a poet whose work had been the object of critical
debate for almost two decades; one of the book's opening
promises had been to settle 'the long continued controversy
concerning the true nature of poetic diction' (BL I 5). Coleridge
employed a dual strategy to this end. Seeking to divide the poems
from the *Preface*, as the kernel from the shell, he reconstructed the
Preface's arguments so as to bring them into line with critical
orthodoxy, or at least to show that the reviewers had been pursuing
a shadow, if not entirely of their own making, then at least projected
by Wordsworth's failure to describe adequately the purpose of his
poems. Wordsworth had really sought to define a common idiom, a
'lingua communis' conforming to received notions of poetic
propriety, which he had mistakenly dubbed 'the real language of
men'. Coleridge wishes to present a *Preface* conforming to critical
principles which also sought (successfully, he suggests) to correct
the hyperbole and mannerism of late-eighteenth century poetic
diction. The ghost of a 'jacobinical' Wordsworth is thus laid to
rest, a ghost which had informed Francis Jeffrey's influential
insinuation in 1802; Wordsworth's attempt 'to copy the sentiments
of the lower orders is implied in his resolution to copy their
style.'[1]

Having brought Wordsworth in from the margins, Coleridge
then proceeds to conscript his poetic achievement in the service of
his own revisionist theory of culture. Denigrating the adequacy of
'common sense' as a criterion for poetic value, he emphasizes the
individuality and inimitability of Wordsworth's genius, especially
as manifest in the meditative poems like the *Immortality Ode*. The
'ideal poetry' adumbrated by Coleridge is aloof from the civic
world of the 'lingua communis' and abrogates to itself a quasi-
religious authority.

The first part of Coleridge's reinterpretation depends upon a denial of what Roger Sharrock has called Wordsworth's 'Revolt against Literature'.[2] He is therefore concerned to show that Wordsworth's fierce manifesto was an overreaction rather than a misnomer. In justifiably attacking the false refinement of a particular form of poetic diction he had attacked poetic diction *per se*; why prove that an ape is not Newton before proving that it is not a man? In a sense Coleridge bases his own critical authority on a denial of Wordsworth's critical acumen, whilst at the same time deriving the essence of that authority, namely his distinction between Fancy and Imagination, from his intuitive response to Wordsworth's poetry. Coleridge can know Wordsworth critically better than Wordsworth knows himself, although that knowledge derives ultimately from the poetic *performance* of the latter. The overreaction which the *Preface* typifies is characteristic of the young men of the age, but fortunately for posterity the poet Wordsworth has been the mouthpiece for an impulse purer than that of the critic, whose productions show the tarnish of the times. Had Wordsworth put into practice the precepts of his manifesto, two-thirds of the beauties of his poetry would have been excluded (BL II 106). The 'timelessness' of the poems – and by imputation the authority of Coleridge as 'transcendental' critic grounding his poetics on *principles*, in contrast to the ephemeral and opportunistic polemicizing of the reviewers – must be defended on grounds more absolute than had been attempted hitherto. Coleridge would have had particularly in mind the laborious list of precedents, a canon of poetic geniuses existing in problematic relationship with their times, which Wordsworth had amassed in the 1815 *Essay, Supplementary to the Preface* in order to rationalize his own problems and boost his morale (W Prose III 55–107. Coleridge also describes Wordsworth's fame as 'belonging to another age', despite the 'political' paradigm of the *Preface* which had bound his genius to a particular place and to the 'shadowy flux of time'. Like the poems in Boethius' *Consolation of Philosophy*, the Lyrical Ballads

> might even be referred to a purer age, but that the prose, in which they are set, as jewels in a crown of lead or iron, betrays the true age of the writer.
>
> (BL II 143)

Coleridge approves of the tenor of Wordsworth's project, his attempt to define a language of essential humanity overriding the plethora of specialized jargons which characterizes modernity, but fears that his vehicle is inappropriate in its bid to discover the immanence of the ideal in a politically defined, rather than an aesthetic or religious, community. Upholding the virtues of an agrarian republic betokens a sectarianism which excludes an adequate and genuinely 'representative' cultural ideal.

There is still a civic impulse to Coleridge's replacement of the Freeholder by the poet as cultural paradigm; it is only when the poet assumes an arbitrary and 'traditionalist' language and power at the expense of a communal and representative role that the principle becomes authoritarian. Writing now as a 'metropolitan' critic, based in Highgate rather than in the hills of Cumbria, Coleridge discovers the redemptive agency of 'good orders', mutual interdependence, the balance of the parts and the whole, embodied in poetic symbol rather than in a political or economic community. The radical project of disabusing property, that old Adam of the race, of its corrupting control over the passions of men by political means has been transformed, in this passage from the 1811 Shakespeare Lectures, into an aesthetic and religious project:

> Both poetry and religion throw the object of deepest interest to a distance from us, and thereby not only aid our imagination but in a most important manner subserve the interest of our virtues; for that man is indeed a slave, who is a slave to his own senses, and whose mind and imagination cannot carry him beyond the distance which his hand can touch, or even his eye can reach.
>
> (SC II 147)

A similar idea of the 'desensualizing' agency of imagination informed the 1796 poem *Religious Musings*, but the significant difference here is that the political goal of 'aspheterizing' property had been dropped, leaving the aesthetic aim which had formerly accompanied it standing in all its empty splendour as an *alternative* to political idealism. A significant bifurcation of the agrarian and Pantisocratic ideal is evident in the developing thought of Wordsworth and Coleridge which has been already hinted at. If Wordsworth had adapted it into a feudalistic apologia for the landowning interest, opposed to the apostles of democracy, and had thereby lost the end of egalitarianism in the means, the proportioning of political power to property, Coleridge had maintained the end, the equality of all men in Reason and Imagination, but willingly sacrificed the political means by which equality could be anything more than a metaphor. As Raymond Williams has expressed it, culture thus became a good clause in a bad treaty, and poetry a panacea and consolation rather than a representative and progressive energy.

For Coleridge in the *Biographia*, the *Preface*'s linguistic paradigm produces a 'doubtful moral effect' (BL II 42); far from being dependent on the language and ordonnance of the 'market, wake, high-road or plough-field', the poet must embody the professional, academic values of 'grammar, logic and psychology' (BL II 81). The cultivated canon of Dante, Scaliger and the Italian poets of the Seicento are evoked to demonstrate the perspicuity of Sir Joshua Reynolds' dictum that good taste is contingent upon a submissive study of good models. Coleridge goes so far as to adapt the Burkean argument-by-presumption: '*presume* these to be the best, the *reputation* of which has been matured into *fame* by the consent of ages. For wisdom always has a final majority, if not by conviction, yet by acquiescence' (BL II 36n). Aristotle, Horace and Quintilian are variously cited as classical authorities for this gentlemanly standard, of which Hooker, Bacon, Jeremy Taylor, Burke and even Algernon Sidney (now recuperated into the defence of an establishment which represents the noblest kind of compromise with republicanism) are the English exemplars (BL II 55).

In order to show the 'old School' that Wordsworth's poetry is really only singing an old song in a new way, rather than a new song, according to the Socratic precept cited in his 1817 letter to Liverpool (CL IV 762), Coleridge attempts to place it within a traditional vein of pastoralism, offering an analytic account of the three legitimate orders of pleasure produced by this genre. The first is derived from 'the naturalness, in *fact*, of the things represented', the second from the 'apparent naturalness of the *representation*, as raised by an imperceptible infusion of the author's own knowledge and talent', the third in effect from the sense of superiority with which members of a more elevated class contemplate the rude antics of their social inferiors (BL II 43). Wordsworth manifestly refused all three in his *literal* advocacy of the manners of rustics, rejecting outright the three pastoral modes.

But Coleridge aims, with this typology of pastoral pleasures, to demonstrate the false basis of the *Preface*'s claim to originality and innovation; despite these false claims, the *Lyrical Ballads* themselves are successful to the extent to which they conform to the second order of pastoral pleasure, the 'apparent' naturalness infused by the author's own genius, rather than deriving from his subjects. For this reason they conform to the criteria of a *Lingua Communis*, dependent not upon the accidents of birth or abode, or any set of property-rights, but upon education and the laws of grammar, logic and psychology, values which descend and permeate from a common cultural centre rather than emerging from the manners and language of any part of the whole. For 'Anterior to cultivation the lingua communis of every country, as Dante has well observed, exists every where in parts, and no where as a whole' (BL II 56).

This redefinition has the effect of putting the disinterested wisdom of the 'common language' beyond the reach of the common people; it is now defined *for*, and not *by* them. Coleridge justifies this by demolishing the 'economic' basis of Wordsworth's 1800 argument. The language of rustics, far from being an 'hourly communication with the best objects from which the best part of language derive' is based on a pragmatic and dependent relationship to the object-world which may only be remedied by the educative agency of aesthetic and religious culture. Coleridge's 'metropolitan' argument here assimilates some common current attitudes to country life, the most famous of which must be Hazlitt's opinion that 'all country people hate each other'. 'Their egotism becomes more concentrated, as they are more insulated, and their purposes more inveterate as they have less competition to struggle with', Hazlitt wrote in *The Round Table*.[3] The lack of sympathy for others manifested by country people is the equivalent of the poetical egotism of their champion, Wordsworth. In a similar way, citing the parsimonious dispensation of poor relief by farmers as an example of 'how selfish, sensual, gross and hard-hearted' country people are, Coleridge pours scorn upon the ennobling effects of the 'objects' with which they hourly communicate:

> The few things, and modes of action, requisite for his bodily conveniences, would alone be individualized; while all the rest of nature would be expressed by a small number of confused, general terms.
>
> (BL II 53)

Coleridge imputes that the *Preface* perpetrated a mistaken view of language which limits human culture to the accidents of 'occupation and abode', the trait in Wordsworth which he denounces in an August 1820 letter to Thomas Allsop as 'this inferred dependency of the human soul on accidents of Birthplace & Abode' (CL V 95). He is implying that willing, meditation and reflection are conceptual activities quite unconnected with the practical or social sphere. The passage which follows the above establishes a definition of culture contingent upon a separation from work and economic matters, anticipating his theorization of the Clerisy, a professional intellectual caste at the centre of the 1829 *Constitution of the Church and State*. The difference between freeholders, mechanics or labourers is implicitly elided by 1815; all partake of the designation 'uneducated man', the base of an authoritarian pyramid:

> The best part of human language, properly so called, is derived from reflection on the acts of the mind itself. It is formed by a voluntary appropriation of fixed symbols to internal acts, to processes and results of imagination, the greater part of which have no place in the consciousness of uneducated man; though in a civilized society, by imitation and passive remembrance of what they hear from their religious instructors and other superiors, the most uneducated share in the harvest which they neither sowed or reaped.
>
> (BL II 54)

The irony of Coleridge's closing metaphor of agricultural labour passes a silent comment on this passage. Legitimate consciousness is the exclusive property of those who can afford the leisure and independence for reflection, although as we will see in considering the second *Lay Sermon*, Coleridge increasingly regarded the virtue of conceptual independence as the property of a professional intellectual class (rather than the newly-capitalized gentry) which should be endowed by the nation. Given the 'immethodical' language of 'uneducated man', in contrast to whom the 'man of method' of the 1818 *Friend* is master of the object-world and possessor of the Idea (Friend I 448–57), it follows that the *Preface* has perpetrated a serious breach of critical decorum and good sense by suggesting that poets should imitate 'the rude and unpolished manners and discourse of their inferiors' (BL II 42–3).

The *Preface*'s failure is linked with a more insidious tendency, that of 'literary Jacobinism', a charge from which it is ultimately acquitted. The wilful inversion of social hierarchies and values is discussed in chapter 23 in relation to the drama of *Don John*:

> its popularity, consists in the confusion and subversion of the natural order of things in their causes and effects: namely, in the excitement of surprise by representing the qualities of liberality, refined feeling, and a nice sense of honour . . . in persons and in classes where experience teaches us least to expect them; and by rewarding with all the sympathies which are the due of virtue, those criminals whom law, reason and religion have excommunicated from our esteem.
>
> (BL I 221)

The egalitarianism and exemplary virtue which Wordsworth described in the economy, manners and language of the Lakelanders is shown to be one which the poet *intended* rather than found, the literalization of a poetic metaphor. Coleridge makes no attempt to recuperate the agrarian republicanism of the *Preface* as a fundamentalist example of the virtues of the Tory landowners, in the way that Wordsworth did in the *Guide to the Lakes* or the *Freeholders of Westmoreland*. One exception is made which renders his condemnation of the Lakelanders all the more remarkable. Having declared in chapter seventeen that as a rule rustics are 'selfish, sensual, gross and hard-hearted', he excepts the 'stronger local attachments and enterprising spirit of the Swiss and other mountaineers' which are the result of 'forms of property which beget . . . manners truly republican' (BL II 45). Pointedly omitting to mention Wordsworth's Lakelanders in this obvious connection, Coleridge compares the Swiss exception to the rule, represented here by the peasants of North Wales for whom 'the ancient mountains, with all their terrors and all their glories, are pictures to the blind, and music to the deaf'. He clearly does not wish to embark upon any consideration of 'republican manners' as such, preferring to substitute a different paradigm for Wordsworth's contentious and sectarian model. The Swiss suffice given their foreignness and the anti-jacobin sentiments with which they are associated by the British public due to their invasion by the French.

In the middle of chapter twenty-two, an analysis of the

'characteristic defects of Wordsworth's poetry', Coleridge delivers what is perhaps his most successful recuperation of the *Preface*'s egalitarianism:

> The feelings with which, as christians, we contemplate a mixed congregation rising or kneeling before their common maker: Mr Wordsworth would have us entertain at *all* times as men, and as readers; and by the excitement of this lofty, yet prideless impartiality in *poetry*, he might hope to have encouraged its continuance in *real life*.
>
> (BL II 130)

Coleridge here returns Wordsworth's 'good shepherd' to the heavens, preferring a religious to a civic definition of communal parity. Considering the inappropriateness of appealing to the standards of any given section of society as the paradigm of cultural value, Coleridge seeks to invest the 'republic of letters' with the *spiritual* egalitarianism of a transcendent, religious, sphere. Having shown the literary 'pastoralism' which underscores Wordsworth's misleading desire to emulate 'the real language of men', and therefore the conformity of *Lyrical Ballads* to a literary *Lingua Communis*, Coleridge takes a rather different tack in considering the relationship of Wordsworth's *actual* poetic achievement to this stated norm. To understand the context of this aesthetic point it may usefully be considered in the light of Coleridge's employment of an identical discursive strategy in the socio-economic argument of the second *Lay Sermon*.

Coleridge diagnoses the final, if not efficient, cause of the post-war political and economic crisis as an 'overbalance of the commercial spirit' which is a result of 'the absence or weakness of the counterweight', namely, the permanent, stabilizing influence of the 'vascular' or landed interest (LS 169). Coleridge continues by discussing the manner in which land has been 'undercut' by capital, with the effect of transforming the traditional patronage and paternalism of the proprietors into self-interest; the point is really analogous to the appropriation of the value of 'Common Sense' by competing class-ideologies. What had been claimed to be true for the *whole* is now only true for the *part*. But Coleridge's appeal to the landed class to look to their social responsibilities lacks the conviction which is evident in Wordsworth's *Two Addresses to the Freeholders of Westmoreland* of the following year.

Coleridge considered a landed class which was capable of instigating the protectionist Corn Laws to preserve its partial interests at the cost of the rest of society, to have forfeited its historical role as guardian of the national interest. The 'gentlemanly' virtues of disinterestedness and propriety had been replaced by the acquisitive urge of capitalism, which rendered the claims of this class to embody the 'common sense' of the nation so much cant. The very notion of 'common sense' had come to serve the legitimation of particular interests; not only those of the gentry, but also of the advocates of Thomas Paine's interpretation of 'common sense' and those who played upon the contractural language of the 1688 constitution, 'political rhinoceroses' like Cobbett and Cartwright. It is for this reason that Coleridge argues that the 'overbalance' of commerce can only be remedied by the absolute, quasi-religious authority of 'culture', 'the slow progress of intellect, the influences of religion, and irresistible events guided by Providence' (LS 169).

Only in the light of Coleridge's complex reaction to the 'common sense' ideology of the literary and political establishment can his ambivalent account of the 'beauties and defects' of Wordsworth's poems, and the defects of the Preface, be fully intelligible. The Preface's bid to advocate a very literal interpretation of common sense as the best standard for poetry is refuted, not by an 'external' argument, but by the manner in which such an aim is contradicted by Wordsworth's actual poetic achievement. The prosaic, conversational style which emulates 'the real language of men' and which Wordsworth argues is the correct style for poetry, is not in fact the language of *his* best poetry. Poetry is distinct from prose both in ordonnance and diction, in the 'organic' interdependence of diction and metre, which results from an 'unusual state of excitement' in the poet, so necessary to good poetry (BL II 61–8). Coleridge denies Wordsworth's criticism of the 'arbitrary' authority of poetic diction; surely he was thinking of a fool, madman or 'ignorant phantast' rather than a poet, whose prescriptive wisdom marks him off from other men, when he wrote this (BL II 81). Wordsworth had meant no more by his 'language of men' than the 'milder muse' or neutral poetic style, a sort of minimal or quasi-prosaic poetry in the minor (although nonetheless venerable) tradition of Gellert, Spenser, Waller or Cotton (BL II 90–2). Bowles, Byron, Southey and Thomas Moore are all contemporary exponents of this style; it is clearly not a vehicle for apostles of poetic heterodoxy or literary Jacobins. But nonetheless, Coleridge argues, Wordsworth's manifest desire to emulate it is fundamentally misguided.

Wordsworth's *actual* poetic performance cannot be said to conform to the *Lingua Communis* which he had sought to define in the *Preface*, for after Milton and Shakespeare's, it is 'of all others the most *individualized* and characteristic' (BL II 99). Not only do the poems themselves fail to fit the hypothetical poetic norm of the *Lingua Communis*, they far surpass it and create new standards of perspicuity and poetic propriety. Thus Wordsworth is shown to be an outstanding and inimitable genius despite himself, a genius manifest mainly in the meditative poems like the *Immortality Ode* rather than the dramatic ballads like *The Thorn*. Coleridge considers that Wordsworth's matter-of-factness and tendency to particularize 'repress the force and and grandeur of his mind' (BL II 120).

Chapter twenty-two's account of the faults and beauties of the *Immortality Ode*, a poem which contains a mixture of 'mental bombast' and 'meditative pathos', is typical of Coleridge's ambivalent strategy. On the one hand the poem itself dramatises the dangerous proximity of the 'gift of imagination' to antinomianism, pantheism, even neo-paganism, which will be seen to problematize Coleridge's theory of imagination in chapter thirteen. He makes it clear that the 'common language', the conditions of which he seeks to re-define, is not a spontaneous, unconscious growth from man in a 'natural' state, but rather a highly self-conscious construction of poetic genius, or the professional 'men of research' who determine 'common sense' in chapter four (BL I 86n). Like Newton's gravity working and shaping inert matter, consciousness permeates down to the common or 'natural' man from the pulpit, and to the pulpit from the academy (BL I 226). In contrast to the position adopted in the years before 1800, Coleridge now denies the immanence of the shaping spirit, the 'plastic power' which equally informed and swept through the world of men and nature. For this reason he objects to Wordsworth's description of the child in the *Ode* as 'Thou best philosopher. . . . Thou eye among the blind. . . . Mighty Prophet! Seer blest!' (BL II 138). The child, like the uneducated rustic, must have been subject to 'an unconscious revelation of truth' in order to possess this sort of wisdom and power, which could not have been achieved, Coleridge insists with aggressive literalism, by '*any* form or modification of consciousness' (BL II 138).

Like the Old Cumberland Beggar discussed above, the child's 'insentient wisdom' is a function of its role as a 'silent monitor', a figure of wisdom not from any mystical influx of knowledge, but from its innocent participation in the well-ordered soul of the world (or in the case of the beggar, more specifically of the civic body). Coleridge objects to this identification of philosophical power with a literal 'common sense' for reasons similar to his objection to the *Preface*'s description of rustic language as more 'philosophic' than that of poets. Wordsworthian bathos or bombast (sinking poetic language or raising trivial subjects are two aspects of the same deviation from a legitimate norm) are subversive of established cultural hierarchies. The 'eccentricity' of his poetic experiment is diagnosed as a 'hysteron proteron', 'putting the cart before the horse'; in a metaphor aptly combining philosophy and power, Coleridge warns that we should bow to Antoninus, the Emperor philosopher, before we marvel at the existence of Epictetus, a slave who happens to philosophize, but an exception to the rule (BL II 131). Coleridge is no believer in 'mute inglorious Miltons', having no confidence in the machine of language until it has been blessed and legitimized by men of genius. In 1809 he had summed up his life-work as an attempt 'to expose the Folly and the Legerdemain of those who have thus abused the blessed machine of Language' (Friend II 73), notably those who argued for a human and natural, rather than transcendent and divine, provenance for language and consciousness.

And yet Wordsworth, despite his dangerous tendency to 'subrept' or literalize his poetic metaphors by attributing innate meditative power to the common forms around him, exemplifies in his inimitability and untranslatable quality, language at the very highest point of mental precision. The *Biographia* offers his 'articulate energy' as the source and sanction for its own critical authority. Coleridge's praise of the 'beauties of Wordsworth's poetry' in chapter twenty-two is followed by a simple citation of the most sublime passages, for critical language can do no more than defer in this way to imagination 'in the highest and strictest sense of the word' (BL II 151). The question of *Lingua Communis* is dropped from what has become in effect a 'hierophantic' definition of poetic authority. The *Immortality Ode* need only appeal to those 'as had been accustomed to watch the flux and reflux of their inmost nature, to venture at times into the twilight realms of consciousness, and to feel a deep interest in modes of inmost being, to which they know that the attributes of time and space are inapplicable and alien, but which yet can not be conveyed, save in symbols of time and space' (BL II 147). The project of defining the 'real language of men' in terms of a more adequate 'common language' is replaced by a justification of 'the poem as Mystery':

> A poem is not necessarily obscure, because it does not aim to be popular. It is enough, if a work be perspicuous to those for whom it is written, and 'Fit audience find, though few.'
>
> (BL II 147)

No longer a 'man speaking to men', a 'fellow-sufferer or co-mate', the poet is rather a 'contemplator' or 'spectator, haud particeps' (BL II 150) whose power is the effect of his transcendence. Coleridge allows Wordsworth to step forward out of his pastoral disguise to claim the laurels which await the creator of the FIRST GENUINE PHILOSOPHIC POEM (BL II 156). Like Clifford in the poet's own pastoral, *Song at the Feast of Brougham Castle*, a shepherd boy restored to the estates and honours of his aristocratic ancestors, Wordsworth has been nurtured and humanized by his sojourn amongst common people. But his genius does not derive from the pastoral world, for it carries the noblest of lineages provided that it is shown for what it is, and not just for what it seems:

> Among the heavens his eye can see
> The face of thing that is to be;
> And, if that men report him right,
> His tongue could whisper words of might.
>
> (WPW 163, ll. 134–7)

6

Cultivation, Criticism and Common Sense

The question of Coleridge's relation to the philosophy of Common Sense has been touched upon in connection with his ambivalent handling of the idea of *Lingua Communis* in Wordsworth's theory of poetry. The Scottish Common Sense philosophers, notably Thomas Reid, James Beattie and Dugald Stewart sought to disarm the threat of Hume's sceptical empiricism by proposing an 'instantaneous, instinctive and irresistable impulse' of Truth which might outweigh the solipsistic and divisive principle of reason. Paul Hamilton, who has drawn attention to the neglected importance of this native philosophy of mind for the English Romantics, discusses its role in Burke and Francis Jeffrey, and cites James Mackintosh's description of it as the 'efforts of the conservative power of philosophy to expel the mortal poison of scepticism'.[1] We have already noted how critics in the 'Common Sense' tradition tended to censure Wordsworth not so much for his implicit radicalism as for his idiosyncratic egotism, his refusal to adhere to commonly defined norms of social and linguistic propriety. Social propriety was in fact the lynchpin of Common Sense philosophy, and determined the attack by Beattie in his 1770 *Essay on the Nature and Immutability of Truth* on the pusillanimous temper which seeks rational proof of first principles in religion and philosophy. The analytic impulse which motivates the Humean, or indeed in the context of our argument, Godwinian, brand of scepticism,

> seems rather to be owing to a defect in that kind of sensibility, or sympathy, by which we suppose ourselves in the situations of others, adopt their sentiments, and in a manner perceive their very thoughts; and which is indeed the foundation of good breeding.[2]

Of course the contractual efficacy of this gentlemanly standard was only binding upon 'gentlemen', a characteristic of the 'Whig double standard' which determined its attack by those beyond the social pale like Joseph Priestley. For Priestley, Common Sense embodied 'an exploded doctrine of passive obedience and non-resistance', the hypocrisy of an Oligarchy which falsely claimed representative status by excluding Dissenters and others who fell outside its definition of 'breeding'.[3] Coleridge, like Priestley, attacked Common Sense for its sectarianism, its confusion of Truth with Opinion, but latterly for rather different reasons. Priestley would not have denied this conflation of Truth and Opinion if the latter had been more genuinely democratic, rather than the prejudice of a ruling cabal. By 1817 Coleridge, in contrast, feared the untenability of any civic criterion for Truth precisely because Common Sense was being defined, after Tom Paine, in a literal, democratic fashion. A need had arisen for a more absolute definition of Truth based on transcendental rather than empirical criteria, upon what Kant in the Second Critique had defined as a Categorical rather than Hypothetical Imperative.[4] Coleridge's discussion of Common Sense in the 1812 *Omniana* anticipates his 1815 Wordsworth criticism in its strategy of initially accepting Beattie's common sense proof against sceptics, only to criticize it for confusing proof with 'mere general prejudice' (Om 164). His argument is substantially the same as Kant's in the Fourth Moment of Book One of the *Critique of Judgement*.[5] Coleridge's repositioning of traditional modes of authority in a subjective and 'religious' sphere would have major implications for English criticism, implications which we have already touched upon in relation to the Wordsworth of the *Biographia*.

We may now consider these in a more general way with reference to Peter Hohendahl's important discussion of the relationship of criticism to Habermas's 'Public Sphere' in his book *The Institution of Criticism*.[6] The Public Sphere represents a form of 'Common Sense' and underlies many eighteenth-century critical norms; it is thus identical with the civic court of appeal which Coleridge rejects. Based on the debate of 'a homogeneous circle of informed laymen', it determined the role of even a professional critic as that of 'a speaker from the general audience [who] formulates ideas that could be thought by anyone'.[7] Dr Johnson is the obvious example, with his rejection of the idea of an Academy based on prescriptive French models, and, in his role as compositor of the first English Dictionary, his definition of the lexicographer's task as being descriptive rather than prescriptive. Johnson's definition of the author, in many ways prophetic of the often-savage polemics between Reviewers and authors in the first decades of the nineteenth century, would have been unacceptable to the author of *Biographia Literaria*; he is

> a kind of general Challenger, whom everyone has a Right to attack; since he quits the common Rank of Life, steps forward beyond the Lists, and offers his Merits to the publick Judgement.[8]

As Hohendahl indicates, polemic criticism of this kind is based on 'the idea of restricting the power of authority through the concept of law. In the early bourgeois period, the chief purpose of law, as the epitome of universal abstract norms, was to contest the arbitrary use of authority'.[9] This Whiggish ideal is at the basis of both the 'Common Sense' norm of the establishment and the fundamentalist reinterpretation of 1688 which we have seen embodied in the *Preface to Lyrical Ballads*, where the 'real language of men' is opposed to the arbitrary authority of poetic diction. Earlier observers like the Scottish 'Conjectural Historian' Adam Ferguson had feared that the 'public sphere' was being vitiated by the divided and variegated form of modern society. In the 1767 *Essay on the History of Civil Society* he had commented on the inevitable destruction of the 'ties of commonwealth' by division of labour and increasing specialization, both necessary conditions of 'progressive' society. But these would 'withdraw individuals from the common scene of occupation, on which the sentiments of the heart, and the mind, are most happily employed'.[10]

This fear also conditioned Coleridge's critique of sectarianism, inducing him to abandon a 'civic' court of appeal in his revision of Wordsworth's 'real language of men'. Coleridge's unwillingness to do this will be the subject of our next section, in terms of his fascination with Schelling's essentially civic definition of art. His reluctance to abandon the 'ties of commonwealth' is also dramatized in the account of the genesis of that most significant medium of social exchange, language, in chapter four of the *Biographia*. Describing this genesis in terms of an organic process of verbal differentiation and proliferation which he terms 'desynonymization' (no doubt influenced by William Taylor's recent *English Synonymes Discriminated* (1813) which was attacked by Wordsworth in his 1815 *Preface* as well as by Coleridge), he regards it as motivated by 'an instinct of growth, a certain collective, unconscious good sense' (BL I 82). Even as late as 1825, Coleridge could still describe language as 'the embodied and articulated Spirit of the Race, as the growth and emanation of a People' (AR 235). The 'natural' agency of the development of language is further reinforced by Coleridge's analogy of mitosis in an insect called 'a *minim immortal* among the animacula infusioria' which has neither birth nor death: 'at a certain period, a small point appears on its back, which deepens and lengthens till the creature divides into two, and the same process recommences in each of the halves now become integral' (BL I 83). This illustrates the proliferation of language from 'a few simple sounds'; words with originally the same meaning are naturally or unconsciously desynonymized by changes in pronunciation which affect spelling and thence meaning.

The example Coleridge gives of this unconscious process, however, casts some doubt upon the desirability of this 'collective unconscious good sense'; we should bear in mind while reading the following passage Coleridge's opinion of the consequences of the abandonment of social responsibility by the landed classes in the *Second Lay Sermon*:

> Even the mere difference, or corruption, in the *pronunciation* of the same word, if it have become general, will produce a new word with a distinct signification; thus 'property' and 'propriety'; the latter of which, even to the time of Charles II was the *written* word for all the senses of both.
>
> (BL I 83)

The organic growth of language, like the 'unconscious' wisdom of rustics or children in Wordsworth's poems, tends to make havoc of established hierarchies. It is precisely this appropriation of a 'common sense' criterion of truth which fuels the incendiary arguments of reformers and motivates the confusion of terms properly differing in kind, which Coleridge analyses with reference to the rhetoric of demagogues in the second *Lay Sermon* (LS 142–57). From this point of view, the absence in 1817 of a community which might emanate 'common sense' as a natural growth (a point which is close in spirit to Ferguson's lament for a 'common scene of occupation' as well as being a conservative criticism of a democratic notion of representation), determined its rejection as a practical criterion for Truth.

In mid-argument, Coleridge veers away from the organic model to a redefined account of the agency of 'desynonymization', a redefinition which shadows the shift from a civic *Lingua Communis* to the hierophantic language of poetic genius in *Biographia* Volume Two. Discovering the tendency of the organic model to sketch a 'natural history' of the high emerging from the humble, a confusion of certain hierarchical distinctions in undifferentiated synonyms (or indeed, as in the case of property/propriety, the 'false', unconscious desynonymization by mispronunciation), Coleridge writes,

> Men of Research startled by the consequences, seek in the things themselves . . . for a knowledge of the fact, and having discovered the difference, remove the equivocation either by the substitution of a new word, or by the appropriation of one of the two or more words, that had before been used promiscuously.
>
> (BL I 86)

This form of desynonymization is exemplified by two instances standing at the centre of the later thought, *Imagination* and *Fancy*, and *Reason* and *Understanding*. Depending upon the lucubrations of professional 'men of research' like Coleridge, it is a far cry from 'a collective unconscious good sense' or the 'growth and emanation of the people' in the authority it abrogates to the intellectual. Now arguing consistently with the Wordsworth criticism in the second volume, Coleridge offers a model of language as a coinage struck from a central mint, which is sole determiner of value. Although the term 'common sense' is still used to describe this form of dissemination, the meaning is stretched to the limits of credibility, dependent as it is now upon what the 1800 *Preface* would have called the *arbitrary* power of poets or linguistic authorities. Like the discriminatory skill and 'mental accuracy' of poetic genius, the agency of desynonymization is now described in authoritarian or transcendent terms:

> When this distinction has been so naturalized and of such general currency, that the language itself does as it were *think* for us (like the sliding rule which is the mechanic's safe substitute for arithmetical knowledge) we then say, it is evident to *common sense*.
>
> (BL I 86)

The men of research claim the authority to effect desynonymization and to pass the amended idiom back into common currency, a claim quite distinct from that of the 'public sphere' with its 'evolved' rather than superinduced ideal of cultural values. The fascination of Coleridge's account is not simply the transition from a representative to an authoritarian model, but rather the ambivalence and tension which marks that shift in the argument as a whole. A similar type of ambivalence is evident in the 'be not merely a man of letters' passage in *Biographia* chapter eleven, which begins by criticizing literary professionalism, professing an ideal of literature as an activity integrated with everyday life. As in the desynonymization argument, the 'civic' definition is no sooner ventured than withdrawn, when Coleridge exhorts young men with literary interests to join the Church, a profession uniting 'the widest schemes of literary utility with the strictest performance of professional duties' (BL I 226).

These ambivalences inform not only the *Biographia* as a whole but also other texts of this middle period, as we shall see. The difficulties and the veering toward an authoritarian argument should be considered before we accept Paul Hamilton's contention that the poetics and language theory of the *Biographia* are based upon a 'progressivist' ideal of desynonymization displaying 'a radical openness to human potential'.[11] Coleridge's revisionist version of Common Sense denies that aesthetic and linguistic values are the legitimate outgrowths of a public sphere or contractual system of authority. His 'separation of powers' here is closely akin to his hypostatization of poetic diction from the 'real language of men' in Volume Two. Decisively rejecting Wordsworth's 1800 bid to integrate art and life, culture and politics, or spirit and matter, he shows that the 'Lyrical Ballad' was a mere pipe-dream which in reality separated out into an inferior ballad literature, or an inspired meditative pathos in the noblest traditions of the eighteenth century Ode.

Sometime between the 1800 and 1802 *Prefaces to Lyrical Ballads*, Coleridge embarked on a serious study of Kant and post-Kantian German Idealism: the fruits of this attempt to outflank the cultural impasse of a now-sectarian Common Sense philosophy are still evident in the Theory of Imagination which remains one of the most famous, and certainly most opaque, sections of the *Biographia*. I now wish to consider this involvement with German Ideas in the light of the Coleridgean ambivalence we have traced above, an ambivalence which we will find to some extent anticipated in the relations of Fichte and Schelling to their master Kant. The Kantian subjectification of the art-work which we noted above with relation to the Wordsworth criticism is not necessarily a synecdoche for the influence of German Thought *per se* upon Coleridge. For lodged in the body of the *Biographia* is a remarkable vestige and development of the republican and 'One Life' speculations of the 1790s' radical milieu, evidence of a philosophy in which Coleridge found for a time an answer to the fragmented and sectarian problem of the Common Sense ideology of the establishment. The philosophy of Schelling provided an integrative and essentially civic alternative to the hebetude of a bankrupt native metaphysics, and moreover one whose radicalism was disguised by its manifest bid to graft Christian voluntarism onto a Spinozistic framework.

Part Two
Imagination, the Ruined Tower

7

Reorientations

Turning back from Coleridge's reinterpretation of Wordsworth in the *Biographia*, I will now consider his vexed relationship with German ideas in the years between 1801 and 1820. The theory of imagination presented in chapter thirteen of the *Biographia* represents the real watershed of Coleridge's thought, far more than the 'epistemological conversion' from native empiricism to a German philosophical idiom. A principal concern of the following pages is to show important continuities between the 'One Life' theory of 1796–1800 and the German idealism which Coleridge espoused after that date. Only after 1817 did he attempt a consistent account of the philosophical and religious dualism, and the political and ideological position, which informed his criticism of Wordsworth in the second volume of the *Biographia*. This entailed a series of qualifications of German idealism (rejection is too strong a word given that it continued to constitute the interests – and idiom – of the mature Coleridge), linked to a slackening of interest in imagination and literary criticism.

Any account of Coleridge's indebtedness to German thought must now take on board a formidable body of recent scholarship. The focus upon the German influence has to some extent resulted in a tendency to overlook the importance of his native affiliations and intellectual context; the present study is therefore concerned with keeping in sight the political and ideological themes discussed in Part One. A brief list will suffice to give some sense of the scope of this scholarship. We have a study of Coleridge and the German *Pantheismusstreit* (debate on Spinoza) by Thomas McFarland; accounts of his relation to German Idealism in general (Gian Orsini, René Wellek and Rosemary Ashton); to the Romantic irony associated with the Schlegel brothers and the *Athenaeum* group (K. M. Wheeler); to German 'Higher Criticism' (Elinor Shaffer); to German romantic historiography (Robert Preyer), and to the *Naturphilosophie* of Schelling, Steffens and Oken (Trevor Levere and Raimonda Modiano).[1] There is no longer any excuse for a simplistic account of Coleridge's transition from 'naive'

British empiricism to a 'sophisticated' German Transcendentalism. It will be seen below that the notion of homogeneous, nationally-defined bodies of thought is a myth, and that (to cite an example of great importance here), the sort of differences between Joseph Priestley and his followers and the philosophical establishment at home to some extent mirror those between Kant and the Idealists in Germany. German Idealism and *Naturphilosophie* appealed to the interests of the intellectual group to which Coleridge belonged as a highly-developed articulation of the 'One Life' theory, which (as was shown in Part One) represented their social and ideological aims. To connect ideas with social interests in this way is a reminder that ideas themselves have specific instrumentality, and that their development is not merely a form of parthenogenesis; indeed, that their precise orientation is contingent upon context and historicity.

In this connection, Paul Hamilton's *Coleridge's Poetics* has gone a considerable way towards redressing the situation, a timely critical relocation of Coleridge within a more historicized British context. Hamilton acknowledges the lead given by Marilyn Butler in singlehandedly reviving 'Peacock's awareness of the organizing political principles behind the *Biographia*'.[2] Such an approach, long overdue in Coleridge studies, allows for a more objective account of a writer whose personality has often magnetized his critics, resulting (at the extreme ends of the range) in I. A. Richard's adulatory enthusiasm or Norman Fruman's pious iconoclasm.[3] If the present argument approaches Coleridge in the spirit of Hamilton or Butler, it also questions some of their conclusions in contextualizing Coleridge's German influence. Both follow Peacock's account (in the character of Mr Flosky in *Nightmare Abbey*) of German Transcendentalism as obscurity and intellectual mystification, associated with the reactionary backlash of the Holy Alliance abroad and the authoritarian Liverpool administration at home.[4] Paul Hamilton qualifies this criticism of Coleridge's alliance to German thought in parts of the *Biographia* by teasing out a 'radical' theory of poetry from the Schellingian lucubrations, itself based upon a 'common sense' idea of the progress of language which Coleridge called *desynonymization*.[5] The 'popular, collaborative activity' of the one is contrasted with the 'purloined, sham authority' of chapters twelve and thirteen, portraying Coleridge torn between linguistic and poetic radicalism and increasing political conservatism.[6] Given the doubts raised in

Part One above concerning the 'radicalism' of Coleridge's *desynonymization* (on account of his artful extrapolation of 'common sense' from the contractual domain of a 'public sphere'), the following pages question Peacock's judgement by examining the sociology of the Schellingian ideas presented in the *Biographia*. Coleridge's problematical presentation of German ideas to the Establishment provoked the scorn of liberal critics who easily identified the difficulty of an alien philosophical idiom with political authoritarianism.[7] But this picture is misleading in the context of Coleridge's thought as a whole, and can only be remedied by stressing the continuity of Schellingian 'imagination' with the 'One Life' theory which played such an important part in the radical thinking of Coleridge's youth. Schellingian aesthetics offered Coleridge a chance to preserve a unifying and immanent role for poetic symbol, a role which the rejection of the 'civic' criterion of *Lingua Communis* in volume two had already effectively challenged. This was the significant split which renders the *Biographia* a watershed in Coleridge's thought.

Schelling was by no means the only important German influence on Coleridge. As well as borrowing from Schelling's *System des Transcendentalen Idealismus* (1800) and *Abhandlung zur Erhläuterung des Idealismus der Wissenschaftslehre* (1796–97), the *Biographia* was also indebted to the work of Kant, G. E. Maas and Jacobi. The 1814 essays on the *Principles of Genial Criticism* echo Kant's *Critique of Judgement*, the lectures on Literature (and upon Shakespeare specifically) owe a debt to A. W. Schlegel's *Über dramatische Künst und Literatur* (1809–10), at least after the eighth of the 1811–12 series. Coleridge's 1816 *Theory of Life* leans on Steffens' *Beyträge zur innern Naturgeschichte der Erde*, his *Philosophical Lectures* (1818) upon G. G. Tennemann's *Geschichte der Philosophie* (1798–1819). These are the most prominent cases of close, often word-for-word, borrowing; there is no dispute as to the saturation of Coleridge's public and private writing with German ideas after about 1802, and increasingly after 1812.

The influence of Schelling is given privileged treatment in the following pages for a number of reasons, however. Because of our concern with the genesis of the 'politics of imagination', the Schellingian definition of imagination in chapter thirteen of the *Biographia*, which more than any other part of Coleridge's criticism has assumed a constitutive importance in the English critical canon, must be a central focus of the argument.[8] But in addition

to this important consideration, Schelling's role as the foremost
exponent of post-Kantian Idealism in Coleridge's lifetime meant
that he virtually set the terms of the latter's intellectual interests.
Coleridge's trip to Göttingen in 1798 preceded Schelling's rise to
eminence, but the serious study of Kant, Fichte and Schiller upon
which he embarked in 1801 prepared him for Schelling's early,
Fichtean writings. In 1805 he was able to discuss Schelling with
Ludwig Tieck and other German intellectuals in Rome,[9] and,
by 1811, Crabb Robinson described him as 'very much of a
Schellingianer', although noting Coleridge's scruples about what
he later came to describe as the 'allein selig-machende Philosophie'
(CL IV 792).[10] After a predominately 'Kantian' period around 1814
(the date of the *Principles of Genial Criticism*), he showed a relatively
unequivocal accord with Schelling's ideas in chapters twelve and
thirteen of the *Biographia*. The *Naturphilosophie* of the *Theory of Life*
perhaps owed as much to Schelling as it did to his pupil, Heinrich
Steffens, and the 1818 *Essays on Method* are linked in title and aim
to Schelling's *Über die Methode des akademischen Studiums* (1803).[11]
Although it is perhaps an overstatement to characterize (with
Dorothy Emmet) Coleridge's thought in general as 'a form of
Naturphilosophie',[12] the appendix to the 1829 *Constitution of the
Church and State* bears out John Beer's point that 'it is possible to
trace through all the movements of the later years a fascination
with the ideas of youth, which he tends still to put into footnotes or
asides'.[13]

Schelling himself, although the inaugurator of *Naturphilosophie*,
became increasingly more interested in the mythological and
historical, rather than natural, manifestations of the Absolute, an
interest reflected in his 1815 treatise *Über die Gottheiten von
Samothrace*. The importance of this work for Coleridge's later
thought (especially evident in the eleventh *Lecture on Literature*
1818, and the *Lecture on the Prometheus of Aeschylus* 1825) is the
subject of Part Three below. The intellectual interests which we
saw informing the 1795 *Lecture on Revealed Religion* in many ways
conformed to the hermeneutic, scientific and epistemological
concerns of the German Idealists, at a period preceding Coleridge's
direct acquaintance with them. Nevertheless, his subsequent
intellectual career suggests that in Schelling he found an affiliation
of more significance than the influence of any other single thinker.
Even after 1817, when Coleridge frequently – and scathingly –
attacked Schelling, an increasing public subscription to Kant and

the rigour of the Moral Imperative (evident in *Aids to Reflection*) concealed a carefully-qualified and circumscribed interest in the 'One Life' principle expressed in Schelling's 'Transcendental Idealism'.

It was usual for Coleridge to present German ideas to his countrymen with a certain amount of circumspection and caution. In an 1817 letter to his 'pupil' J. H. Green – himself a student and enthusiast for *Naturphilosophie*[14] – Coleridge wrote 'I am no Zealot or Bigot for German Philosophy, taken without comparison' (CL IV 793), and in perhaps his most revealing statement on the subject, in another 1817 letter to Green, he concluded with the following disclaimer:

> As my opinions were formed before I was acquainted with the Schools of Fichte and Schelling, so do they remain independent of them: tho' I con- and pro- fess great obligations to them in the development of my Thoughts – and yet seem to feel, that I should have been more *useful*, had I been left to evolve them myself, without knowledge of their coincidence.
>
> (CL IV 792–3)

Coleridge's ambivalence here – a simultaneous statement of coincidence with an independence of the German Idealists – was echoed in the mode and style of his appropriations of the Germans elsewhere in the writings, appropriations which Norman Fruman has taken pains to expose. It would certainly be easier to describe Coleridge's engagement with the Germans as affiliation rather than plagiarism if it were not for the censorious tone he adopted in condemning other men's unacknowledged intellectual obligations.[15] Fruman has dispelled an attitude of sentimental sufferance amongst Coleridge's apologists by exposing his disingenuousness in, for example, accusing Schelling of concealing his intellectual debt to Jakob Boehme, whilst simultaneously concealing his own obligation to Schelling.[16] Fruman's expose still poses a challenge to Coleridge's critics, and has certainly sobered the eulogists; at the same time it is only to be regretted that the *Damaged Archangel*'s crude psychologism and moralistic tone contribute little to an understanding of Coleridge's literary relations with Germany. Fruman's book is undermined by a positivism which denies the importance (arguably of more significance than the *originality*), of Coleridge's theory of imagination, because it can scarcely 'be said to have added to the sum of human knowledge in any objective sense'.[17]

The following pages suggest rather that Coleridge's ambivalence is a result of the history and ideological connotations of German Idealism in England, and Coleridge's difficulty in presenting it to an Establishment whose formation had been based upon Lockean and Newtonian norms. Explanations based on Coleridge's psychological problems, upon his 'mosaic method' of composition, or any more ingenious apologetic, all seem to fall short of the mark; as Elinor Shaffer has written, 'a movement of this significance and scope cannot be reduced to the mechanics (or the moralities) of transmission'.[18] The social connotations and values of the ideas themselves determined Coleridge's ambivalence and obfuscation of his sources.

Rosemary Ashton, in her study of *The German Idea* in early nineteenth-century England, has portrayed an almost complete disregard for, and ignorance of, German culture in the war years (until 1815), emphasizing Coleridge's intellectual isolation: 'Coleridge alone in the period between 1800 and 1820 fully knew and drew upon German culture for his own intellectual life.'[19] Both Tories and Whigs shared the antipathy; the *Anti-Jacobin Review* had parodied the 'Jacobinical Art of Poetry' in Schiller as well as Wordsworth, Southey and Coleridge; Francis Jeffrey dismissed the latter group as 'those *dissenters* from the established systems in poetry and criticism',[20] and his *Edinburgh Review* carried only one article on German literature (on Lessing) between 1803 and 1813.[21] Coleridge's translation of Schiller's *Wallenstein* (in 1800), must have cemented the 'Jacobinical' connection in the eyes of reviewers.[22] The situation was somewhat mitigated by the publication, in 1813, of a translation of Mme de Staël's *De l'Allemagne* and in 1815, of A. W. Schlegel's *Lectures on Dramatic Art and Literature*, both conservative works which must have laid the spectre of German Jacobinism to rest.[23] But the suspicions of a liberal critic like Sir James Mackintosh were now aroused, and German culture was seen to partake of the religious bigotry and obscurantism of the post-war reaction.[24] Kantian philosophy appears to have made the leap from a marginal illuminism to a marginal absolutism without ever having come to rest in the centre.

There is perhaps a danger in assessing English attitudes to German literature and thought in this period to concentrate on the Establishment at the expense of the highly-intellectualized milieu of 'rational dissent' from which Coleridge's thought emerged. Coleridge's 'advanced circle of Bristol friends' helped to stimulate his German interest, providing a milieu which must challenge the image of a lonely transcendentalist and consequently of the unintelligibility of the Schellingian sections of the *Biographia* to any significant intellectual group in England.

The playwright Thomas Holcroft, William Taylor of Norwich (author of *English Synonyms Discriminated*, p. 70 above) and Henry Crabb Robinson, all mentioned by Rosemary Ashton, were, like Coleridge, enthusiasts for German thought, and Dissenting intellectuals. Exceptions to the general 'black-out' on German culture in the Reviews were eight articles by Taylor in the radical *Monthly Magazine* between 1805 and 1809, articles by Crabb Robinson in the *Monthly Register* on Kant and the post-Kantians (1802–3), and in the Unitarian *Monthly Repository* in 1808 and 1832.[25] A glance at René Wellek's *Kant in England* provides further evidence in support of the predominantly radical and dissenting interest in German thought. Although the early dissemination of Kant was initiated by Willich, Von Baader and Niebuhr around the famous medical school at Edinburgh University, another disciple of Kant, F. A. Nitsch, lectured on the philosopher in London in 1794–96 and published the first book on him in English.[26] The lectures seemed to have appealed mainly to radicals and dissenters like the painter H. J. Richter, the friend of Blake, and John Thelwall.[27]

In the ultra-reactionary *History of Jacobinism* (1798), the Abbé Barruel propagated a conspiracy-theory concerning an international underground of Jacobins and Illuminists who looked to Kant as one of their intellectual mentors.[28] Barruel surprisingly portrayed Kant as an atheist and Jacobin, the philosophical equivalent of Robespierre; but clearly there was some contemporary basis for such a misinformed opinion. When Crabb Robinson discovered Kantian philosophy in Frankfurt in 1801 he was surprised that 'a philosophy so mystical in its fundamental principles', and one moreover which championed voluntarism in contrast to the necessitarian orthodoxy prevalent in radical English circles, should be 'anti-christian and suspected to be elaborate infidelity'.[29] Robinson was attracted to Kantianism because it 'freed the Mind of all shackles of prejudice' and because Kant and his pupil Fichte had apparently 'avowed Republicanism, not indeed in Paine's language but with all the formalities of scientific demonstration'. It is not difficult to see why this view of Kant would have aroused Coleridge's interest in the same period. Such interest is in contrast to the circumspection or indifference of the English and Scottish philosophical establishment with regard to Kantianism, however, or at least of those of its members who condescended to notice the German philosopher. Wellek has shown how the 'Common Sense' philosophers tended, despite a superficial resemblance between the Kantian categories and common sense 'conditions underlying experience', to dismiss the stylistic 'pusillanimity', the 'mysticism' and neo-scholasticism which they discerned in Kant.[30]

Coleridge's presentation of German Idealism in the *Biographia*, the *Lay Sermons* and other works was thus an attempt to mediate a philosophical idiom associated with a marginalized Dissenting culture to a more mainstream 'reading public'. Despite his appeals to statesmen and cabinet ministers like Lord Liverpool (CL IV 757–63), his exhortations to the landed interest not to abandon their social responsibilities, and his cultivation of the patronage of the aristocratic Sir George Beaumont, Coleridge's real ideological importance lay in his role as representative and conscience of a professional (as opposed to commercial) middle class. His influence upon this group (which Harold Perkin has called the 'forgotten middle class'[31]) was that of a regenerate dissenter seeking to 'moralize' his peer group and return them to the fold of a threatened church and state, and to graft their social and ideological vision onto traditional social hierarchies. The 'spiritualized politics' of the *Statesman's Manual*, for example, represents just such a mediation of the civic idealism of the 1795 *Lectures* with the interests of the 'old society', against the democratic and secularizing forces perceived to be threatening the as-yet unreformed Establishment. German Idealism provided the vehicle for this Quixotic venture as a sophisticated expression of the 'One Life' theory which we followed through the late 1790's. The 'civic' enterprise would culminate in the awkward (and yet vastly influential) Schellingian passages in chapters twelve and thirteen of the *Biographia*, and Coleridge's re-direction to the impulse to unity in the later cultural politics.

Coleridge's engagement with German philosophy did not emerge from an ideological vacuum, nor was it a 'reactionary' alternative to the spiritualized republicanism of the Unitarian period. German *Naturphilosophie*, Higher Criticism and aesthetics, on the contrary, had provided the bourgeois milieu of 'advanced dissent' with a more palatable social, epistemological and cultural radicalism than the secularizing French school popular in Plebeian radical circles. In the 1795 *Lectures on Revealed Religion*, Coleridge had already been influenced by the German J. D. Michaelis's *Introduction to the New Testament*, and as Elinor Shaffer points out, was involved with a Unitarian circle which included one Alexander Geddes, himself in touch with the 'higher critics' Michaelis and Eichhorn. In 1797, Thomas Beddoes advised Coleridge to drop his plan to study at Jena, 'a cheap German University where Schiller resides' (CL I 209), and also, ironically, the as-yet unknown Schelling who took the Chair of Philosophy at the age of the twenty-three. Coleridge was urged to go instead to the Göttingen of Blumenbach, a physiologist and comparative anatomist, of Heyne and Tychsen, philologists or 'philosophical linguists' (BL I 208), and of Eichhorn, scholar, historian and critic.[32] At Göttingen, Coleridge attended lectures on 'Physiology, Anatomy & Natural History' (CL I 518), and although his German was not up to studying Kant and Fichte, he ordered copies of their works to take back to England, as well as imbibing their ideas, which were very much 'in the air'. It was from this very intellectual milieu, and the highly-charged and sublimated nationalism of the German universities, that Schelling's expansive philosophy emerged.[33]

In his study of Coleridge's 'polar philosophy' and science, Trevor Levere has suggested that during the war years, 'science in Britain was less insulated from Germany than has been generally thought' and indicates that the *Philosophical Magazine* and *Quarterly Journal of Science and Arts* 'published regular notices of foreign researches'.[34] Indeed Thomas Beddoes had 'an extensive German library' in Bristol in the period of his friendship with Coleridge, and Levere notes an 'extensive overlap between Beddoes' German review list and Coleridge's scientific reading as it appears in the notebooks of his productive middle age.'[35] Clearly Coleridge and his circle were no strangers in the seventeen-nineties to the interest in Spinoza absorbing German thinkers (especially Schelling) in the same period – indeed Coleridge himself records in the *Biographia* how Sidmouth's spy feared that the two young poets Coleridge and Wordsworth had 'blown his cover' because the perpetual subject of their conversation was one 'Spy-nozy' (BL I 194). Despite Coleridge's bid to salvage Spinoza's reputation in the *Biographia* (Spinoza, as Rosemary Ashton suggests, may count as a 'German' thinker for the purposes of a discussion of German philosophy in early nineteenth-century England), he came to argue that Spinozism and its various current forms was more subversive of the authority of church and state than any of the treasonable pronouncements which the Spy had hoped to hear.[36]

The 'Spinozistic' discussions of the early years, absorbed with the connections between pantheism, naturphilosophie and imagination, were continued into Coleridge's Highgate years, a period in which, as Levere has pointed out, 'many of the sixty or more physicians and surgeons among his acquaintances were interested in powers, in the theory of life, in zoo-magnetism and in psychosomatic diseases'.[37] It would appear that these were still 'extra-establishment' interests, however, the Royal Society and the London Philosophical Society being as suspicious of the 'One Life' theory, the identity of powers in nature and in the mind, as the cultural and literary establishment were of Coleridge's aesthetic and theological engagement with German thought.[38]

The 'dynamic philosophy' presented by Coleridge in the *Biographia* was characteristic of the intellectual interests of a small but significant and increasingly influential professional group. The awkwardness attending his mediation of German thinkers to a wider public was a result of the ideological heterodoxy of their ideas and the dissenting and radical milieu which had originally championed them in England, a fact of which the public could not have been entirely unaware. If German thought really served a reactionary establishment as effortlessly as liberals like Peacock implied, it is hard to see why an increasingly conservative Coleridge should have suggested to Green in 1817 that a society for the propagation of German naturphilosophie and idealism in England should be called 'The Friends of Northern Literature, Swedish, Danish and German' (CL IV 794). Coleridge was trying to break what he considered to be a salvific heterodoxy to the intellectually misguided and threatened establishment.[39]

German naturphilosophie represented a more sophisticated articulation of the 'philosophy of identity' characteristic of the Priestleyan, dissenting intelligentsia discussed in Part One above. By privileging the 'spiritualized materialism' manifest in poetry, theology and natural science rather than the Lockean and

Hartleyan epistemological foundations, the customary picture of Coleridge's 'philosophical conversion' to German Idealism in the years 1801–4 is somewhat qualified. In the essay 'The Peculiarities of the English', E. P. Thompson has warned of the danger of 'confusing an intellectual *idiom*, which for various historical reasons he become a national habit, with an ideology. Bacon and Hazlitt, Darwin and Orwell, may all have employed this idiom, but they can scarcely be said to have been attached to the same ulterior ideological assumptions'.[40] The 'idiom' is of course empiricism, which Coleridge began to reject in 1801–2 by accepting a version of Kantian transcendentalism in place of the mechanistic metaphor or 'physical analogy' of Locke, Hartley or Priestley.[41] This was not simply in order to replace a 'passive' by an 'active' theory of mind; Priestley's theory of matter had already proposed the plasticity and vastness of the 'intellectual breeze' infusing matter with the energy and vitality of spirit, as Coleridge well knew. Rather, Kant's synthetic a priori judgement and Fichte's idealist interpretation of this synthetic theory of mind articulated a considerably more sophisticated version of the philosophy of identity than had been possible using the empiricist's 'machinery', a dialectical doctrine of powers for the corpuscles, vibraticuncles and monads of the native idiom. Coleridge's lifelong struggle against philosophical dualism, his attempt to formulate an identity between spirit and matter (increasingly in conflict with his need to postulate a transcendent and personal deity), found common cause with the idealist's bid to overcome Kant's dualistic 'distinction of powers'.

In 1825, Coleridge was to liken Priestley's reduction 'of the Creator to a mere Anima Mundi' with the Spinozism he increasingly discerned underpinning Schelling's philosophy (AR 395). In the *Biographia*, the physiologist Richard Saumarez, indubitably working within the 'native philosophical idiom'; was praised for being the 'English Schelling', in substituting 'life and progressive power, for the contradictory inert force' of the Newtonians (BL I 162–3n). The discussion of Priestley's *Disquisitions* in Part One above showed how he had imbued matter with the powers of attraction and repulsion in an attempt to ultimately reconcile science and religion. In an analogous attempt to overthrow dualism, in this case the 'nescience' represented by Kant's noumenon, Schelling regarded matter as the product or 'indifference' of the twin polarities of expansion and restraint. This followed the 'Copernican' strategy of Transcendentalism, regarding phenomena as the product of powers, rather than vice versa.

In chapter eight of the *Biographia*, the 'Schellingianer' Coleridge poured scorn upon the epistemological crudity of Priestley's attempt to 'refine matter into a mere modification of intelligence' (BL I 136) but not upon his former master's attempt to outstrip 'the common rank of soul-and-bodyists' (BL I 135). Chemistry was of especial significance for the philosophy of identity, standing as it does between the life-sciences and the sciences of inorganic nature: in 1817 Coleridge regarded it as the only hope for reforming modern science and 'Psilosophy' ('from the Greek psilos slender, and Sophia wisdom, in opposition to Philosophy, the love of wisdom' (CL IV 922)) because it 'forces on the very senses the facts of mutual penetration & intus-susception which have supplied a series of experimental proofs, that in all pure phaenomena we behold only the copula, the balance or indifference of opposite energies' (CL IV 760). Coleridge's friendship with Humphry Davy put him close to the vanguard of current chemical research. As Thomas McFarland has pointed out, Schelling also was remarkable for seeing 'the metaphysical possibilities of the discoveries made in late eighteenth century physics and chemistry'.[42] Again, it is little wonder that Coleridge found in Schelling's system a focus and continuation of his abiding intellectual interests, at least until his 1817 qualifications.

In Chapter 2 we discussed the idea of a 'plastic immaterial nature' in the 1795 'Eolian Harp', a power which Coleridge associated with the vitalistic theory of Alexander Monro; the term 'plastic power' suggested a continuity between seventeenth-century Neoplatonic notions of *anima mundi* and the eighteenth-century 'One Life' theory represented by Priestley's theory of matter. Coleridge changed the original text of his 1795 poem in 1796, 1803 and 1817, a series of revisions which allow it to be read, in the words of M. H. Abrams, as 'a palimpsest that can serve as an index to Coleridge's evolving thought and imagination over a period of 22 years'.[43] The final addition was integrated in the text in 1828, but was supplied in the errata of the 1817 version in *Sibylline Leaves* (PW I 101n), demonstrating the contemporaneity of these added lines with the Schellingian concerns of the *Biographia*:

O! the one Life within us and abroad,
Which meets all motion and becomes its soul,
A light in sound, a sound-like power in light,
Rhythm in all thought, and joyance everywhere –
Methinks, it should have been impossible
Not to love all things in a world so fill'd.

(PW I 101, ll. 26–31)

The central drama and tension of the poem remains that between the poet's hubristic and visionary egalitarianism, and Sara's 'mild reproof' (l. 49); a constructed opposition between a 'Meek Daughter in the family of Christ' (l. 53) and the pantheistic 'shapings of the unregenerate mind' (l. 55). Of particular interest here is the development of the 'One Life' theory from the corpuscular and monadic terms of 'Soul of each, and God of all' (l. 48) to the dynamic philosophy of powers, namely the creative power of *light*, described by Schelling as 'the first phenomenon of the universal force of nature, through which motion is increased and maintained', and its synaesthetic interpenetration with *sound*.[44] The 'Eolian Harp' provides evidence for the continuity between Schelling's dynamism and the theory of powers formulated throughout the eighteenth century by British scientists like Robert Greene, Hutton, J. Michell, Priestley and Davy, a tradition which Rom Harré has described as 'existing, although hardly flourishing, alongside the dominant but paradoxical sensationalism and atomism of the Newtonians and their "official" philosopher John Locke'.[45] Coleridge's 1795 poem reveals the importance of this tradition for the early English romantics, showing that the doctrine of powers preceded direct knowledge of *Naturphilosophie*, a precedence which must be extremely troubling for any reading of Coleridge which seeks to make an issue of the 'separability' of German thought from his native preoccupations.[46] This has been noted by Kelvin Everest, as well as M. H. Abrams; the former writes that the 1817 additions represent 'a seamless reconciliation of opposed philosophical positions', providing 'an important case in the argument for the essential continuity of Coleridge's philosophical development towards the idealism of his mature prose writings'.[47]

Coleridge's increasingly competent grasp of the more sophisticated and totalizing German doctrine of powers did however coincide with criticism of manifest Unitarianism and the associationist and necessitarian language of his native philosophical idiom (common to both dissenting and establishment circles). In March 1801 he wrote to Poole claiming not only to have 'completely extricated the notions of Time and Space; but [to] have overthrown the doctrine of Association, as taught by Hartley, and with it all the irreligious metaphysics of modern Infidels – especially the doctrine of Necessity' (CL II 706), displaying a rudimentary knowledge of Kant's categories. He continued 'I shall be able to evolve all the five senses, that is to deduce them from *one sense* & to state their growth, & the causes of their indifference' (CL II 706). This shows a garbled understanding of Fichte's idealistic interpretation of Kant's Transcendental Ego and suggests that Coleridge, right from the start of his acquaintance with Kant, took the idealists' view of their master. Such a surmise is supported by Coleridge's claim to have arrived at his insight by the quite un-Kantian means of 'intellectual intuition', for the deduction he tells us, 'came to me almost as a Revelation' (CL II 707).

In theological matters, Coleridge still displayed in December 1802 a 'religious Deist's' pantheistic impatience with the anthropomorphism and idolatory of orthodox, and even sometimes Unitarian, christianity:

> Even the worship of one God becomes Idolatory, in my convictions, when instead of the Eternal & Omnipresent, in whom we live, & move, and *have* our being, we set up a distinct Jehovah tricked out in the *anthropomorphic* Attributes of Time and *Successive* Thoughts – & think of him, as a PERSON *from* whom we *had* our *Being*.
>
> (CL II 893)

By identifying God in this way with the pre-phenomenal or transcendental powers informing and sustaining the material world, Coleridge was performing the 'Copernican' trick of replacing Priestley's 'spiritualized matter' ('the refinement of matter into a mere modification of intelligence' (BL I 136)), with the Transcendentalist's reorientation, 'spirit does not arise from matter, but rather matter arises from spirit'. This priority had been stressed by Kant in his seminal *Metaphysische Anfangsgründe der Naturwissenschaft* (1786) and was a pillar of Schelling's naturphilosophie.

The same letter to J. P. Estlin shows, however, Coleridge's concern for the emotional poverty of pantheism, a concern which would lead him increasingly to a qualified acceptance of a personal God, and the articles of orthodox Christianity:

We we dismiss *three Persons* in the Deity, only by subtracting *two*, we talk more intelligibly, but I fear, do not feel more religiously – for God is a Spirit & must be worshipped in Spirit.

(CL II 893)

The spirit worshipped by Coleridge informed both mind and nature, and not just mind, as in the 'subjective' idealism of Berkeley and Fichte; doubtless this important condition (which Coleridge shared with Wordsworth, Beddoes and Davy) made Schelling's 'completion' of the Fichtean system more congenial, with its concern to show that 'if nature coexists with thought, or even precedes it, then the *first* task of philosophy is not to chart the realm of the self's unconditioned reflective experience [as in Fichte's subjective idealism] but to understand the nature of the original relationship between the self and nature'.[48]

Before looking more closely at the German Idealists themselves, we may conclude this account of the native 'philosophy of identity' with a survey of the genesis of Coleridge's relationship with Humphry Davy. In 1800 Davy had sought the identity of powers in mind and nature, pursuing the analogical, deductive method characteristic of the romantic scientist:

> . . . here in my kindling spirit learn'd to trace
> The mystic laws from whose high energy
> The moving atoms, in eternal change,
> Still rise to animation.[49]

It should be pointed out with reference to these verses that, according to Barry Gower, the 'dynamical atomism' of the above lines was common to both Davy and the Germans, including Schelling, and should be distinguished from the mechanistic, passive atomism represented by the Daltonian chemistry of the scientific establishment.[50] Coleridge attacked the Daltonians in his 1817 letter to Lord Liverpool (CL IV 760). Davy's analogism led him to the 1807 'March of Glory' when (in Coleridge's words) 'by the aid and application of his own great discovery, of the identity of electricity and chemical attractions, he has placed all the elements and all their inanimate combinations in the power of man' (CL III 38). Coleridge hoped the scientific breakthrough could be the occasion for a new metaphysical synthesis, an extremely 'Schellingian' programme characteristically checked by his moral scruples which link the following passage (in a November 1807 letter to Dorothy Wordsworth) back to the 'Eolian Harp' and forward to the strained articulation of Schellingian aesthetics in the *Biographia*:

> Davy supposes that there is only one power in the world of the senses; which in particles acts as chemical attractions, in specific masses as electricity, & on matter in general, as planetary Gravitation. Jupiter est, quodcumque vides; when this has been proved, it will then only remain to resolve this into some Law of vital Intellect – and all human knowledge will be Science, and Metaphysics the only Science. Yet after all, unless this be identified with Virtue, as the ultimate and supreme Cause and Agent, all will be a worthless Dream.
>
> (CL III 38)

But Coleridge's admiration for Davy did not survive the latter's spectacular success and lionization by the establishment. Levere has shown how Davy came increasingly to identify with the experimental emphasis and cautious scepticism of scientific orthodoxy regarding the deductive method and enthusiastic analogism of romantic science.[51] In an 1810 Lecture, Davy denied the 'One Life' theory itself:

> To be attracted to mere speculation, is to be directed by a dream. Knowledge can only be acquired by the senses. Nature has no archetype in the human imagination. Her empire is given only to industry and action, and governed by experience.[52]

Coleridge's disappointment at his friend's betrayal of the cause is evident in a marginal note to Boehme cited by Levere and dated 1812: 'H. Davy is become Sir Humphry Davy and an Atomist!'[53] Coleridge felt that knighthoods were hardly compatible with the 'One Life' ideal, and Davy's compromise with the scientific establishment, and its conservative dualism and 'nescience' was still a cause for disillusionment. And yet Coleridge himself will be

seen to have trod a similar path just five years later when he
checked and sublimated his theory of the unifying agency of
imagination, publicly adopting a rigorous moral imperative and a
Kantian dualism. The scruples which had all long accompanied
his statement of the 'One Life' and its visionary civic idealism
finally got the better of him; in response to the murmurings of the
private voice Coleridge would henceforth 'walk humbly with his
God'.

8

The Kantian Foundation and the 'Distinction of Powers'

An understanding of the philosophy of Kant and his idealist followers, so important to Coleridge after 1801, is an essential prerequisite for an adequate interpretation of the *Biographia's* theory of imagination. So far the identification of intellectual and aesthetic positions with ideology has been a relatively unproblematical task, given the self-consciously oppositional culture of Coleridge in the 1790s, and his politicization of poetry, theology and science in this period. But because Coleridge's engagement with German idealism was partly motivated by an impulse to disguise as well as to deny that knowledge was a function of what would be named, in a late reflection upon romantic idealism, the 'will-to-power', such an identification will be by no means so straightforward in the following pages. The privilege of claiming an ideologically unsituated idea of freedom, the transcendental idea, as a fulcrum with which to wield the chaos of desire and historical determinations to the ends (I will argue) of social cohesion and collective purpose, now needs to be scrutinized in the light of its formation and motivation. Part Three below will show some of the ways in which the 'idea' itself became diverted from its role as an enabling device and appropriated as a strategy of containment.

Yet an account of the context and internal development of post-Kantian idealism is beyond the scope of the present study of Coleridge's critical thought. All that can be ventured here is an awareness of some of the issues underpinning Coleridge's presentation of German ideas. It might be useful to bear in mind Edward Said's account of the responsibilities of critical consciousness in re-locating what he calls 'travelling theory', especially pertinent in a discussion of Coleridge and German thought: 'theory has to be grasped in the place and the time out

94

of which it emerges as a part of that time, working in and for it, responding to it; then consequently that first place can be measured against subsequent places where the theory turns up for use'.[1] Undoubtedly the 'strangeness' of German transcendentalism in England had the advantageous effect of essentializing its authority and suppressing the ideological motives so palpably obvious in the native idiom of the dissenting philosophy. If the Idealism of Fichte and Schelling represented the sublimated cultal unity of politically divided Germany, it was championed in England by members of a highly educated and professional middle-class (like Coleridge) in the process of transition from a marginal to a culturally-central social position. As *Blackwood's Magazine* complained in 1825, 'the Philosophers . . . are getting up what they are pleased to call a New Aristocracy – an Aristocracy of Science [which] is to be the enemy and ruler of the old one'.[2] However much Coleridge's holistic social theory paid lip-service to a traditional aristocracy (increasingly less so after 1817, as we shall see), the significance of transcendentalism lay in its unique power to support the claims to social centrality and 'disinterestedness' of this '*New* Aristocracy'. Coleridge's mediation of German ideas in the *Biographia* to a wider public than the social group associated with 'advanced dissent', was the first of its kind and still compares favourably with the next attempt, Carlyle's enthusiastic but misconstrued 1827 article on German thought in the *Edinburgh Review*.[3] Coleridge's bid to discover in imagination a centralizing and unifying alternative to the dualistic forms of traditional cultural authority, a split between temporal and spiritual power, is of enduring significance and value, not least because the attempt already bears the marks of its failure.

German idealism is best understood in relation to the Kantian 'distinction of powers' against which it rebelled. Kant's crucial separation of Reason ('Vernunft') and Understanding ('Verstand') may be usefully regarded in the light of his 1784 article *Was ist Aufklärung?* (*What is Enlightenment?*). The celebrated definition of enlightenment, 'Man's release from his self-incurred tutelage' and the rationalist slogan *Sapere Aude* are somewhat qualified by Kant's distinction between the public and private functions of knowledge.[4] The public function is associated with a realm of constraint, a 'civil post or office' in which the diligent servant of the state finds satisfaction in uncritical obedience. The private function, however, is what could be described as a cultural sphere within the boundaries of which the individual is free to argue or criticize 'without hurting the affairs for which he is in part responsible as a passive member'.[5] In the interests of functional efficiency and consensus in the state, value judgements are sublimated from a practical to a putative theoretical realm (a 'public sphere' in Hohendahl's terminology[6]), which, it is hoped, has some feedback to the executive realm from which they have been expurgated. This is of course in the faith, as Kant optimistically put it, that 'Caesar non est supra grammaticos.'[7] This 'emptying' of the practical sphere is inevitable if a functional consensus is to be maintained. Kant's 'distinction of powers' anticipated the social function of Coleridge's 'National Church' and the liberal credo of Arnold's maxim in *The Function of Criticism* (1864), 'Force till right is ready; and till right is ready, force, the existing order of things, is justified, is the legitimate ruler.'[8]

As David Simpson has pointed out, there is a distinction between Kant's 'rationalism' in the *Critique of Practical Reason*, in which the Categorical Imperative 'directs the individual to act as if he were prescribing a law for universal behaviour' and the historical and anthropological writings in which it is evident that Kant 'did not foresee such prescriptions as ever being empirically effective. The essence of the judgement consists . . . in its being delivered in despite of the fact'.[9] This effectively qualified the enlightenment dictum *Sapere Aude*, for, 'as things now stand, much is lacking which prevents men from being, or easily becoming, capable of correctly using their own understandings in religious matters with assurance and free from outside direction'.[10] Kant's caution was easily diverted into a highly conservative appeal, as will be evident in my discussion of Coleridge's post-1817 theory of Knowledge as *Mystery* in Part Three below. Having achieved so much in overcoming the vestiges of absolutism and Feudal power, and with the *prospect* of achieving so much more, bourgeois reason seeks a firm resting-place in a 'distinction of powers', as a buttress against a political 'enthusiasm' which might take the enlightenment ideal of rational self-determination to its literal conclusion in social egalitarianism and the socialization of property. Kant wrote in 1784 as the apologist of enlightened despotism and opponent of republicanism, the Abbé Barruel notwithstanding.

Certain common themes are evident both in Kant's 1784 remarks and the 'distinction of powers' inaugurated by the *Critique of Pure*

Reason (1781). The monumental 'bureaucratization' of philosophy undertaken in the First Critique, and continued and qualified in the Second and Third, sought to establish for once and for all the distinction between what could and could not be the legitimate objects of rational inquiry, but the 'Copernican' strategy of grounding the distinction in an analysis of the transcendental conditions, rather than the empirical objects, of experience. Coleridge believed that the First Critique would have been more accurately entitled 'An Inquisition respecting the Constitution and Limits of the Human Understanding' (CL V 421). Kant's *transcendental* system was a critique of *transcendent* thought which confused scientific and metaphysical modes of inquiry. Coleridge criticized Dr Johnson for failing to discriminate the terms, unlike 'our elder divines and philosophers' who had been aware of the distinction long before Kant (BL I 237). Notwithstanding the unsubstantiated nature of this claim, Coleridge did offer, in the *Philosophical Lectures*, a cogent account of Transcendental Critique:

> [Kant] examined the faculties critically before he hazarded any opinions concerning the positions which such faculties had led men to establish. He entered into a real examination of the balance before he would suffer any weights to be put in the scale, and thus he did as alone could be done at that time upon the ground of reflection, taking the human mind only as far as it became an object of reflection.
>
> (Ph L 388)

But in contrast to this, *transcendent* inquiry, exemplified in the 'flights of lawless speculation' of mystics like Boehme or Bruno, transgressed the bounds and purposes of our intellectual faculties (BL I 237). Coleridge valued Kant's Critique more for the limits it imposed upon the scientific understanding, preventing its critical forays into the metaphysical sphere, than for its putative 'enlightened' aim of expelling the Ideas of Pure Reason from philosophy. Coleridge's real sympathy lay with the mystics rather than the scientific atheists who believed that Kant's title *Critique of Pure Reason* supported their aims. Like the other idealists, he was concerned to argue for a form of direct knowledge of the noumenal *ding-an-sich*, different in kind from that available to the intellectual faculties of the analytic understanding, but nevertheless fulfilling a constitutive role in human experience. Coleridge accordingly interpreted Kant's *ne plus ultra* of the understanding as the dawning of a spiritual wisdom (Pure Reason) rather than as the limit of human possibility.

In the first part of the *Critique of Pure Reason*, Kant maintained a respectful silence regarding matters not subordinate to the Table of Categories of the Understanding, notably the Ideas of God, Freedom and Immortality. The presence of such ideas in the scientific realm had substituted a dogmatic, anthropomorphic knowledge for a sober and rational evaluation of experience, impeding the progress of scientific research. This attitude is comparable with Humphry Davy's cautious scepticism regarding romantic science in the years after 1808. In his apparent reduction of the Ideas to good order by denying them a constitutive role in understanding and experience, Kant anticipated his 1784 division of knowledge into public and private realms.

But limitation was only part of Kant's philosophy. In the later sections of the First Critique, he admitted that the noumenon had a heuristic or regulative function in relation to the understanding, and in moving from the epistemological to the ethical and aesthetic concerns of the Second and Third Critiques, the function of the Ideas grew in importance to the point at which they operated as if constitutive, in the moral imperative and the aesthetic judgment. The self-enclosure of Kant's system seemed to open out as both moral behaviour and art offered access to the noumenal realm, although in the latter case merely in the limited and subjective sphere of Taste, incapable of being translated into objectively communicable knowledge.[11] The gains and losses of Kantian imagination would profoundly influence Coleridge's post-1817 'Promethean' cultural vantage-point; our immediate concern, however, is with the Schellingian metaphysics which Coleridge presented in the *Biographia*, building upon the constitutive, unconditioned knowledge afforded by imagination, in a broad interpretation of 'the most astonishing of Kant's works', the *Critique of Judgement*.[12]

Kant's 'distinction of powers', the laying-aside of the Ideas of Pure Reason, thus freed the executive efficacy of understanding from theological dogma and the prerogative power of absolutism, whilst at the same time preserving the authority of traditional modes of power as an unassailable court of appeal exempt from the rationalizing spirit. Kant's distinction represented a treaty between old and new, between the achievements of understanding and the theistic power of the Ideas of Reason. In the *German Ideology* Marx and Engels described the historical conditions for just such a 'treaty' in the case of the analogous political 'separation of powers':

> In an age and in a country where royal power, aristocracy and bourgoisie are contending for mastery and where, therefore, mastery is shared, the doctrine of the Separation of Powers proves to be the dominant idea and is expressed as an 'eternal law'.[13]

The notion of treaty is the most useful key to an understanding of Kant's philosophy in the context of the present argument. But Coleridge, like Fichte and Schelling, believed that Kant had gone further, and that the distinction of Reason and Understanding disguised a covert idealism which he had laid aside in response to ideological repression. Many of Kant's followers had been quite mistaken in limiting the possibilities of metaphysics. Coleridge was claiming to have seen behind Kant's 'scientism' when he wrote in the *Biographia*:

> I could never believe, it was possible for him to have meant no more by his *Noumenon*, or THING IN ITSELF, than his mere words express: or that in his own conception he confined the whole *plastic* power to the forms of the intellect, leaving for the external cause, the *materiale* of our sensations, a matter without form.

> (BL I 155)

Thus Fichte and Schelling saved Kant from his so-called disciples, who 'had adopted his dynamic ideas, only as a more refined species of mechanics' (BL I 163). Kant could be seen either to have limited dogmatic knowledge and expelled metaphysics from the field of science, or to have freed the Ideas of Reason from the clutches of the critical understanding. Coleridge's Kant was clearly the latter; showing the value of the Pauline assertion 'that by wisdom (more properly translated by the powers of reasoning) no man ever arrived at the knowledge of God' (BL I 202), he had cleared the way for an idealization of the 'unearthly' (and yet human) power of imagination. If in his later years Coleridge employed Kant's philosophy in defence of a mystificatory fideism, ultimately limiting and constraining to human potential, it was under the aegis of Schelling's system that he found for a time a more creative interpretation of transcendental critique. Kant himself has seemed to warrant such a broad understanding of his purpose in the celebrated preface to the 1787 second edition of the *Critique of Pure Reason*:

I have therefore found it necessary to deny *knowledge*, in order to make room for *faith*. The dogmatism of metaphysics, that is, the preconception that it is possible to make headway in metaphysics without a previous criticism of pure reason, is the source of all that unbelief, always very dogmatic, which wars against morality.[14]

9

Post-Kantian Idealism

The ambivalent reception of Kant's philosophy by a whole generation of Germans is well represented by Goethe in his essay *Anschauende Urteilskraft*, in a passage cited by Rosemary Ashton:

> When I tried, if not to penetrate, then at least to make use of the Kantian doctrine, I often began to think that the dear man was dealing ironically, for he seemed intent on limiting the faculty of Knowledge, but then began to suggest, as it were with a sideways gesture, ways of crossing the boundaries he himself had set.[1]

The licence Coleridge took from the 'sideways gesture' way typical of the romantic generation, who questioned the philosopher's 'nescience' and humility with regard to the noumenal realm, seeking to incorporate its inviolable prerogative within the terms of experience and knowledge, and demanding that the dynamic spirit of Reason be made its own.

This desire to overthrow the dualism of Kant's 'treaty' and to take possession of the absolute in the 'here-and-now' can be viewed as the sublimated self-assertion of a new class of bourgeois academics in socially backward Germany, in Marilyn Butler's words 'the bitterest and probably the best-educated middle-class in Europe'.[2] Rigid social divisions between a nationally-minded burgher class and a Francophile aristocracy, the fragmentation of the German-speaking peoples into numerous duchies and principalities, both enforced the construction of a unified, national culture at the level of wish-fulfilment, a 'republic of letters' in the formation of which the universities played a prominent part. Mme De Staël wrote in 1813 that 'the want of a political career, so fatal to the mass, affords a freer scope to the thinking part of the nation . . . [In] Germany a man who is not occupied with the comprehension of the whole universe has really nothing to do'.[3]

A detailed account of the context of German idealism is clearly outside the scope of the present argument, but we may mention in passing the connection of the new school of thought with the radical student groups or *Burschenschaften*, and the efforts of natural philosophers like Schelling and Lorenz Oken to carry over 'a unifying philosophy in science as a unifying philosophy in culture and politics'.[4] Ben Knights has stressed the importance of the German apotheosis of the scholar, as mediated by British Germanists like Coleridge and Carlyle, for the native 'Clerisy' tradition of the nineteenth century. This emphasis on the social mission of the German universities is evident in the very titles of publications like Klopstock's *On the German Republic of Scholars* (1774), Fichte's *On the Vocation of the Scholar* (1794) and *Addresses to the German Nation* (1807), or Schelling's *On Method in University Studies* (1803).[5] A parallel is evident between the cultural predicament of the German bourgeois intelligentsia and the English Unitarians and 'rational dissenters' who found themselves excluded from civil power in a similar way; the fact that it was this very social group which pioneered the introduction of German ideas in England is far from fortuitous.

The efforts of Fichte and Schelling to re-state the ambivalent and conciliatory dualism of their master should be regarded in this social context, the ideological goal of incorporating the noumenon, which Schiller in 1786 described as 'a torch in a dungeon', into the dialectical structure of their philosophical systems.[6] Accordingly Fichte's *Wissenschafteslehre*, a seminal work for the idealists, set out to deny the dualism of Kant's *ding-an-sich*, which, it asserted, was based on a paralogism of the sort which Kant had himself condemned in the section of the *First Critique* entitled 'Transcendental Dialectic'. If Kant had asserted causality as one of the categories of understanding by which the mind constitutes experience, then how could it be legitimately applied to the 'thing-in-itself' as the *cause* of our experience, without perpetrating the paralogism? How could causality condition the unconditioned? The supposition that the noumenon is the cause of experience is an illegitimate application of a category of understanding to a non-empirical object, the objection which we saw Coleridge raising on page 99 above.

Fichte accordingly replaced the 'thing-in-itself' by the self-positing activity of consciousness, considering (in the words of Mme De Staël) 'the exterior world only as a boundary of our existence, on which thought is at work . . . [This] boundary is created by the soul itself, the activity of which is constantly exerted on the web it has formed'.[7] Mind and nature are, in Coleridge's words, 'different modes, or degrees in perfection, of a common substratum' (BL I 130). The Idealists replaced the unconditioned noumenal realm by Self-Consciousness, a 'subject which becomes its own object'. In one of his 'sideways gestures', Kant had argued for the self-presence of consciousness, a bundling-together of diverse representations as objects of an identical subject which he he termed 'Transcendental Unity of Apperception'. This assertion of an active, self-identical mind was levelled against Hume and the sceptical empiricists who denied that the Mind (the I-consciousness) was anything other than 'an "epiphenomenon" or an end product, a pale reflex or residue of repeated impressions'.[8] But characterisically suspicious of dogmatism, Kant asserted the noumenal status of self-consciousness, denying it could be the basis of absolute or unconditioned knowledge; because it was limited to the same empirical procedures as knowledge of the phenomenal world all we know about ourselves we have 'to learn the hard way'.[9] The only Idea of Reason which could be manifest in experience was the Practical Reason, the Idea of the good, and this only at the cost of a stoical suppression of the feelings and desires of the empirical self to the stern maxim of duty.

The Idealist interpretation of Self-Consciousness endowed it with the unconditioned power of a 'substantial ego' (in the tradition of the Cartesian *Cogito*), affording it immediate knowledge of its own ground, a principle which came to be called 'intellectual intuition'. For the elderly Kant this was a scandalous return to dogmatism, a form of Spinozism which denied the human freedom preserved in his carefully-wrought dualism.[10] In the *Biographia*, Coleridge (at his most Schellingian) took a typically idealist view of Kant, having satisifed himself – for the time being – that Schelling's 'polarization' of human consciousness and the Absolute 'ground of being' preserved the possibility of human freedom. Only Kant's fear of persecution by the Prussian authorities on charges of irreligion had motivated his refusal to 'liberate transcendental self-consciousness' (BL I 154–5). Kant had left it to Fichte to 'complete his system', a task which, predictably enough, had cost the latter his chair at Jena in 1798 (BL I 154–5).

But Coleridge followed Schelling, the 'completer' of the 'Dynamic System' (BL I 163) beyond Fichte, whose 'Transcendental Ego' was basically a subjective, 'sciential' principle. Although

Fichte's dynamic monism, 'commencing with an *act*, instead of a *thing* or *substance*' (BL I 158) overthrew materialism and mechanistic philosophy, as well as dualism, by 'having its spring and principle within itself', Coleridge needed a broader base for the 'One Life' theory. He criticized the Fichtean *Ich* as 'a crude egoismus, a boastful and hyperstoic hostility to NATURE, as lifeless, godless, and altogether unholy' (BL I 158–9). Schelling elevated Fichte's dynamic Self-consciousness by identifying it with Spinoza's pantheistic deity, concerned to show the 'plastic power' at work in both mind and nature. In his 1797 and 1799 treatises on *Naturphilosophie*, the increasing influence of Spinoza was realized in Schelling's identification of the 'objective', 'real' principle of Spinozistic *substance* with the 'subjective', 'ideal' principle of Fichte's *Ego*, an objectification of the Fichtean dialectic into a polar philosophy of mind and nature, a 'philosophy of identity'. In the words of Joseph Esposito,

> The Self's dual positing of itself and nonself became primordial 'tendencies' within the universe itself – the active tendency to impose limitations (Sphäre) and the passive tendency to let them be imposed (Grenz).[11]

From the relative equilibrium, predominance or subordination of these powers (in chapter twelve of the *Biographia* Coleridge described them as Centrifugal and Centripetal forces, BL I 286), Schelling constructed a series of *Potenz* or potencies. The term derives from Bruno, like so much else in Schelling, perhaps via Jacobi;[12] Coleridge translated it as the verb 'potenziate', 'the combination or transfer of powers', and claimed it as his own (BL I 287). Schelling's 'Odyssey of Spirit' is an *a priori* construction of the history of self-consciousness through the three principal potencies; undifferentiated identity of the Absolute, separation into opposite poles in ceaseless antagonism, and reconciliation at the highest level of self-consciousness, the so-called 'intellectual intuition' which (as we shall see) Schelling found 'objectified' in the art-work. The proximity of this system to the aims of the 'One Life' theory is evident in the identity proposed between mind and nature; because these are but two stages of the trajectory of the absolute, rather than discrete realms, it is quite legitimate to deduce *a priori* the forms of the laws governing nature, and conversely, to find in nature symbols for the laws of mind.

Knowledge of self, far from being the private, solipsistic experience which the modern consciousness so often takes it to be, affords an insight into the rationality and purposiveness of the whole universe.

For methodological purposes, Schelling divided his early philosophy into two poles, the 'real' pole expounded in the *Systems der Naturphilosophie* (1799) and the 'ideal' pole in the *Systems des Transcendentalen Idealismus* (1800). Coleridge made a similar division in his presentation of the subjective and objective poles of the 'Dynamic Philosophy' in the *Biographia*, but like Schelling denying the 'reality' of the distinction: 'I must necessarily set out from the one, to which I give therefore hypothetical antecedence, in order to arrive at the other' (BL I 255). *Naturphilosophie* begins with the real pole of nature and arrives at the Ego as the highest potency, demonstrating the proposition – so subversive of orthodox christian dualism – that 'body is but a striving to become mind, – that it is mind in its essence!' (Bl sh II 258). Transcendental Idealism begins with a Fichtean construction of the Ego to arrive at the highest potency of self-consciousness, 'intellectual intuition' and its objectification in the work of art. The 1800 *System* culminated with a treatise on art as mediator between the two poles of Being and Consciousness, a unique and miraculous means of presenting, in Coleridge's words, the 'repetition in the finite mind of the eternal act of creation in the infinite I AM' (BL I 304).

Schelling's identification of mind and nature, based upon a form of intuitive knowledge (*gnosis*) which claimed an immediate and direct comprehension that would unlock the secrets of nature,[13] more characteristic of poets than philosophers in the post-Cartesian tradition, derived partly from Neoplatonic hermeticists like Giordano Bruno, and partly from the new understanding of 'mythic' consciousness which had emerged in late eighteenth-century Germany. The refusal of myth to distinguish between a symbolic and a rational experience of reality inspired Schelling, in the words of E. Cassirer, to aim 'not at analytical disintegration but at synthetic understanding . . . striving back towards the ultimate positive basis of the spirit and of life itself'.[14] What Coleridge wrote of Humphry Davy he might equally well have said of Schelling: 'the Father and Founder of philosophic Alchemy, the Man who *born* a Poet first converted Poetry into Science and *realized* what few men possessed Genius enough to *Fancy*' (CL V 309). Like Bruno's, Schelling's 'pantheistic materialism' envisaged a new philosophical religion, a dream shared by Lessing, Novalis and Friedrich Schlegel[15] – the Nolan heretic had envisaged, in his 1584 *Spaccio della Bestia Trionfante* a universal revival of learning based upon civic and republican, rather than priestly authority. In his 1796 manifesto *Das älteste Systemprogramm des deutschen Idealismus*, Schelling proposed a 'mythology of the Ideas – an eventual mythology of Reason', the symbolic representation of which would provide a religion for the masses as well as for the philosophers.[16] The all-encompassing 'Dynamic Philosophy' would overcome dualism and 'distinction of powers' in the name of 'universal freedom and intellectual equality'; 'no more contemptuous glances, no more blind trembling of the people before their wise men and priests'.[17]

The flourishing of this Idealism, based upon the doctrine of polar powers, which Thomas McFarland has described as the essential characteristic of romantic thought,[18] found expression in other areas of German intellectual life. The renewed interest in Vico (and important influence on Coleridge after 1825, as will be evident in Part Three), the historicism of Herder and of Niebuhr, the aesthetics of Schiller and the Schlegels, the new hermeneutics of Eichhorn, Michaelis and Schleiermacher, in all cases represented a counter-enlightenment tradition rejecting the analytic, a-historical standpoint and asserting the 'polar' doctrine that 'like may know like'. Rather than being limited to empirical inquiry and debarred from knowledge of the 'thing-in-itself', the inspired mind was afforded an immediate insight into the transcendental powers which constituted the phenomenal product. In his 1807 *Über das Verhältnis der bildenden Künste zur Natur*, Schelling expressed the key presupposition of the idealists: 'that which contained no intelligence (Verstand) could not serve as an object for the intelligence either; what was without Knowledge could not itself be known'.[19] In the field of hermeneutics, this principle is described by Elinor Shaffer as 'the recreation of alien experience, the experience of the author within his historical milieu'.[20] The confident ebullience of romantic hermeneutics stands in marked contrast to the subsequent prestige of a tradition which according to H. G. Gadamer (its principal modern proponent) has been reduced to the defensive strategy of seeking the 'experience of truth that transcends the sphere of the control of scientific method wherever it is to be found, and to inquire into its legitimacy'.[21] The deductive, *a priori* method which Coleridge amongst many others believed could seriously challenge the experimental paradigms of Bacon's *Novum Organum* and the mathematical propositions of Newton's *Principia* was increasingly qualified after the 1818 *Essays on Method*, and outside a narrowly-defined aesthetic sphere was in general decisively defeated. The reaction against *Naturphilosophie* in Germany, for example, is summed up by Justus von Liebeg's 1840 verdict that it had been 'the black death of our century'.[22]

10

Aesthetics and Idealism: Kant, Schelling and Coleridge

The reconciliation of opposite qualities, a 'manifold in unity' which Kant's aesthetic judgement discovered in reflecting upon the beautiful in art or nature, became the great productive principle of Schelling's idealism, freed from the formalism and subjective limitations which Kant had imposed upon it. Coleridge's theory of imagination is best approached via the German debate concerning the power and scope of the aesthetic faculty, although it was also clearly influenced by a native debate concerned with Fancy and Imagination which had been current throughout the eighteenth century.[1]

In his *First Critique*, Kant had limited the agency of imagination to gathering the manifold of sense data and presenting it to the Concept (Begriff). It was therefore a constitutive element in perception and experience, but had no role beyond this subordination to the understanding. In the *Third Critique*, however, Kant elevated imagination to the status of an autonomous and self-conscious principle, the aesthetic judgement of the Beautiful, independent of any concept of Understanding. Within the limitation of this act of judgement, imagination discovered a harmony between the mind and its object; in the words of Paul Hamilton, 'the autonomy of imagination in aesthetic judgement, in giving a law to itself, means that in judging an object to be beautiful, we are judging how the imagination works'.[2] The feeling for the harmony of this autonomous principle (Taste) was entirely subjective and thus contingent upon its distinction from objective knowledge. Therefore poetry might provide a sense of our powers of apprehension and of the harmonious integration of all our faculties in a way which was not possible for philosophy, a point which the 'Kantian' Schiller elevated into the pedagogic and cultural principle of 'disinterestedness' in his *Letters on Aesthetic Education*, an important influence on the young Schelling.

The power of Kant's aesthetic judgement of the beautiful was contingent upon the fact that it was set aside from the realm of objective knowledge. The fact that imagination gave a law to itself rather than to the 'purposive' understanding (in the art work) conciliated and mitigated Kant's otherwise harsh dualism. It allowed for the 'Idea' of beauty as being constitutive within experience, on the condition that it could not be specified or argued about, but rather *felt* as an impalpable and subjective certainty. This limited integration of the noumenal and phenomenal realms contributed, in the second division of the *Critique of Judgement*, to the heuristic efficacy of organicism (or teleological judgement) in the scientific investigation of nature. This purposive, anthropomorphic Idea of Reason (relegated from the realm of the understanding in the *First Critique*) allowed the scientist to see system and order in the natural world, in an analogy with the harmony of his own mind, without being able to render this insight a dogmatic law in the manner of Spinoza. The systematic unity of nature, according to Kant, was *created* by the natural scientist rather than *discovered* in nature itself. As Barry Gower has indicated, Schelling regarded the Kantian claim that 'unity was injected by hypothetical Reason' as 'equivalent to the claim that it has source of nature itself', an obvious consequence of his denial of Kant's dualism and *ding-an-sich*.[3] Kant's 'sideways gesture' with regard to the 'constitutive' efficacy of the aesthetic imagination should be interpreted in the context of his need to introduce the organic principle into natural scientific research.

Kant's need to palliate the severity of his dualism in the ethical field is perhaps harder to grasp, given that he had assigned constitutive status to the Categorical Imperative in the *Second Critique*. This was nevertheless the goal of the aesthetic judgement of the Sublime.[4] The dualistic separation of the noumenal and phenomenal realms was not so much mediated as enforced in the Practical Reason, however, the moral Imperative giving the rule of Reason to conduct by means of a harsh subordination of the desires of the empirical self to the maxim of freedom 'the universal conformity of action to law in general'. As early as 1803 Coleridge had followed Schiller in his antipathy to Kant's moral rigour, still evident in 1817 but growing into qualified acceptance after that date.[5] Geoffrey Barnouw has argued that the intransigence of

Kant's 'Stoic Principle' (CL IV 791) determined the 'palliation' effected in the aesthetic judgement of the Sublime:

> Kant recognized that moral motivation – doing something simply because it is right, out of respect for the law prescribed by its own rationality – required an impulse from feeling in order to be effectual as motivation. His problem was to identify a source in human sensibility that could give energy to moral rationality without linking it, through natural concepts and motives drawn from experience, to the environing 'phenomenal' world. He found this source in the sublime.[6]

Thus if the Beautiful mitigated the dualism of the *First Critique*, the Sublime performed a similar task in relation to the *Second*; a somewhat deceptive conciliation, however, given that the formal, subjective harmony of the Beautiful is actually undone by the Sublime. Only formlessness in art and nature provides sensibility with the experience of Reason, and that in a violent and negative manner. The reciprocity of the senses and the intellect established by the imagination in the Beautiful is 'short-circuited' in the Sublime, as the understanding fails to comprehend any unity in the boundless abyss revealed to it by the struggling and thwarted imagination. The understanding is baffled by the 'presentation of the infinite – albeit a negative presentation' which has the effect of expanding its respect for the noumenal realm.[7] Here is no mitigation of dualism, no harmony of reason and experience, but a powerful impulse from the thwarted sensibility towards acknowledging the authority of the Idea of Practical Reason. Kant's Sublime was of great importance to A. W. Schlegel's theory of Tragedy, teaching us respect for 'the divine origin' of the mind and leading us 'to estimate the earthly existence as vain and insignificant'.[8] Schelling refused to admit 'a true objective opposition between beauty and sublimity: the true and absolutely beautiful is invariably also sublime, and the sublime . . . is beautiful as well'.[9] It is significant that Coleridge adopted the 'devotionalism' of Schlegel's tragic paradigm after his rejection of the 'One Life' theory and the temporalizing medium of Schellingian imagination.[10]

Kant's formulation of the aesthetic faculty, while seminal to the art theories of Schiller, Schelling and Coleridge, seems in itself to be subordinate to ulterior motives which ultimately denied the significance of experience and the empirical realm in general. As Barnouw points out, the 'disinterestedness' which 'frees the aesthetic sphere from the practical and moral' was paradoxically a freedom 'not from but for a formative influence on convictions and conduct'.[11] Viewed in the context of Kant's philosophy as a whole, the theory of imagination with its formulation of a harmony between rationality and experience in art was a very brief concession no sooner posited in the realm of the Beautiful than retracted in that of the Sublime, enforcing a radical discontinuity between the rational and empirical faculties of mind. Kant's 'saturnalia of imagination' fell far short of satisfying the expansive demands of his idealist successors.

We saw above Schelling's aspiration for the new philosophy, a 'mythology of the Ideas', and it was this very concern to relocate the aesthetic in civic and collective terms which determined his bid to free imagination from the subjective limits which Kant had imposed upon it. Freeing Kant's torch from its dungeon meant defining an all-embracing 'mythological' world-view the highest articulation of which was a temporalizing and integrative theory of culture. Schelling's quest for a modern epic or mythology was evident in his 1803 lecture *Über Dante in philosophischer Beziehung*, which evoked the archetypical verity of the *Commedia*, a work providing a clearer insight into the evolving powers of nature and history than could be discerned by empirical methods, 'confused and obscure' as these always are. The eternal significance of the poem was binding.

> not only as outward form, but also as sensuous (sinnbildlich) expression of the inner paradigm of all scientific knowledge and poetry, and is capable of containing within it the three great domains of science and culture; nature, history and art. Nature, as the birthplace of all things; is eternal night, and as that unity through which they have their being in themselves, it is the aphelion of the universe, the place of distance from God as the true centre. Life and history, whose nature is a succession of step-by-step advances, is simply a refining process, a transition to an absolute state. This is present only in art, which anticipates eternity, and is the *Paradiso* of Life, truly at the centre.[12]

The knowledge derived from art is constitutive and 'objective'; the *Commedia* symbolizes the structure of reality itself, for the world is made for the word rather than vice versa as the empirical mind would suppose. Art affords a privileged knowledge of the Absolute, the whole prior to the parts, but this knowledge is the fruit of experience, the dialectial engagement of reason and existence. Coleridge explained this 'hermeneutic circularity' at the heart of Schelling's thought in an 1820 letter to his son Hartley:

> tho' as One can never be *known* but as it is revealed in and by the Many, so neither can the Many be *known* (ie. reflected on) but by its relation to a *One*, and therefore, *Ones* being = Many, only by reference to THE ONE, which includes instead of excluding the Alter. The Aleph, say the Rabbinical Philologists, is no Letter; but that in and with which all Letters are or become.
>
> (CL V 99)

The 'Absolute' perception objectified in the aesthetic experience is not a mystical vision of a noumenon independent of experience (the whole is nothing if not the sum of its parts) but rather a reorientation of the phenomenal world, according to which the object is filled with the significance accruing from its participation in a universal process, rather than its existing as a discrete entity. The world of experience is no longer dependent upon a translation into rational terms for significance, precisely Coleridge's meaning in Appendix C of the *Statesman's Manual* when he distinguished the Symbol from other forms of representation: it is not 'a metaphor or allegory or any other figure of speech or form of fancy, but an actual and essential part of that, the whole of which it represents' (LS 79).

The 'secret wonderful faculty' which affords this philosophical or aesthetic intuition (the distinction will be examined below), although ostensibly turning the mind away from contingency to contemplate the purposiveness of the Absolute, does so only in order to transfigure the contingent, in contrast to the dualistic experience of the Kantian sublime. Symbolic perception never loses sight of the parts in its contemplation of the whole, just as it never loses the whole in its contemplation of the parts. In 1796 Schelling had defined the 'philosophy of the spirit' as 'an aesthetic philosophy', adding sensuous interest to the ideas of the philosophers and philosophical rigour to the popular mythology'.[13] The 'worldly' orientation of imagination is exemplified by E. D.

Hirsch in his typological study of *Wordsworth and Schelling*, in the Simplon Pass episode in book six of Wordsworth's *Prelude*. The vision of 'woods decaying, never to be decay'd' and 'the stationary blasts of waterfalls' which follows the rise of 'imagination is characterized by Hirsch as a vision of the immortality of the present' rather than an evocation of the 'invisible world' interpreted as the city of God.[14] The quality of transfiguring rather than transcending experience is the key to comprehending Schellingian and Coleridgean symbol, one which has been designated by Georg Lukács as the intensification of the world of experience, the saving grace of an otherwise 'anti-rational' and (for Lukács) reactionary organon of philosophy. The 'immediate knowledge' dismissed by Kant as a philosophical scandal was still oriented to an enhanced knowledge of this world for the young Schelling rather than devotion (Andocht) towards another:

> For the world which intellectual intuition was supposed to render accessible was, as Schelling then conceived it, by no means inimical to reason, not even meta-rational. On the contrary: it was precisely here that the real forward movement and development of the universe was supposed to be revealed in all its rationality.[15]

The major claims made by Schelling for the importance of imagination at the climax of his *Transcendentalen Idealismus* were the basis of Coleridge's attempt to work out a metaphysical foundation and rationale for his theory of imagination in chapters twelve and thirteen in the *Biographia*. The connection (in both writers) between philosophical intuition and aesthetic imagination was important as a transposition from a ratiocinative discourse to an existential 'grounding' of the system as a whole. The movement from philosophy to art preserved the metaphysician from speculative hubris and reintegrated the speculative intellect within a community in which the Idea could find its fulfilment.

At the climax of his transcendental deduction of self-consciousness (part six of the *System*) Schelling arrived at intellectual intuition, the philosophic imagination, a 'wonderful power' at once means and end, 'whereby in productive intuition (so the philosopher claims) as infinite opposition is removed', revealing the identity of mind and nature in the absolute.[16] Schelling's parenthetical qualifier is highly significant. The incommunicability and paradoxical nature of intellectual intuition might be a problem for the philosopher who has reached the apogee of self-consciousness; in a note to corollary three, Schelling described his insight as 'itself merely an internal one, which cannot in turn become objective for itself'.[17] The solipsism of his insight threatens to empty it of communicable meaning and its status as *event*; the philosopher, thus divided from the community whose ideal experience is the object of his reflection, would fit the image of Schelling himself which Shawcross inaccurately propagates in his 1907 introduction to the *Biographia*.[18] The contemplation of the Absolute in Schelling's thought is precisely *not* 'the arid abstraction of the speculative intellect' (Bl sh 1xxi) because of the paramount significance of art in the Transcendental Idealism. Art grounds the highest epoch of self-consciousness in a collective universality which guarantees the communicability and authority of intellectual intuition:

> This universally acknowledged and altogether incontestable objectivity of intellectual intuition is art itself. For the aesthetic intuition simply is the intellectual intuition become objective . . . that which the philosopher allows to be divided even in the primary act of consciousness, and which would otherwise be inaccessible to any intuition, comes, through the miracle of art, to be radiated back from the products thereof.[19]

Aesthetic imagination identifies knowledge with the ground of being, really a Schillerian point that whereas philosophy can bring only a fragment of man to the highest epoch of self-consciousness, art can bring him whole, given its access to an undifferentiated community of existence. Schelling described intellectual intuition as relevant only to the particular orientation involved in philosophizing, and therefore absent from ordinary consciousness, whereas *aesthetic* intuition, 'nothing else but intellectual intuition given universal currency, or become objective, can at least figure in every consciousness'.[20]

Schelling's aesthetic intuition reconciled the conscious, intending mind with the constitutive and unconscious power of the Absolute, a 'being-moved' (Rührung) in the tradition of the *pati deum* of Plato's *Ion*.[21] Just as Vico's providence works through history in a way 'quite contrary, and always superior to the particular ends that men had proposed to themselves',[22] the 'infinite I AM' is only manifest in all its intelligibility in the aesthetic attitude, in the cultures or collective belief-systems whereby men create (in the etymological sense of poiésis, a 'making' (CL IV 545)) their identity and destiny. Schelling's transcendental deduction of imagination challenged the historical exclusivity of christian belief, or at least a rationalist apologetic which based belief upon such an historical event, a point to which we will return in Part Three. Art (and not exclusively Christ) 'is the one everlasting revelation which yields that concurrence, and the marvel which, had it existed but once only, would necessarily have convinced us of the absolute reality of that supreme event'.[23] The mediation of imagination is figured by the redemptive agency of Christ in the logic of the Trinity, but for Schelling this is but one, albeit the highest, articulation of a 'mythology of the Ideas'. Imagination offers a perpetual redemption, an integration of the absolute principle within the present and the community of experience, in contrast to the historical and sacramental exclusivity of christian dualism. Accordingly Schelling appended to his 1800 apotheosis of the role of aesthetic imagination an appeal for a new poetic mythology to authenticate the partial achievement of his philosophical system, to 'objectify . . . with universal validity what the philosopher is able to present in a merely subjective fashion'.[24]

Three years later, in the 1803 essay *Über Dante in philosophischer Beziehung*, Schelling repeated his challenge for a modern 'mixed epic' in the mould of the *Commedia*, synthesizing science, religion and art, combining allegorical and symbolical figures; the poet must create 'lasting shapes out of the confusion of the age, and into the arbitrarily produced forms of the images of his poetry he must again impart universal validity'.[25] This anticipated Coleridge's hopes for Wordsworth's 'FIRST GENUINE PHILOSOPHIC POEM' (BL II 156), a polymathic epic in the Lucretian mode, an ideal which the *Excursion* clearly failed to live up to (CL IV 574–6). A central tenet of Schelling's projected epic (more so than Coleridge's highly 'prescriptive' poem) was its openness to experience, and to forces which the philosopher himself could not prescribe. It would be the 'creation, not of some individual author, but of a new race, personifying, as it were, a single poet'.[26] True to the nature of myth, it will be a collective representation, the product not of poet or philosopher, but created by 'the future destinies of the world and in the course of history to come'.[27] Behind this may be discerned the Vicchian and Wolffian theories of epic according to which the *Iliad* and *Odyssey* were not the creations of individual poets (representing an occult 'wisdom of the ancients'), but rather 'civil histories of the first peoples, who were everywhere naturally poets'.[28]

Behind this view, which Coleridge himself endorsed (TT I 128–9) was a sense that authentic mythic art was the issue neither of philosophy nor priestcraft, but the outgrowth and exponent of civic experience. David Simpson defines romantic 'mythology' as 'a unifying body of representations held in common by an artist, his public and the idea which he objectifies; i.e. a body of materials from which art may emerge and in whose terms it may be understood'.[29] Schelling would later modify this definition of mythology in his work on the Mystery Cults, 'hermetic' vehicles of truth set against the civic, sacerdotal religions. But the notion of culture expounded in the conclusion of *Transcendentalen Idealismus* and elsewhere challenges the case which H. G. Gadamer has made for the overriding dominance of Kantian aesthetics in this period, the limitation and subjectivization of art which we noted above. Schelling's theory of art, like Coleridge's definition of symbol in *The Stateman's Manual*, attempted to formulate imagination in the civic terms of *Sensus Communis* in the face of social and historical forces which increasingly vitiated the possibility of such an ideal:

> In Germany, the followers of Shaftesbury and Hutcheson did not, even in the 18th century, take over the political and social elements contained in *sensus communis* . . . in the removal of all political content it lost its real critical significance. *Sensus Communis* was understood as a purely theoretical faculty, theoretical judgement, on a level with moral consciousness (conscience) and Taste. Thus it was fitted into a scholasticism of the basic faculties.[30]

11

Art and Nature

In the finale of *Transcendentalen Idealismus*, as important a source for Coleridge's pronouncements in *Biographia* chapters twelve and thirteen as was the 1807 *Verhältnis der bildenden Künste zur Natur* for the 1818 lecture *On Poesy or Art*, Schelling distinguished two different activities simultaneously at work in artistic creativity. These are identical in kind, although different in degree, from the constitutive polar powers of nature:

> If we are to seek in one of the two activities, namely the conscious, for what is ordinarily called *art*, though it is only one part thereof, namely that aspect of it which is exercised with consciousness, thought and reflection, and can be taught and learnt and achieved through tradition and practice, we shall have, on the other hand, to seek in the unconscious factor which enters into art for that about it which cannot be learned, nor attained by practice, nor in any other way, but can only be inborn through the free bounty of nature; and this is what we may call, in a word, the element of *poetry* [Poesie] in art.[1]

Perhaps contrary to expectations, this 'inborn gift' is not the exclusive property of hierophantic genius, as so many later interpreters of romantic 'inspiration' have taken it to be, but a common property of all men. 'It is not easy for a man to be by nature wholly without poetry [Poesie], though many are wholly without *art*', wrote Schelling, adding that it was given to few to balance the technical achievement with the natural insight, to capture the 'inexhaustible depth' of *poesie* in the work of art.[2]

Schelling's key notion of *poesie* was the quality he found lacking in Kant's formalist aesthetics. In the 1807 *Verhältnis* he implied that the Kantian art-work was limited to *art* devoid of *poesie*, a superficial arrangement of one component 'beside and outside the other', unconnected with the productive essence of nature.[3] Kant limited imagination to representing a subjective harmony of the faculties, and in his doctrine of the sublime, asserted moral power at the cost of imaginative vigour, form and matter had thus been separated, emphasis falling upon one or the other (in the Beautiful or the Sublime) without figuring the indifference of the two.

> Once everything positive and essential had been mentally eliminated from form [Form] it was bound to appear restrictive and, so to speak, hostile to essence [Wesen] and the same theory which had conjured up the false and feeble idea inevitably operated in the direction of the formless in art at the same time.[4]

For Schelling, form and essence were co-determinants in both art and nature, in paintings and crystals alike. The stellar system showed 'the most sublime art of number and mensuration', animals manifested unconscious artistry in 'their simple architectural works', and the song-bird, 'intoxicated by music, surpasses itself in soulful notes'.[5] The dialectical struggle between Form and Essence, the limiting and expansive powers, was anticipated in the mineral world, developed in the animal kingdom to the higher potency of consciousness, and reached its highest stage in the work of art, the polar indifference of the 'Shapely' and the 'Vital' (Bl sh II 257). Art is the 'reconciliation of infinite contradictions', a miraculous abridgement of nature's unlimited process; in Coleridge's words, the 'whole (of nature) *ad hominem*' (Bl sh II 262).

Schelling's identification of art with the creative agency of the Absolute in nature mapped with the analogical ease characteristic of the 'Constructive Philosophy' on to the field of art-history in a manner anticipating Hegel's *Aesthetics*. The formal proclivities of primitive organisms are compared with the Greek emphasis on the statuesque; the development of the ideal faculties in more sophisticated organisms with the 'Christian' art which prefers formlessness and chiaroscuro, the picturesque.[6] Although wary of a facile primitivism, Schelling admired the classical ideal (like Schiller's inclination to the *Naive* in his essay *On the Naive and Sentimental in Poetry*), which, in contrast to the modern art characterized by Kant's theory, was brimming over with unconscious *poesie*: 'besides what he has put into his work with manifest intention, the artist seems instinctively . . . to have depicted therein an infinity, which no finite understanding is capable of developing to the full'.[7] Schelling also lamented the 'debauching' of the sculptural by the 'painterly' ideal, and in the

Philosophie der Kunst (1802–3) desired a more 'representative' tendency than the highly individual characters of Protestant art. Shakespeare, compared unfavourably to the catholic Calderon, 'knows the highest beauty *only* as individual character';[8] Schelling demands a regeneration of what risks becoming an effete, spiritualized culture by a rekindling of the classical aesthetic attitude. Schelling's search for a civic religion in mythic art has much in common with the 'One Life' theory and the symbolic programme of the 'Lyrical Ballad', although its bias towards classicism should be regarded as a dialectical strategy rather than an absolute preference. Like Schiller's 'playdrive' (Spieltrieb) in the *Aesthetic Education*, Schelling's imagination redressed an overbalance of either the *form* or the *sense* drive (the Christian and the classical respectively) by means of a 'bracing' or 'melting' beauty.[9] That is to say, in the modern period, Schelling sought to 'brace' the highly-spiritualized, moral culture of christianity, just as Plato (in an antithetical manner) had 'melted' the sensuous Greek world in preparation for christianity.[10] It is significant that after 1817, Coleridge had no sympathy with Schelling's 'bracing' beauty in his defence of protestant individualism and devotion to a personal God; 'Schelling is a zealous Roman-Catholic, and not the first Philosopher who had adopted this sort of Plotinized Spinozism for the defence of the Polytheism and Charms of the Church of Rome' (CL IV 833; see also Ph L 391).

Coleridge's assimilation of Schelling's aesthetic philosophy was, as has been mentioned, a long and problematic process. In the 1814 essays *On the Principles of Genial Criticism* Coleridge presented a Kantian doctrine of aesthetics, in contrast to the Schellingian lecture of 1818, *On Poesy or Art*. Concerned primarily to overthrow the associationism of the current aesthetic theories of Archibald Alison, Dugald Stewart and Richard Payne Knight, Coleridge equated beauty with disinterestedness and characterized it as a subjective harmony of all the faculties in the object. The pleasure deriving from frost-patterns on a window-pane, for example, is contingent upon the formal arrangement of parts to whole, quite independent of any pleasant or unpleasant associations which the representation might evoke in the viewer (Bl sh II 232). Coleridge echoed Kant's definition 'The Beautiful arises from the perceived harmony of an object . . . with the inborn and constitutive rules of the judgement and imagination' (BL sh II 243). The Kantian bias evident here and in the Wordsworth criticism in volume two of the *Biographia* (composed only ten months after the *Principles of Genial Criticism*) should also be connected with the influence of A. W. Schlegel, whose criticism was more Kantian and 'dualistic' than his friend Schelling's.

The influence of Schelling on *Poesy or Art* is unmistakable in the following sequence:

> For of all we see, hear, feel and touch the substance is and must be in ourselves; and therefore there is no alternative in reason between the dreary (and thank heaven! almost impossible) belief that everything around us is but a phantom, or that the life which is in us is in them likewise; and that to know is to resemble, when we speak of objects out of ourselves . . .
>
> (BL sh II 259)

Coleridge's definition of art as 'the mediatress between, and reconciler of, nature and man', his account of 'unconscious activity' as 'the genius in the man of genius', of beauty as 'the union of the shapely (formosum) with the vital', of a pantheistic theory of matter 'body is but a striving to become mind'; all represent a decisive rejection of the Kantian criteria of the 1814 essays (BL sh II 258; 257; 258). Beauty is still defined as existing independent of assocation, as universal, intuitive and disinterested (as in Kant and Schelling), but the Schellingian increment is added whereby formal harmony is subordinate to essential vigour or *poesie*:

> [If the artist proceeds] only from a given form which is supposed to answer to the notion of beauty, what an emptiness, what an unreality there always is in his productions, as in Cipriani's pictures! Believe me, you must master the essence, the *natura naturans*, which presupposes a bond between nature in the higher sense and the soul of man.
>
> (BL sh II 257)

The unity of the creative mind with the 'germinal cause of nature' (BL sh II 258–9) necessitates a momentary abandonment of the outer forms of nature, the *natura naturata* which exists in separation for self, in order to master the common essence of both.

A note of qualification in Coleridge's treatment of the moral connotations of Schelling's system is already apparent in his re-working of one of the German's sentences. (The lecture is perhaps the most notorious case of plagiarism in the Coleridge canon, much of it being an unacknowledged translation of Schelling's *Verhältnis*). In distinguishing the conscious from the natural realm, Schelling is more concerned to stress continuity than distinction. Coleridge qualifies Schelling's account of 'the wisdom in nature' by adding the moral dimension absent from the undifferentiated natural realm in which 'there is reflex act, and hence there is no moral responsibility' (BL sh II 257). This qualifier is typical of the public scruples Coleridge developed with regard to the pelagianism of Schelling's system, which increasingly forced him to identify it with Spinozism. Schelling's 'world system' was itself morally purposive, the self-generation of the Absolute leading inexorably to the good, however obscure that destination often seemed to the finite mind. Schelling's optimistic determinism implied a rejection of the orthodox doctrine of original sin, which E. D. Hirsch has compared to the Wordsworthian attitude of 'wise passiveness', the moral probity of 'the impulse from a vernal wood'.[11] Although Schelling does evoke a 'fall into consciousness', a separation implicit in the whole polar doctrine, the freedom afforded by self-reflection is fulfilled in a reunification with the 'germinal causes of nature' rather than in an ascetic renunciation of the world. Schelling's Absolute is manifest in the world of nature and history rather than being a principle which transcends it.

In the 1809 treatise *Über das Wesen der menschlichen Freiheit* Schelling disguised the determinism of his system by considering the origin of evil as a Platonic 'fall' from the plenitude of the Absolute, entailing a sense of alienation at the very roots of consciousness. The choice of finitude or 'false imagination' led to guilt-consciousness and a false, dualistic knowledge and practice, 'the very fact of sin itself'.[12] Evil is thus an illusion rather than an original fact, and man is linked to a primordial goodness which constantly reveals itself in experience:

How could anything except truth be real, and what is beauty if it is not full and complete existence? . . . What higher purpose could art have other than to depict that which exists in nature and in fact?[13]

Imagination wrests the mind from its separative condition, its finitude and self-limitation, and integrates it with the 'natural' purposiveness of the Absolute. The *engagement* of the Schellingian symbol rather than the *asceticism* of Kant's moral proof establishes the road to the Absolute, 'the one everlasting revelation'.[14]

In Appendix C of the *Stateman's Manual*, written at the time of his most uncritical acceptance of Schelling, Coleridge also subscribed to a notion of 'non-radical evil'. Considering the melancholy which accompanies the contemplative observation of nature, he commented:

> From this state hast *thou* fallen! Such shouldst thou still become, thy Self all permeable to a holier power! thy Self at once hidden and glorified by its own transparency, as the accidental and dividuous in this quiet and harmonious object is submitted to the life and light of nature which shines in it, even as the transmitted power, love and wisdom, of God over all fills, and shines through, nature! But what the plant *is*, by an act not its own and unconsciously – that must thou *make* thyself to *become*!
>
> (LS 71)

But Coleridge's later (undated) note to this passage in Copy G reads:

> At the time I wrote this Work, my views of *Nature* were very imperfect and confused. But for this whole passage . . . una litura [an erasure] would be the best emendment. STC.
>
> (LS 71 n6)

Coleridge's specification of 'moral responsibility' came to involve an emphasis quite distinct from Schelling's, with which he is evidently struggling in the delivery of the Schellingian imagination in chapter thirteen of the *Biographia*. For the Will, the Promethean faculty in man, increasingly finds itself at odds with nature, conceived latterly as 'the Devil in a strait-waistcoat' (LS 71 n6). As Coleridge grew away from the immanence of the 'One Life' ideal towards a sterner dualism, the path of redemption drew further from the social idea of art and from the natural world. This is summed up in a late marginal note in Schelling's *Über Dogmatismus and Kriticismus*, in its unqualified praise for the Hebrew idea of the World as at emnity with God, and of the continual warfare which calls forth every energy, both of act and endurance, from the necessary vividness of worldly impressions, and the sensuous dimness of faith in the first struggles! Were the impulses and impresses from the faith in God equally vivid, then indeed all combat must cease, and we should have Hallelujahs for tragedies and statutes.

(BL sh lxxxv)

12

Art and Knowledge: Chapters Twelve and Thirteen of the *Biographia Literaria*

Chapters five to thirteen of the *Biographia*, composed in August and September 1815 after most of the rest of the book was completed, represented at once the most sophisticated articulation of the 'One Life' ideal, but also its evanescence and practical failure.[1] The theory of imagination which Coleridge expounded in these chapters, along with a metaphysical justification of the theory, should be connected with both the *Statesman's Manual* (December 1816) and the letter to Lord Liverpool (July 1817) which accompanied his gift of the recently-published *Biographia* to the Tory prime minister.[2] The first of these sought to combine two major strands in Coleridge's thinking; his advocacy of poetic symbol as focus for national community (presented in the 'polar' terminology of Schellingian idealism), and a complementary vision of the state modelled upon the Jewish Theocracy, consistent with the 'republic of God's own making' which he had presented in the 1795 *Lectures on Revealed Religion*. The Jewish commonwealth, vehicle of divine providence and a nation in which politics and religion were one, was here proposed as a model for the statesmen of the English ruling class. The commonwealth republicanism of the younger Coleridge, shedding the egalitarian agrarian law and its animosity to aristocrats and priests, had blended with a well-established Tory apologetic which essentially based its concept of citizenship upon an idealization of propertied independence, opposed to the caprice and corruption attendant upon the commercial order.

And yet the tensions which exhausted Coleridge's theory of imagination in *Biographia* chapter thirteen are palpably present in the *Lay Sermons*. Written shortly after the introduction of the protectionist Corn Laws, published in the same month as the massive demonstration for parliamentary reform at Spa Fields, the *Stateman's Manual* was an exhortation to the 'Higher classes' of society (rather than the professional clergy, as Coleridge later sought to maintain[3]), not to abandon the social duties attendant upon proprietorship which seemed, from the vantage point of 1816, to have been the condition of the 'organic' unity of the 'old society'. The very fact that *three* 'Lay Sermons' were proposed, each an 'ad hominem' address to a particular social class, itself symptomized the crisis of values and language in which the *Sermons* intervened; in the second *Lay Sermon* especially, the socially-unifying, organic values have themselves to be spelt out as it already half-forgotten. Because of an overbalance of the 'commercial spirit', which has vitiated the civic humanism of the landed classes, Coleridge appealed to a new kind of 'public-spiritedness' called 'cultivation': 'the slow progress of intellect, the influences of religion, and irresistible events guided by Providence, (LS 169). The role of Schellingian aesthetics in Providing a 'civic' (as opposed to orthodox Christian) appeal for political community, now detached from any available political identification, whether radical or Tory, is the subject of the following pages. But as we saw in connection with Coleridge's 'revision' of Wordsworth in *Biographia* volume two, Schellingian idealism of the imagination co-existed with an alternative theory of culture involving a paradoxical recourse to what might be termed the 'separation from separation'; this grew out of Coleridge's increasing sense of inexorable social and civic fragmentation.

Coleridge's ambivalent opinion of Schelling in the period immediately following the publication of the *Biographia* provides an instructive context for a reading of the problematic of chapters twelve and thirteen. The lecture *On Poesy or Art* was delivered probably in early 1818;[4] with the slight qualification noted on p. 121 above, it represents a full acceptance of Schellingian aesthetics. Less than a year later, however, in the penultimate *Philosophical Lecture*, Schelling was publicly denounced as a Catholic and Polytheist (Ph L 391) and in late September and mid-November 1818, Coleridge's objections to the German were explained in letters to J. H. Green and C. A. Tulk (CL IV 873–6; 883–4). In the following October, he wrote, regarding naturphilosophie, that he must henceforth be content 'with caressing the heretical Brat in private' (CL IV 956). Coleridge's opinions of the 'metaphysical sections' of the *Biographia* are predictably enough tied up with his loss of public faith in Schelling. Writing to his publisher on the 17 September 1815, Coleridge gave a high rating to the recently-expanded chapters five to thirteen (CL IV 585–6); later in life, however, he feared that the 'metaphysical disquisition' was 'unformed and immature', containing 'fragments of the truth, but it is not fully thought out' (TT II 335, 28 June 1834).

Despite the fact that German idealism had offered Coleridge a 'safe' alternative to the 1800 cultural paradigm of 'the real language of men' as vehicle for *Sensus Communis* (the latter increasingly tainted by sectarian political connotations), the post-1818 criticisms of Schelling echoed the earlier objections to Wordsworth. Evidently Coleridge was more dissatisfied with the project of grounding a theory of culture on a civic basis as such, than he was with either of his own former influences as individual thinkers. The 'plotinized Spinozism', ethical determinism and systematic hubris of Schelling echoes, in a finer tone, the 'nature worship', 'pious fraud' and confusion of established hierarchies which taints the poetry of Wordsworth (CL IV 883; V 95). The *Biographia* articulates a fundamental contradiction between the 'One Life' theory we have traced through Wordsworth and Schelling, and Coleridge's developing will towards a 'distinction of powers' evident in the second volume, a contradiction which determines the strained equivocation at the heart of chapter thirteen's theory of imagination, the exhaustion attendant upon its delivery.

Many critics have perceived the division between the two volumes of the *Biographia* as a suture which conveniently preserves a continuity between two fundamentally irreconcilable positions. The sudden transformation of idiom from the metaphysics of volume one to the 'practical criticism' of volume two has been described as a 'miraculous recovery' as the literary sensibility reassuringly finds itself freed from 'the viscous integument of metaphysics'.[5] But this discontinuity goes beyond critical idiom to contradictory ideological positions, the co-existence of the 'One Life' ideal with a dualistic definition of culture which we will see shaping Coleridge's later thought. Paul Hamilton, attacking a recent impulse to read the *Biographia* as a hermetic unity, has rightly discerned an absence at the heart of the book, a 'genuine hiatus in [Coleridge's] thought, and not the mask worn by his super-subtle philosophy'.[6] But this hiatus is not a gap between the Schellingian 'tertium aliquid' preceding chapter thirteen's 'letter', and an intrinsically Coleridgean desynonymization of imagination and fancy, inaugurating a separation between critical theory and 'practical criticism' which has dogged English criticism ever since. The hiatus is rather a discontinuity between the Schellingian chapters twelve and thirteen (taken as a whole) and the dualistic definition of poetic authority emerging in the Wordsworth criticism in volume two. Coleridge neither adds to, nor subtracts from, the German's idea of imagination here, although certain ambivalences dog its presentation; but the Schellingian sections are far from being consistent with the *Biographia* taken as a whole. Only in the wider implications of these contradictory positions will their co-existence become intelligible, for aesthetic arguments have no privileged exemption from ideological problematics, despite the disguise of immunity inaugurated by the historical distinction of cultural and political power which is the object of our study.

Despite all the hedging exposed by Fruman and others, Coleridge admits the German provenance of his ideas, seeking only to render 'the system intelligible to my countrymen' and acknowledging the importance of 'my German predecessor' (BL I 163–4). The greater part of chapters twelve and thirteen is concerned with establishing a metaphysical basis for imagination (or rather the dependence of metaphysics upon imagination). Imagination is announced at the beginning of chapter ten, in the words of the latest editors, as 'an abortive or false start on what finally becomes chapter thirteen, "on the imagination or esemplastic powers"' (BL I 168n). Ninety-six pages later (in the new edition) it resurfaces, in the statement that the results of the 'Ten Theses' 'will be applied to the deduction of the imagination, and with it the principles of production and of genial criticism in the fine arts' (BL I 264).

Coleridge offered his readers a general synopsis of Schelling's philosophy whilst concentrating (for the aesthetic purpose to hand) upon 'the *subjective* Pole of the Dynamic Philosophy; the rudiments of *Self*-construction' (CL IV 767). James Engell's and Jackson Bate's contention that 'a strong case' could be made for the Fichtean, rather than Schellingian provenance of these chapters is really a quibble; the 'subjective pole' of Schelling's system underpinning Coleridge's transcendental deduction of imagination subsumed Fichte's *Ich-philosophie* into a more expansive metaphysical framework, the imagination mediating between Fichtean self-consciousness and the polar powers of nature. The role in which Coleridge cast imagination as productive essence of the 'world-system' went far beyond Fichtean subjectivism and 'hyperstoic hostility to NATURE' (BL I 159). Chapter twelve's 'subjective pole' is only intelligible in the light of the 'objective' pole of naturphilosophie which Coleridge expounded in his *Theory of Life* the following year, and in a September 1817 letter to Tulk (CL IV 767–76). Coleridge's (failed) attempt to 'christianize' naturphilosophie[7] in these works and in subsequent notebooks is paralleled here by his bid to dress up the Schellingian Absolute as the traditional Christian god (p. 256) and as Jehovah (p. 275n). In the first of these instances, Coleridge's identification of nature and self-consciousness is qualified by an orthodox scruple, whereby Schelling's equation ('so-called DEAD Nature in general is an unripe intelligence') is replaced by a verse from Psalms 19.1 'the heavens and the earth shall declare . . . the glory and the presence of their God'.[8] To the later Coleridge, even this qualification of Schelling's monism, containing an implication that natural science could offer a revelation similar in kind to that of the Logos, would be quite unacceptable as public doctrine.

I do not wish to follow Coleridge's 'construction' of self-consciousness in detail since it follows the lines of Schelling's system already considered at some length. All the components are there: refutation of philosophic dualism ('sensation itself is but vision nascent, not the cause of intelligence, but intelligence itself revealed as an earlier power in the process of self-construction' (BL I 286)); a defence of 'intellectual intuition' with an attack on Kant's limitation of the noumenon (BL I 288–9); the syncretic design of the 'Dynamic Philosophy' (BL I 244–7); the introduction of the Brunonian/Schellingian *Potenz* (converted to the English verb 'potenziate' (BL I 287)), and of course the narrative of ascending potencies of self-consciousness in the 'Ten Theses'. Philosophy is divided into *real* and *ideal* poles, the methodological rather than existential nature of the division being stressed (BL I 255), and the philosophical expression of intellectual intuition is stated to be an impossibility: 'while I am attempting to explain this intimate coalition I must suppose it dissolved' (BL I 255).

In the 'Ten Theses' themselves, Coleridge gets down to a

systematic deduction of self-consciousness the 'highest principle of knowing . . . at once the source and the accompanying form in all particular acts of intellect and perception' (BL I 282).[9] In Thesis VI, a sensitive issue is touched upon in the relationship between transcendental self-consciousness (the highest expression of the polar powers) and the orthodox deity. The appended footnote shows just how close Coleridge is here to a form of pantheism, the assertion of an immanent, self-evolving power rather than a transcendent creator. A parallel is drawn between the fiat of Jehovah 'I am that I am' and the idealist's interpretation of the 'Transcendental Unity of Apperception', highly dangerous to the transcendent God of Christian orthodoxy; it is in this transcendental Ego (rather than the 'conditional finite I'), defined as 'the absolute I AM', that 'we live, and move, and having our being' according to the Pauline text (BL I 277n). According to this view, God is an 'Out-birth of the World-System', the expression of a human sublime, rather than a transcendent creator set over against a fallen world of consciousness and nature as in traditional christian dualism (CL IV 883). Coleridge had accepted Schelling's system as mitigated or 'Plotinized' Spinozism, in the faith that his concern to maintain human freedom (especially in the eponymous 1809 treatise) saved it from pantheistic determinism. In chapter twelve Coleridge argued that 'Pantheism is . . . not necessarily irreligious or heretical; tho' it may be taught atheistically' (BL I 247n), echoing the earlier Unitarian argument that sought to spiritualize the phenomenal (and political) world in the most literal way without accepting materialism or atheism. Coleridge had sought a deity at once immanent and transcendent (or, as he wrote in an August 1818 marginal note in Boehme's *Aurora* 'as if God were a Whole composed of Parts, of which the World was one!', by 1818 regarded as an intoxication 'with the vernal fragrance & effluvia from the flowers and first-fruits of Pantheism, unaware of its bitter root' (MI 602–3)). Coleridge was now subordinating the vestigial radicalism of the earlier position to an idea of the necessary separateness of God from the world.

But Coleridge's pantheism in the *Biographia* was, like Schelling's in the *Transcendentalen Idealismus*, mitigated by the separation of consciousness or knowledge from the ground of being, the Absolute. However close he may have been (as in the above passage) to identifying God with human self-consciousness, thereby committing the Fichtean heresy of deifying a 'mere Ordo

Ordinans' (BL I 160), Coleridge stressed that consciousness had itself fallen from the plenitude of the Absolute, and was therefore independent and morally responsible. Some commentators have (mistakenly) affirmed that the distinction here between *being* and *knowing* was Coleridge's attempt to render Schelling's system compatible with orthodox Christianity, apparently in ignorance of the German's attempts to enforce such a separation in both *Transcendentalen Idealismus* and *Der menschliche Freiheit*.[10] As is evident from Coleridge's ensuing disaffection with Schelling, even this mitigated pantheism came to seem heretical, in its identification of the Absolute with the 'germinal causes of nature' and the priority it affords the aesthetic imagination (over the Logos) as a salvific medium reconciling the finite intellect with the ground of being. In chapter twelve, Coleridge located the genesis of self-consciousness within a larger, all-encompassing system created by the *divine* self-consciousness, the *Absolute*, rather than the *finite*, I AM. Finite self-consciousness is a sub-set of the Absolute, merely a complete system of knowledge set within god's complete system of existence. The system of the Absolute is beyond the philosopher's reach because it surpasses knowledge, although it is the privilege of 'intellectual intuition' (and its 'objectification' in the work of art) to identify with the divine ground of being, reorientating and upholding the speculative mind; as Coleridge expressed it in *Church and State*, 'Not without celestial observations, can even terrestial charts be accurately constructed' (CS 48). Only faith in a supernatural existence and destiny can give meaning to natural knowledge.

Self-consciousness is thus not the *ne plus ultra* of the mind for either Schelling or Coleridge because it may be 'explicable into something, which must lie beyond the possibility of our knowledge' (BL I 284–5). This 'something' is the *cause* of which knowledge is merely the *effect*; the very act of self-consciousness implying the prior existence of the mind which thinks. Only the Absolute self-consciousness (the infinite I AM) is 'causa sui et effectus', identity and simultaneity of being and knowing (BL I 285).

The importance of maintaining this separation was impelled by the importance of human freedom to both thinkers; a moral act for both Schelling and Coleridge in 1815 was one which independently chose identity with the Absolute. By this definition art was the symbol of a moral act, it being the agency of art to overcome the separative finitude of consciousness and to integrate *art* with *poesie*, or knowledge with being; herein lay the superiority of art to philosophy for Schelling.

> For the aesthetic intuition simply is the intellectual intuition become objective . . . that which the philosopher allows to be divided even in the primary act of consciousness, and which would otherwise be inaccessible to any intuition, comes, through the miracle of art, to be radiated back from the products thereof.[11]

The aesthetic core of Schelling's and Coleridge's thought determined it as a system based on belief rather than ratiocination, exempting it from that hubristic brand of pantheistic system-making and 'consequent reasoning' in which 'the Intellect refuses to acknowledge a higher or deeper ground than it can itself supply, and weens to possess within itself the centre of its own System' (Friend I 523n). Hence the context of Coleridge's metaphysical construction within a 'biographia literaria' (rather than a philosophical treatise) assumes great importance in determining its interpretation. Chapter twelve's argument is an essential preliminary to the 'chapter on imagination', now clearly established as 'the vision and the faculty Divine'.

The rhetorical effect of this 'self-effacing' philosophical disquisition, set within its literary and biographical context, engineers a subtle distinction between the figure of the philosopher and the 'genial' author of the *Biographia*. While the philosopher doggedly ploughs on with his transcendental deduction, the author's figure lies in wait for him (in a manner of speaking) springing forward with the chapter thirteen letter to slice off the aspiring dialectic in mid-sentence. This device really dramatizes Schelling's account of art as the 'objectification' of intellectual intuition, for Coleridge's 'philosopher' overreaches himself (perhaps the point is that philosophers always do) by borrowing material from mathematics 'the only province of knowledge, which man has succeeded in erecting into a pure science' (BL I 297–8), in order to pacify 'the unsettled, warring and embroiled domain of philosophy' (BL I 298). Coleridge offers an exegetical clue to his strategy just before the point at which his text breaks off, his intention to 'elevate the Thesis from notional to the actual, by contemplating intuitively this one power with its two inherent indestructible yet counteracting forces' (BL I 299). The textual rupture following the annunciation of the *tertium aliquid* dramatizes not only Schelling, but also perhaps Schiller's introduction, in the thirteenth of his *Aesthetic Letters*, of the Play drive, also a completely unthinkable concept.[12]

The chapter thirteen letter, for all its irony and rhetorical caprice, shows a certain awkwardness or unease with its own artifice. On the one hand, it seeks to remind the author of the limitation of human knowledge in relation to the divine, anxious to avoid the hubris of Bishop Berkeley's 'Essay on tar-water, which beginning with Tar, ends with the Trinity, the *omne scibile* forming the interspace' (BL I 303). At the heart of Coleridge's device is discernible the guilt of evasion; his limitation of knowledge simply replaces the hubris of the philosopher with that of the artist. Art usurps the prior place of the Logos in this daring revision of traditional Christian apologetic, a *poiēsis* of the creator. The letter gives priority to the poet, as it replaces a metaphysical with a rhetorical idiom, translating the deduction into a gothic cathedral. The correspondent alludes to Wordsworthian epic (Coleridge's hope for the modern 'myth') by citing lines from the poem *To William Wordsworth*, written after the first hearing of the *Prelude*. But the lines are altered to describe the *Biographia*'s (omitted) 'chapter on imagination':

> . . . An orphic tale indeed,
> A tale *obscure* of high and passionate thoughts
> To *a strange* music chaunted!

> (BL I 302)

The divinity of Wordsworth's orphism compares favourably with the harsh obscurity of the overreaching philosopher, a speculative hubris which tempts beyond the legitimate bounds of knowledge.

The point is that although the device of the letter excuses Coleridge from perpetrating the philosopher's hubris (the 'link' with the heavens being removed, the missing chapter on imagination), the rhetorical artfulness, and the existential identity which artfulness affords with the Absolute, repeats the hubris, albeit in a finer tone. Art symbolizes the immanence of the Absolute, the power constitutive of phenomena, literally 'embodying' the 'aeternitas mundi' of the civic ideal. Art permits a dangerous proximity to, and identity with, the creator. In the subsequent development of Coleridge's thought we will see this represented as the primal (and perennial) sin of mankind, the recuperation of power, the tendency of natural intellect or imagination to assert 'man as the measure of all things', satisfying the fallen consciousness's will-to-power by denying the transcendence of God. This metalepsis of the origin is traditionally figured in the myth of Babel, Nimrod's endeavour (like the philosopher's) to link up earth and heaven by means of a miracle of human construction, the Tower. In the 1825 lecture *On the Prometheus of Aeschylus*, Coleridge described this pantheistic impulse as 'the first apostasy of mankind after the flood, when they combined to raise a temple to the heavens' (LR II 350). The chapter on imagination, and indeed the whole project of establishing the divine power of art as an archetype of the Logos, repeats the profane attempt to 'raise a material temple to the heavens' – as the chapter thirteen correspondent indicates, Coleridge's construction resembles 'fragments of the winding steps of an old ruined tower' (BL I 303). Babel is cast as a haunting figure for the 'politics of imagination', now a ruined vestige of the brave edifice which had been Coleridge's 'One Life' ideal, the 'republic of God's own making'. The mythic allusion reverberates with the pathos of John Milton's appeal to the citizens of the English commonwealth, in the 1660 *Ready and Easy Way to Establish a Free Commonwealth*, as the shades of Restoration were already moving in. What has happened, Milton asks, to 'this goodly Tower of Commonwealth, which the *English* boasted they would build to overshadow Kings, and be another *Rome* in the West?'[13] The 'civic religion' of the republic has been fragmented into a confusion of tongues, the 'errors of party-spirit', and the spirit of faction presiding over the literary no less than the political realm (much of the *Biographia* is a counterblast to the faction of Reviewers), now threatens the very possibility of political and symbolic unity. Within its immediate historical context the theory of imagination presented in the *Biographia* is thus aptly emblematized by the 'old ruined tower'; Coleridge himself increasingly identified with the blind and alienated Milton, revenging himself upon the Restoration with his *Paradise Lost* (LR I 178).

Coleridge's device of the letter, translating the *Biographia* from a philosophical to a literary-critical idiom, sought to overcome the hubris of an 'Intellect [refusing] to acknowledge a higher or deeper ground than it can itself supply' (Friend I 523n). But the artful project of theorizing imagination as a copula with the Absolute, however 'secondary' and 'finite' its products might be in relation to the 'infinite I AM', was fraught with anxiety. The civic provenance of the 'One Life' ideal came increasingly to seem like a satanic substitute for the salvific mediation of the Logos; despite the checks imposed upon the secondary imagination and its ambivalent 'co-existence' with the conscious will, the perilous metalepsis can still assert itself in the identification of creative power with the Creator, the self-creation of origins. Coleridge's theory of imagination stands as a (ruined) monument to the antinomianism of the 'spiritual politics' of the 1790s, and its continuation into the manifestly *un*political symbolism of the 1815–17 period. But imagination came to seem like a 'rebellious principle of monism', as Coleridge abandoned the civic tradition and sought a redefinition of culture based upon an absolute separation between the Absolute and 'the things that are seen'. The 'metaphysical disquisition', once given pride of place in the *Biographia* as a whole, came to be identified with the hubristic aims of Wordsworth's 1800 Preface, or the 'immanent' spirit of Schelling's system, confusing the hierarchies of heaven and earth by the interpenetration of spirit and matter. Returning to the fold of Christian devotion and asceticism, Coleridge increasingly subscribed to an exclusive faith in 'the Moral Being only, which the Spirit and Religion of Man can alone fill up' (Friend I 523n). Devotion must precede creation, Mystery take priority over illumination, entailing a stoical suppression of experience to the dictates of Kant's moral Imperative. Coleridge's unfinished tower remains pointing to heaven as a standing rebuke to the proponents of political, philosophical and aesthetic idealism.

13

Coleridge's Theory of Primary and Secondary Imagination

A principal stumbling-block to a contextual understanding of Coleridge's theory of imagination has been a confusion concerning the meaning of the Primary/Secondary distinction, perhaps partly caused by his tendency, in other writings, to stress the Secondary whilst omitting the Primary or 'divine' imagination.[1] This is a pity, because it is a critical distinction of far more significance than the conventional Fancy/Imagination one, the eighteenth-century genesis of which must be one of the best-documented areas of literary history.[2]

A consideration of the chapter thirteen definitions in the light of the Schellingian distinction between *art* and *poesie* makes more sense of the precise differential between Coleridge's two categories of imagination. How does art reconcile the primary, unconscious being of the Absolute with the secondary, conscious activity of the intellect? A juxtaposition of Schelling's definition, in part six of *Transcendentalen Idealismus*, with Coleridge's celebrated passage, clarifies the issue:

> It is the poetic gift, which in its primary potentiality constitutes the primordial intuition, and conversely, what we speak of as the poetic gift is merely productive intuition, reiterated to its highest power. It is one and the same capacity that is active in both, the only one whereby we are able to think and to couple together even what is contradictory – and its name is imagination . . . that which appears to us outside the sphere of consciousness, as real, and that which appears within it, as ideal, or as the world of art, are also products of one and the same activity.[3]

> The IMAGINATION then I consider either as primary, or secondary. The primary IMAGINATION I hold to be the living Power and prime Agent of all human Perception, and as a

135

repetition in the finite mind of the eternal act of creation in the infinite I AM. The secondary I consider as an echo of the former, co-existing with the conscious will, yet still as identical with the primary in the *kind* of its agency, and differing only in *degree*, and in the *mode* of its operation. It dissolves, diffuses, dissipates, in order to re-create; or where this process is rendered impossible, yet still at all events it struggles to idealize and to unify. It is essentially *vital*, even as all objects (*as* objects) are essentially fixed and dead.

(BL I 304)

It is quite impossible to separate Coleridge's definition from its context in Schellingian idealism in the way Thomas McFarland has suggested;[4] there is a direct link between Coleridge's 'Ten Theses' in chapter twelve and the chapter thirteen definition, a link endorsed by the similarity of the two passages cited above. To extrapolate the chapter thirteen definition is to make imagination do duty in the service of any critical theory which might choose to appropriate it. The fact that Coleridge's abandonment (and elision[5]) of these terms after 1817 coincided with his critical qualification of Schelling's system is not fortuitous. Both Wellek and Orsini offer a more fruitful contextualization of the theory of imagination, however, the latter comparing Primary imagination with Schelling's productive intuition and Kant's *Anschauung* (in the *First Critique*), mediating between sense and understanding, figurative synthesis of the Many and the One.[6] Coleridgean Primary imagination, unlike Kant's, however, repeats the productive activity of the Absolute rather than merely presenting to the understanding all that may be known of the noumenal *ding-an-sich*. Schelling's idealism replaced cognition with creation in the manner examined above.

Primary imagination is not specifically connected with art except insofar as the perceived world is the creation of the Absolute, or, as Schelling put it, 'what we speak of as nature is a poem lying pent in a mysterious and wonderful Script'.[7] Secondary imagination, on the other hand, is the creative power of art in the more usual sense, operating in a similar manner to the Primary, but within the framework of consciousness and will. The redemptive agency of art is *chosen* in a manner which distinguishes it from the unconscious realm of nature, placing human reflection (a moral act) both within the terms of, and apart form, natural spontaneity. Consciousness betokens a 'fortunate fall' preserving human freedom, the correct orientation of which is the choice of submitting the finite will to the Absolute necessity: 'what the plant *is*, by an act not its own and unconsciously – *that* thou must *make* thyself to *become*!' (LS 71). The poet is offered the unique privilege of overcoming the limits of consciousness and finding within the world of experience the means of transforming finitude and embodying unconscious *poesie* within the conscious forms of art. Secondary imagination is the essential copula between Primary imagination (unconsciously creative perception and nature, both of which 'repeat' the divine creativity), and fallen consciousness. Its reconciliations of these polarities partakes of the great productive synthesis of the 'world-system' and 'the eternal act of creation in the infinite I AM'. Without the copula, consciousness remains oblivious to the divine ground of being – unable to 'see all things in God', it perceives only 'fixities and definites', the dualistic limits of the conditioned finite self. The latter condition is manifest in art as *Fancy*; a necessary component of imaginative art, but as an end in itself, limited and derivative. Only secondary or aesthetic imagination locates consciousness in the correct orientation to the Absolute, at once the archetypal moral act and 'the sole and eternal revelation'.

In *Poetry or Art*, Coleridge referred to unconscious activity (*poesie*) as 'the genius in the man of genius' (Bl sh II 258). The artist has the power to retire from an image of the world which may be described as 'false consciousness' to rediscover the master-currents below the surface, 'the germinal cause of nature'. Willed abandonment of conscious intention paradoxically reveals a higher intentionality, for Schelling's Absolute is a teleological and morally purposive principle; art breaks open false consciousness by revealing the subordination of all things to the creative power of the infinite I AM. In the 1807 *Verhältnis*, Schelling demanded

> How can we, so to speak, spiritually melt this apparently hard form, so that the unadulterated energy of things fuses with the energy of our spirits, forming a single cast?[8]

Coleridge's chapter thirteen definition of secondary imagination answered Schelling's rhetorical question: it 'dissolves, diffuses, dissipates, in order to re-create; or where this process is rendered impossible, yet at all events it struggles to idealize and to unify' (BL I 304). Art represents the purpose and progress of the

Absolute, the creative power to dissipate the hard form of 'separated' consciousness, revealing the factitious nature of reality seemingly 'fixed and dead'. Imagination transforms experience not to the end of transcendence, but to show the underlying purpose, value and unity of the contingent world. In an 1815 letter, Coleridge described art as a miraculous foreshortening of the divine order in nature and history:

> The common and of all *narrative*, nay, of *all*, Poems is to convert a *series* into a *Whole*: to make those events, which in real or imagined History move on in a *strait* Line, assume to our Understandings a *circular* motion – the snake with it's Tail in it's Mouth. . . . Now what the Globe is in Geography, *miniaturing* in order to *manifest* the Truth, such is a Poem to that Image of God, which we were created into, and which still seeks that Unity, or Revelation of the *One* in and by the *Many* . . .
>
> (CL IV 545)

Imagination explicates the purpose of experience not by destroying it and replacing it with something preferable but by unveiling the beautiful as 'full and complete existence'.

We saw above the aspiration to a modern mythology which impelled Schelling's definition of imagination, a dissipation of the rigid forms of social and political division in an epic form, gathering together the fragments of the age, gleaning from science, history and philosophy to create a unifying symbol for a community in the process of self-construction. In the 1817 letter to Lord Liverpool, Coleridge complained that the prevailing mechanical philosophy had rendered such an 'organic' sense of historical community and destiny a virtual impossibility, having inaugurated a process of secularization and 'demythologization' threatening the possibility of civic integrity (CL IV 761–2). His disappointment with Wordsworth's *Excursion* has already been commented upon; in a May 1815 letter he had regretted the poet's failure to dissipate the 'hard form', 'the sore evils, under which the whole Creation groans', and to indicate 'a manifest Scheme of Redemption from this Slavery, of Reconciliation from this Emnity with Nature' (CL IV 575). Wordsworth had failed to achieve the 'inexhaustibility' of Schellingian *poesie*, the authenticity of a communal voice, in his adhesion to the recondite and refined 'how can common truths be made permanently interesting but by being *bottomed* in our common nature' (CL IV 576). It will be evident from our discussion of Coleridge and the republication of Southey's *Wat Tyler* in Part Three that the practical non-existence of such a community (or at least its appropriation by a political rhetoric based on class interests determined Coleridge's) redefinition of the cultural idea in the direction of a specifically Christian unity and tradition. Schelling's civic epic reappears in *Aids to Reflection* and *Constitution of the Church and State* as the Christian church, a 'traditional' structure of authority already polarized and insulated from the flux and fragmentation of the political world.[9] But already in the definition of Secondary imagination, Coleridge was having difficulties preserving a unifying authority for imagination, necessarily based upon an openness to changing qualities of collective experience.

Whilst sceptical of attempts to establish Coleridgean imagination as an anticipation of Marxist dialectic (on the grounds that it was the very failure of romantic imagination to engage squarely with social and economic reality which determines its inadequacy as a radical critique of capitalism), I consider R. F. Storch's comparison of the 'Polar' philosophy with Lukács' account of mediation one of the most fruitful to date.[10] The comparative vantage-point allows Storch to detect an implicit ambiguity in Secondary imagination: Coleridge does not define a single *modus operandi* for the artist, but rather two, which are, moreover, mutually exclusive. *Either* the imagination 'dissolves, diffuses, dissipates in order to recreate' *or* 'where this process is rendered impossible', it 'struggles to idealize and to unify' (BL I 304). The tension and resistance met by imagination (which may simply overwhelm its struggle to 'spiritually melt the hard form') is simply not present as a problem in Schelling's account of aesthetic mediation. Although Schelling's artist might be aware of a contradiction between his 'unmotivated' representation of reality and the 'false forms of consciousness', they are no more than 'poles apart'; and as poles subsumable within the progressive dialectic of the Absolute. Schelling's polarity permits freedom, an unconditioned point from which the artist may wield the errant realm of consciousness, inaugurating an interplay between reason and experience. Schelling's poet seems to have history on his side, seems to inhabit a purposeful universe, his 'freely-chosen' artwork miniaturing the 'unconscious' purpose of the absolute. There is no sense that the master-currents below the surface might sweep him in the wrong direction or that change might be intrinsically meaningless. Coleridge also subscribed to this view when he wrote 'unconscious activity is the genius in the man of genius', but soon came to regard the relationship between the artist and the 'natural' world of process and experience as being essentially tragic in character. These two contradictory views coexist in the chapter thirteen definition of Secondary imagination.

The first option entails an active engagement with the realm of history and community, 'dissolving, diffusing, dissipating in order to re-create'. The 'energy of our spirit' expressed in the critical work of imagination is a match for the stubborn resistance of established cultural and political forms. Each verb is posed as a provisional strategy, an intervention, rather than a totalizing opposition to the given. Like the 1809 account of the progress of Truth as a 'gentle spring' turning icy obstacles into its own form and character (Friend II 54), literally gathering strength from adversity, imagination engages with the obstacles of embodied error. Unashamed of polemicizing, imagination fights its battles in the here-and-now, its recreationary power constantly subject to principled revision.

The second option, in contrast, gathers power by withholding, a secession of imagination from the world of practical ends. The strategy is a response to opposition, a calculated retreat 'when this process is rendered impossible, yet still at all events it struggles to idealize and unify'. Art may now offer a totalizing and ideal *alternative* to the world, in a way which echoes A. W. Schlegel's designation of poetry as an imaginary reconciliation of real contradictions 'when there is an internal dissonance which poetry cannot remove, it should at least endeavour to attempt an ideal solution'.[11] A related (but in fact antithetically opposed) passage in Schelling contemplates this 'internal dissonance' as an unthinkable event, unthinkable because if it *were* the case, the artistic intervention which would cancel it would itself constitute dialectical resolution, given the status of imagination as constitutive *act* rather than subjective reflection in Schelling's system:

> If the real were indeed the opposite of truth and beauty, the artist would not have to exalt or idealize it, but to eliminate it (aufheben) and destroy it in order to create something good and beautiful.[12]

Idealization and unification in Coleridge's later thought became the recourse of an idea of culture which made a virtue of the opposition of the real to 'truth and beauty', a form of *contemptus mundi*. This shift in perspective is one we encountered in the ambivalence of Coleridge's theory of desynonymization, in which the 'self-construction' of the Absolute (a 'certain collective unconscious good sense working progressively to desynonymize' (BL I 82)) had metamorphosed into a chaotic and forceful slippage over which the imagination could wield no control. The disassociation of value from history, of culture from the political realm resulted in the inevitable impoverishment of the work of imagination, as the ideal took refuge in a timeless transcendence, which Ben Knights has described, in his account of the negative influences of the nineteenth-century 'Clerisy', as 'drawing the conceptual net over reality'.[13]

This consideration of the pejorative tendency of Coleridge's 'second option' for aesthetic imagination would be incomplete without a brief survey of its consequences for poetic symbol, and for its social and ideological co-ordinates. In the 1816 *Stateman's Manual* the influence of the 'One Life' theory is still evident in Coleridge's direct appeal to the Statesmen, rather than to the 'new aristocracy' of professional intellectuals, the 'Clerisy'. In a letter of 8 August 1823, Coleridge believed that, despite its title, the work had been aimed at 'Metaphysicians and Theologians by Profession . . . *es*pecially to the Ministers of the established Church' (CL V 289). In the 1818 *Essays on Method* (still structurally dependent on Schelling's *Methode des akademischen Studiums*), the emphasis upon art as the copula between consciousnesss and the Absolute has been superceded by a more Kantian emphasis on Practical Reason. The 'method of the will', an internalized devotional principle expounded at length in the 1825 *Aids to Reflection*, was now theorized as a 'satisfactory solution of all the contradictions of human nature, of the whole riddle of the world' (Friend I 524). In the *Essays'* hierarchy of knowledge, art was the middle ground between the 'higher' relations of Law, and the lower, empirical relations of Theory, only Shakespeare seeming to survive the general demotion as an exemplary 'man of method' (Friend I 464; 457). The materials which the artist receives and with which he must work inevitably blunt the efficacy of his Idea. Coleridge illustrated this by the case of music played upon a harmonica ('Clagget's Metallic Organ') which soon tires the ears on account of the harsh obtrusion of materiality upon the formal proportion of the notes, the proper source of beauty (Friend I 464–5). Regarded in the light of the Symbol/Allegory distinction made in the *Statesman's Manual*, it is as if the vehicle has been separated from its tenor, so that the spirit no longer partakes of the Reality which it renders intelligible, and (of course) which renders *it* intelligible (LS 30). In an 1818 *Lecture on Literature*, Coleridge privileged the characteristic of post-Christian poetry as 'an underconsciousness of a sinful nature, a fleeting away of external things' (LR I 177). Certainly, as Paul De Man has pointed out in *The Rhetoric of Temporality*, this evanescence of the symbolic vehicle was already implicit in the *Statesman's Manual* definition, in which the symbol was described as 'translucent', the Jewish histories as 'educts' of imagination.[14] But the word 'educt' has its origin in chemistry, and is defined in Watt's *Dictionary of Chemistry* as 'a body separated by the decomposition of another in which it previously existed as such, in contradiction to *product*, which denotes a compound not previously existing, but formed during decomposition'.[15] Coleridge's knowledge of chemistry permits us to suppose a precise application of the term, perhaps even in the context of the distinction from *product*. In fact the distinction is as narrow as its consequences were broad, given that it parallels the twin options prescribed for Secondary imagination in the *Biographia*.

The transcendence of the second option, product of 'material decomposition', was an increasingly predominant trait in definitions of romantic symbol, according to De Man:

> The spiritualization of the symbol has been carried so far that the moment of material existence by which it was originally defined has now become altogether unimportant; symbol and allegory alike now have a common origin beyond the world of matter.[16]

For De Man this moment of materiality is 'but a negative moment . . . a temptation that has to be overcome'.[17] More significant is 'the rediscovery of an allegorical tradition beyond the sensualistic analogism of the eighteenth century'.[18] Of course only Coleridge's thought *after* 1817 would support De Man's point, in its recuperation of a form of allegory as the dominant public or devotional figure, exemplified by his 1825 comparison between the symbolic 'tautegory' of Aeschylus's *Prometheus* and the (privileged) allegorical mode of the Biblical myth of origins (LR II 336). De Man describes allegory as 'a language defined in the void of temporal difference'; in Coleridge's case, deconstructive scepticism easily translates into the terms of 'negative' theology, if we add the theistic 'anchoring point' unavailable to De Man '. . . in opposition to the Self-Presence of God'. De Man's revisionary interpretation of romantic symbol (no doubt aimed at the reificatory tendencies of American 'New Critics') entails an *ad hoc* rejection of cultural intervention, a relegation of the civic ideal we saw informing the 'One Life' theory to the status of a mere 'negative moment', a foolish infatuation with the political realm. The separation of the cultural and political which this attitude enforces, the discovery of the 'non-being' of the Absolute in the contingent world, undoubtedly entails the 'painful knowledge' that symbolic identification with the world is illusory. The problem is that cultural melancholy of this order is *itself* a covert intervention, a strategy of containment which has its own ideological provenance and work; certainly since Coleridge's declaration of the 'Promethean' attitude it has held hegemonic sway, disguising its Titanic kinship with a political realm of domination.

The 'bifurcation' of Coleridge's Secondary Imagination in the *Biographia* shows that he had already decided in theory, if not in practice, in favour of the 'distinction of powers' against which his earlier thought had addressed itself. Translating culture from a civic to a religious sphere entailed the rejection of imagination as mediator between reason and experience, a forum in which values could have been presented and contested. The 'politics of imagination' became authoritarian, static, and class-defined inasmuch as they were construed in resistance to democracy and even mass education. Values withheld as a form of spiritual capital lost the power to confront change to the extent to which they abandoned accountability. The critical acumen of the 'One Life' theory, engaged with the whole complex of social relations defining the commercial order and possessing the symbolic tools to challenge a traditional 'distinction of powers', was itself recuperated into the cultural hegemony of the new social order. One might say, with Gramsci, that the 'organic' intellectuals of the emergent middle-class, their critical enthusiasm dampened by the spectre of the powers which their struggle for social ascendency had unleashed, were rapidly assimilated into the 'traditional' forms of cultural power, notably the established church. This very process is incarnated in Coleridge's personal and ideological trajectory.

The political ferment of the period 1816–20 profoundly involved the 'righteous apostates' Wordsworth, Coleridge and Southey (to name but a few) in a manner which will be further explored in Part Three. Although there has been much debate amongst historians as to the precise significance of the post-war social crisis, one of its salient features seems to have been the development (at a *manifest* level), of what Harold Perkin has described as a perceived shift from the *vertical* relations of eighteenth century corporatism to *horizontal* distinctions of social class.[19] Clearly such class-consciousness was anathema to Coleridge's holistic social idealism and might itself be interpreted as constitutive of the *Biographia*'s re-definition of a common culture. Coleridge's social philosophy, which from its earliest days had been opposed to urban capitalism, progressively seeking to rekindle the 'spirit of the state' by means of (firstly) agrarian communism and then aesthetic idealism, was driven by a fear of the triumph of industrial democracy to develop its cultural appeal in a realm which stood in self-conscious separation from the political.

Henceforth the *propriety* afforded by 'cultivation' would precede the threatened property qualification as the criterion for social authority, preserving a traditional hierarchy against the democratic inundation. The cultural politics of the *clerisy*, which Raymond Williams and Ben Knights have shown to have originated in a 'humanistic' reaction to the alienation of the new social order, came instead to offer a bulwark against the threat of a broad-based social structure. The extended Franchise of 1832 could be a relatively minor concession to ease class tension, providing that real power (control of the cultural, legal and religious establishment) remained in the hands of those whom 'cultivation' had rendered politically responsible.

The 'Promethean' posture of the hegemonic intellectuals in the Coleridgean tradition masks a political strategy. As long as we discriminate between a valueless and contingent political world and a sacrosanct aesthetic realm, we need to remind ourselves – to paraphrase Michael Fisher – that the choice between culture and politics is not between evasion and power, but between two kinds of power.[20]

Part Three
The Binding of Prometheus: the Role of the Mysteries in Coleridge's Theory of Culture after 1817

14

Poetry and Mythology: the Coleridges and the Classical Revival

In February 1822, the *London Magazine* published an article by Coleridge's elder son, Hartley, entitled 'On the Poetical Use of the Heathen Mythology'.[1] The article shows unmistakable signs of the father's influence; for the previous year Hartley had sought to vindicate himself in the eyes of his father, after having been deprived of his Oriel fellowship for 'sottish behaviour', by attempting an epic poem on the subject of Prometheus. Coleridge had supplied him with material for the poem, 'a small volume almost . . . containing all the materials & comments on the full import of this most pregnant and sublime Mythos and Philosopheme', attesting to his own interest in classical mythology in this period. These notes on Prometheus contained 'the sum of all my Reading & reflection on this vast Wheel of the Mythology of the earliest & purest Heathenism' (CL V 142–3).

Hartley's article was concerned with the post-war literary vogue for classical mythology and paganism, described by Marilyn Butler as the 'Cult of the South';[2] he named the main practitioners of the new style as Keats, Shelley and Barry Cornwall. Byron, Peacock and Leigh Hunt also championed the aesthetic and political values of classical and Italian renaissance civilization at this time; as Hartley indicated, even the parochial Wordsworth had celebrated the classical spirit in book four of *The Excursion* and the Hellenistic *Laodamia*.[3] The tendency to discern a conflict between a classical and romantic, post-Christian spirit as constitutive of the history of European culture had become a commonplace in the criticism of A. W. Schlegel, Mme. De Staël and Coleridge. As Marilyn Butler has noted, the classical revival, with its preference for 'naturalistic' polytheism in religion, for republicanism in politics, for the comic rather than tragic mode in literature, and for eroticism or 'nympholepsy', 'conveniently fortified the post-war liberals' wish to challenge a resurgent, institutional, politically reactionary Christianity'.[4] Hartley Coleridge (like his father, as will become evident in the following pages) took up the classical 'topos' in order to defend traditional Christian values against the neo-pagans; his article accordingly seeks to dampen the enthusiasm of the second romantic generation, going so far as to question the continuing possibility of imaginative literature in the modern epoch. His doubts were similar to those we saw expressed by his father in the period following the *Biographia*. Some of Hartley's cultural pessimism doubtlessly derived from the failure of his own *Prometheus*, hardly surprising in the light of the complexity of his father's elaboration of the 'sublime philosopheme'. As Derwent Coleridge wrote in the introduction to his brother's posthumous fragment, it was little wonder that the 'youthful Telemachus shrunk from the attempt to bend his father's bow'.[5]

But the interest of Hartley's article lies not so much in the bitterness of personal failure, as in the fact that it is in reality a sensitive appraisal of the contemporary literary scene disguised in the garb of late Augustan Rome. Hartley offered nothing less than a historical and social theory of poetry, showing up the deep links between the cultural and political realms. What was the future for a national culture in the transition from a republican to a cosmopolitan era? How could a new basis be found for the arts when the moral nutriments and the common language upon which they depended had been fragmented or marginalized? Like his father, Hartley was concerned with the problem of achieving authenticity of poetic voice in an epoch of cultural decadence, when the adequacy of traditional values had been questioned by political and social change.

The poetry of the late Augustans, according to Hartley, shared the empty mannerism which he discerned in much of the current 'nympholepsy'; more trenchantly (and the implicit allusion was to the 'Lyrical Ballad'[6] with its bid to discover 'the high in the humble') he criticized in it a discrepancy between form and content, between character and sentiment. Hartley sketched the poverty and insincerity of the late Augustans, the effeminacy of their classical figures, producing a 'frigid Dutch painting' quite inferior to the mythic vigour of their originals, the symbolic art of the Greek and Roman republics.[7] Debased Platonism and a crude materialistic pantheism were put in the mouths of characters like 'the shade Anchises' and other figures from the heroic canon, resulting in an absurd incongruity between the noble actions of the Homeric heroes and the Epicureanism of their sentiments and language.[8] This superimposition of a superficial modern philosophy onto the exhausted forms of the traditional culture represented the vain attempt of the pagan philosophers – champions of the decadent Roman state – to resist the powerful challenge of cosmopolitan Christianity, so threatening to the civic foundation of the old world, with its limited, national religions. Coleridge the elder elsewhere cited Apuleius' treatment of the Cupid and Psyche myth in the *Golden Ass* as an instance of the Classical world's bid to rival Christianity (AR 278).

Wordsworth's project of regenerating the 'republican' founding-myth of 1688 in the *Lyrical Ballads* clearly finds a historical parallel in the adoption, by the 'unbelieving' Roman philosophers, of the popular polytheism, which, in Coleridge's opinion (we shall see) was employing deception in defence of a lost cause. Hartley's account of the Roman philosophers evokes Gibbon's image of the Augustan 'savant', disguising 'a smile of contempt under the mask of devotion' whilst worshipping the local tutelary deities.[9] The expedient piety of the Epicureans is compared to the contemporary example of the 'German illuminati [who] have ranged themselves under the banner of popery' in order to expiate the spirit of Jacobinism rampant amongst the people.[10] Hartley echoes his father's attack on Schelling, who had sought 'to justify the worship of saints by endeavoring to convince the world that god consisted in Saints' (Ph L 390). Coleridge probably believed that Schelling had converted to Rome, although, as the philosopher told Crabb Robinson in August 1829, there was no truth in the allegation.[11] The obscure and garbled remark in the *Philosophical Lectures* should be interpreted as an attack on Schelling's intuition of the Absolute in nature and in the symbols of art and civic community, connecting his imputed Catholicism, 'nature-worship' and classical bias with Coleridge's own theory of imagination, the 'old ruined tower' of the *Biographia*, chapter thirteen. Hartley's connection of the late Augustan philosophers with the polytheistic 'German illuminati' casts some light on Coleridge's rejection of the civic provenance of the 'One Life' theory after 1817. The chapter thirteen definitions and his identification of the unreformed British polity with the Jewish Theocracy – both vehicles for the 'Divine Humanity' – in the *Stateman's Manual* (LS 29), thus represented a final dalliance with Schellingian idealism as a public position, and one which by 1819 would be severely qualified.

Hartley's account of the fraudulent piety of the philosophers would seem to connect his father's appeal in the *Lay Sermons* with the defaults of Wordsworth or Schelling, a connection borne out by Coleridge's praise for Socrates' 'expedient' courage in standing up to the Sophists, in the 1818 essay 'On the Origin and Progress of the Sophists'.

> To the zeal with which he counteracted this plan [the Sophist's bid to separate ethics from the religion of the 'polis'] by endeavors to purify and ennoble that popular belief, which, from obedience to the laws, he did not deem himself permitted to subvert, did Socrates owe his martyr-cup of hemlock.
>
> (Friend I 441)

Coleridge is less positive in his generosity to Socrates in the *Philosophical Lectures* the following year, however, when he is censured for an over-reliance on 'the UNCOMMON excellence of common sense' (Ph L 136); Coleridge converts the civic impulse of Socrates' dying words, the 'cock to Asclepius' into a tragic, 'Promethean' relationship with the 'polis', increasingly identified with the profane.

Hartley associated the cultural malaise of the later Augustans with their abandonment of the republican virtues (derived from the Greeks) in favour of the luxury and ostentation of an imperial power.[12] The national character of their religion was incompatible with economic and political cosmopolitanism; popular reverence for local and tutelary deities had diminished, despite the best efforts of the philosphers to uphold 'the institutions of commonwealth' and national pride. Such is the general fate of mythologies and 'belief-systems' in 'corrupt and unimaginative ages', when 'a respect for words and forms survives the notions or feelings which gave these words and forms a meaning'.[13] Ingenuity was employed by the apologists of the old order to render 'primitive' beliefs adequate to sophisticated intelligence 'some would allegorize and labour . . . to convert the toys of childhood into tools and weapons for maturity'.[14] Meanwhile, sceptics and atheists explained away these traditions as mere mystification employed in the service of domination, 'enigmatical representations of natural philosophy'.[15]

Hartley's own critical apologetics, really an extension of his father's work, sought to salvage the guiding principle of transcendence from the meagre defences of the purveyors of 'pious fraud' in order to offer a better defence against the hostile allegorizers. Native apologetic argument was dominated by the work of William Paley, whose *Evidences of Christianity* sought a rational defence of revelation by means of external evidences and miracles as proof of 'extraordinary providence'. Ironically, Coleridge had himself drawn upon Paley's 1794 work in the 1795 *Lectures on Revealed Religion*, as well as Joseph Priestley's prolific writings and William Warburton's *Divine Legation of Moses* (1738–41), a work about which we will have more to say below. The basis for all these arguments from external evidences had been effectively demolished by David Hume, praised by Coleridge in the *Philosophical Lectures* for having exposed the false, 'Lockean' friends of revealed religion (Ph L 203). The vacuity of the rationalist defences of Christianity has been described thus by James Boulger: 'the blindly orthodox considered them unnecessary, and the philosophically-minded doubted the premise upon which they were based'.[16]

The sceptical assault upon religion and the symbols of the traditional culture against which the evidence-writers marshalled such a feeble defence was the fruit of an 'atheistical' interpretation of Christianity in the light of comparative mythology, going back to Spinoza, Hobbes and Bayle. The ideological ferment of the French Revolution produced a spate of such attacks, perhaps the most important of which were Paine's *Age of Reason* (1794–95), criticized by Coleridge in the 1795 *Lectures* (Lects 1795 149n), Volney's *The Ruins: or a Survey of the Revolutions of Empires* (1792), attacked in the fourth *Lecture* (Lects 1795 183) and Dupuis' *Origine de tous les Cultes, ou religion universel* (1794–95), singled out for criticism in the 1825 lecture *On the Prometheus of Aeschylus* (LR II 323).[17] In his 1822 article, however, Hartley was more concerned to pour scorn upon a group of scholarly Whig sceptics who were currently 'inventing new meanings for old words' from *within* the establishment; men like Richard Payne Knight, author of *An Inquiry into the Symbolical Language of Ancient Art and Mythology* (1818), the comparative religionist Sir William Drummond, author of *Origines: or, remarks on the origin of several Empires, States and Cities* (1824), and Sir William Hamilton, British ambassador in Naples and co-author of *An Account of the Remains of the Worship of Priapus* (1786). These scholars pointed out the mythological parallels between Christianity and the pagan cults, tracing a 'natural history' of religious myths which they interpreted, in the exegetical tradition of Bacon's *Wisdom of the Ancients*, as arcane representations of natural philosophy. Marilyn Butler has re-emphasized the influence of these critics upon Shelley and his circle, an influence confirmed by a glance at the notes to *Queen Mab*, a pastiche of the works of Lucretius, Pliny, Bacon, Spinoza, Helvetius, Rousseau, Hume, Gibbon and Drummond.[18] Hartley's article parodied the 'reductive' exegesis of these sceptics; one ingenious allegorizer would employ 'perverse and unprofitable industry' to discover in the deity Janus 'only a prudent King, who calculated correctly upon consequences'; another, in Prometheus, 'a great astronomer, who had an observatory on Mt Caucasus, and induced a liver complaint by intense application'.[19] Hartley's indictment of the fashionable vogue for comparative mythology amongst scholars of the establishment echoed his father's attack on the 'perilous stuff ' of the philosophy of the ruling class in the 1817 letter to Lord Liverpool (CL IV 761). Hartley marvelled that 'a baronet of the 19th century, a man of no small learning and ingenuity, and not a Frenchman, takes pains to assure us, that the twelve patriarchs were neither more nor less than the twelve signs of the zodiac'.[20] This was the same reductive literalism which Coleridge had criticized in his attack on allegorizers in *The Stateman's Manual*, the 'translation of abstract notions into a picture-language which is itself nothing but an abstraction from objects of the senses' (LS 30).

Hartley clearly regarded his attack on current 'uses of the Heathen Mythology' as more than mere scholarly logomachy, a defence of Christian culture itself. But his argument does reveal some of the 'progressivist' ambivalence of his opponents concerning the possibility of poetry in a post-mythological age, evident in works such as Peacock's *The Four Ages of Poetry* (1821) or Payne Knight's poem *The Progress of Civil Society* (1796). The pursuit of a 'naive' poetic voice in a period of cultural senility is pure self-delusion, 'as if there were no dark misgivings, no obstinate questionings, no age to freeze the springs of life, and no remorse to taint them'.[21] Hartley regretted a 'mythic' youth which seemed to have flown forever: 'we are grown up to serious man-hood, and are wedded to reality . . . the *moral* being has gained a religion and the imagination has lost one'.[22] Payne Knight's didactic poem, written in the Lucretian mode made fashionable in the 1790s by Erasmus Darwin, made a similar point in its lament for the loss of the poetic mythology which had characterized the republican Greeks:

> Each abstract cause to form substantial sprang,
> Assumed a local dwelling, and a name.[23]

The progress of society has left poetry and myth behind, a childlike idiom superceded by the more articulate, but less impassioned language of science, a view which Knight shared with Rousseau and Adam Ferguson.[24] Poetry is to be justified now only as an ornamentation of fact, reflected in the didacticism of Knight's own poem:

> Thus, of ideal images bereft,
> The Muse's humbler task is only left,
> Dry fact and solid argument to strew
> With flowers refresh'd in Heliconian dew;
> And the light flow of narrative to trace
> With just expression, and with easy grace.[25]

This was of course precisely the 'poetic jargon', the empty, mannered style superimposed upon a didactic content which Wordsworth and Coleridge had attacked in the Preface and poems of *Lyrical Ballads*. But Hartley, unlike the elder poets, possesses a 'modern' sensibility which precludes the integrative idealism of the 'One Life' theory, poised between knowledge and nostalgia:

> The sage of antiquity was like a child, who thinks there are many moons within his reach. We know, that there is but one, high above our heads, whose face is mirrored in a hundred streams. Yet the shadow remains not the less because it is known to be a shadow.[26]

Although this sophisticated awareness was certainly present in the poems of Coleridge the father, a despair at cultural exhaustion 'after the life and shaping power was gone',[27] dejection was always tempered by the possibilities of the 'One Life'. The *Biographia* figured this very ambivalence in the attempt, in the first volume, to define an 'immanent' and unifying aesthetic inspired by Schellingian idealism, juxtaposed with the second volume's denial of a genuine 'common culture' in Wordsworth's poetic theory. For Wordsworth, like Hartley's late Augustans, had placed his 'lofty didactick poem' in the mouth of a pedlar in order to idealize the values of an 'organic' society (BL II 118). Coleridge's criticism of Wordsworth should be seen in the context of a more general attack upon the poet's espousal of a disguised civic idealism (and a form of 'neo-paganism' described as 'natural piety') as part of his bid to reinvigorate an exhausted and effete culture. In a letter to Thomas Allsop on 8 August 1830, Coleridge delivered his most scathing attack to date on Wordsworth's poetry. 'This inferred dependency of the human soul on accidents of Birth-place & Abode together with the vague misty, rather than mystic, Confusion of God with the World & the accompanying Nature-worship' was the trait he most disliked in Wordsworth (CL V 95). This anticipated Hartley's 1822 attack on the 'pious fraud' of the Epicureans, striving to maintain popular reverence for the tutelary deities and the local habitations of the national pantheon. Coleridge continues by arguing that Wordsworth had espoused an exploded Toryism and combined his pantheism with an evangelical, vulgar Anglicanism:

> the odd occasional introduction of the popular, almost the vulgar, Religion in his later publications (the popping in, as Hartley says, of the old man with a beard) suggests the painful suspicion of worldly (at best a justification of *masking* truth (which in fact is a falsehood substituted for a truth withheld) on plea of Expediency) carried into *Religion*. At least, it conjures up to *my* fancy, a sort of *Janus*-head of Spinoza and Dr Watts, or "I and my Brother, the Dean."
>
> (CL V 95)

Wordsworth is charged with a quixotic refusal to acknowledge the fragmented and disparate nature of modernity in his appeal to exhausted values, and his obdurate insistence on 'being all things to all men'. This marks Coleridge's rejection of the 'One Life' project, the appeal to imagination as mediator between the finite self and the Absolute, an integration of experience and consciousness with the collective purposefulness of social community. The lofty role afforded to the imagination in the *Biographia* was overscored by Coleridge after 1817, as value and experience appeared to co-exist as mutual contradiction rather than symbolic unity. Coleridge increasingly withdrew poetry from the centre, placing it in subordination to religious doctrine, valid only as a 'prophecy of forthcoming redemption' or as a figure of repetition glorying in the reflected, 'derived' power attendant on its belatedness. Coleridge was radically dissatisfied with Wordsworth's bid to integrate the perilous 'higher critical' knowledge of romantic Spinozism with Watt's evangelism; and yet it was a concern to define a culture adequate to different levels and classes of men, without forfeiting the (at least nominal) claim to community, which preoccupied Coleridge's later years. Coleridge's solution had striking similarities with the Hegel whose motto, according to Crabb Robinson, was 'as old as the Greek mysteries – Lasst uns Filosofen den Begriff, gibt dem Volke das Bild! (Leave us philosophers the true idea, give to the multitude the symbol!)'.[28] The following pages attempt to show how Coleridge set about this task in the context of the crisis of cultural tradition which is so evident in Hartley's 1822 article, taking our understanding of his cultural politics beyond the scattered fragments in public and private writings, and articulating the silence recorded by Crabb Robinson in June 1824:

He metaphysicized à la Schelling while he abused him, saying the Atheist seeks only for an infinite cause of all things; the spurious divine is content with mere personality and personal will, which is the death of all reason. The philosophic theologian unites both. How this is to be done he did not say.[29]

15

Wat Tyler and Political Embarrassment

Coleridge's increasing scruples regarding the impiety of poetry were closely associated with his reaction to the Reform agitation of 1816–17, which rekindled all the political passions of 1795 after the relative unanimity of the war years. His correspondence of 1817 reveals a 'mea culpa' attitude which saw its own former ideals echoed (and in his opinion caricatured) by the republican rhetoric of the Reformers; an attitude which drove Coleridge to work out a complex and somewhat tortuous apology for his imputed political apostasy. In a letter to Daniel Stuart of 2 April 1817, Coleridge outlined his plan for such a work: he would distinguish the 'philanthropic hopes of thousands just at the very commencement of the French Revolution' (hopes, he added, which were often expressed in the 'patriotic' civic humanist rhetoric of 1688) from the ideals and aims of the 'wretches' of post-war Reform whose sophistic appeal to Liberty and Patriotism should have had 'it's brains knocked out by the Charger of Buonaparte' (CL IV 718–19).

His argument is tortuous in both thought and style as he seeks simultaneously to commend and condemn the 'patriot' ideology, to both excuse his youthful republican ardour and attack its contemporary champions. The constitutionalist language of 1688 – based on Locke's political writings (CL IV 719) – represented a 'positive criterion of Loyalty' to the Hanoverian dynasty, the pride not merely of Whigs or Tories, but of Englishmen *per se*. But these principles no longer represented a valid symbol of national community for Coleridge in 1817, notwithstanding the efforts of a Tory partisan like Wordsworth to prove otherwise. Experience had shown the insubstantiality of their tenets, and the inadequacy of the sensationalist empiricism which had accompanied them. The new philosophers, with their transcendentalist separation of Reason and Understanding, had been anticipated by '*a very very*

few, obstinate Metaphysicians and Theologians of the old School
(CL IV 719).

Coleridge's apologia revealed a complex ideological manoeuvre
with two principal aims. The first sought an alternative set of
terms by which Englishmen (not Tories, Whigs or Radicals) might
define national community. The political rhetoric of 1688 had
been appropriated by the apologists of the landed order, and,
more effectively, by the Reformers, whom it served well, given
that it was constructed on the libertarian tenets of the Glorious
Revolution. As such it could no longer serve as a defence of the
establishment. In Coleridge's view the 'founding myth', whether
interpreted in the 'Neo-Harringtonian' manner of Burke,
Wordsworth and Southey, or in the democratic–republican style
of Cobbett, Cartwright and Hunt, had accordingly forfeited all
claims to cultural centrality, on account of this usurpation by
party-politics, increasingly underpinned by class-interests. Both
the *Lay Sermons* and the *Biographia* had sought to regenerate the
tired rhetoric. The unreformed constitution was imbued with the
spirituality of the Jewish Theocracy, the secular and rational
manner of traditional Whig political language traded for the
prophetic style of the Old Testament, a development of the
'spiritualized politics' of Coleridge's Unitarian youth.

But 1817 shows Coleridge's concern to elevate the spiritual
commonwealth from the earth to the heavens, a concern in part
motivated, as a March 1817 letter to T. G. Street makes evident, by
political embarrassment. Coleridge here compared his predicament
with that of Sir James MacKintosh and Robert Southey, alike
branded by the liberals with the mark of apostasy. He cited the
feelings of disgust with which a Lincoln's Inn audience had heard
MacKintosh's testimony: 'I *recant, abjure,* and *abhor* the principles'
i.e. of his own Vindiciae Gallicae' (CL IV 713). Southey had been
similarly embarrassed by a pirated edition of his revolutionary
poem, *Wat Tyler*, in 1817, and had been driven to a similar
recantation. Coleridge's letter to Street supplements the four
articles he wrote in the same month for the *Courier*, defending
Southey from the charge of apostasy (EOT II 449–78). Southey has
set about his vindication in the wrong way, he argued, in simply
abjuring the political views expressed in his poem, thereby laying
himself open to charges of inconsistency and political opportunism.
He should rather have denied that poetry was a vehicle for
political truths at all. Following his strategy of separating the

poetic tenor of Wordsworth's *Lyrical Ballads* from their 'political'
vehicle, Coleridge argued that *Wat Tyler* expressed moral and
spiritual, rather than political, truths, a 'distinction of powers'
which might exempt Southey from the charge of apostasy and
shift the blame onto the inflammatory literalism of those
responsible for the pirate edition.[1]

In his *Second Lay Sermon*, in the press at the time, Coleridge
accused the demagogues of propagating 'verbal' rather than
'moral' truths, that is to say, uttering undeniable truths in a
context which determined their misinterpretation as incendiary,
radical slogans (LS 153). Coleridge's unifying theory of symbol
and of imagination struggled against this disassociation of word
and meaning, which he regarded as cant. But the fissure of
language and 'common sense' at which we have been looking, a
growing belief that what had once been true of the whole was
now only true of the part, of a contradictory relationship between
signs and the social values determining significance, all added up
to an abandonment of the schismatic political realm by the baffled
secondary imagination. Henceforth Coleridge's 'Promethean'
cultural stance would be determined by a 'struggle to idealize and
to unify' where mediation was 'rendered impossible' (BL I 304).
The fate of *Wat Tyler* was a symptom of a society which had lost
hold of the 'sovereign principle':

> For who in the Devil's Name ever thought of reading Poetry for
> any political or practical purposes till these Devil's Times that
> *we* live in? The *publication* of the work is the wicked thing.
> Briefly, my dear Sir! everyone is in the right to make the best
> . . . of a bad business. But the Truth is the Truth. The root of
> the evil is *a Public* . . . this will wax more and more prolific of
> inconvenience, that at length it will scarcely be possible for the
> State to suffer any truth to be published, because it will be
> certain to convey dangerous falsehood to 99 out of a hundred.
> Then we shall come around to the *esoteric* (interior, hidden)
> doctrines of the Ancients, and learn to understand what Christ
> meant when he commanded us not to cast Pearls before Swine.
>
> (CL IV 713)

Coleridge's 'making the best of a bad business' is the keynote of
his cultural theory after 1817, in basing authority on the Mystery
doctrines of the Ancients. The recuperation of 'Mystery', a term

which he had savagely attacked in the 1790s, was largely motivated by the apostate's sense of guilt and a sense of alienation from the community, which he could now dismiss as *'a Public'*. Coleridge's articles in the *Courier* did not fool his old enemy Hazlitt, who observed in April 1817 that 'the author of the *Conciones ad Populem* and the author of THE *Wat Tyler*, are sworn brothers in the same cause of righteous apostasy'.[2] Coleridge answered Hazlitt by republishing part of the *Conciones* in the 1818 rifacciamento of *The Friend* (Friend I 326–38). Unfortunately, Coleridge's indignant self-righteousness was qualified by the fact that he was obliged to omit approximately 250 lines of the original text on account of their radicalism.

Coleridge's scholarly lucubrations on the Mysteries and the religious mythology of the ancients, the principal subject of the following pages, should be considered in tandem with the political expedients of the Tory government in the same period. Coleridge's opinions concerning censorship anticipated those of Lord Liverpool in a speech to the Lords two months later; he blamed the 'extensive circulation of seditious and blasphemous publications' for weakening popular respect for the constitution and 'law, morality and religion amongst the lower orders'.[3] When Southey proposed strict press censorship in the Tory *Quarterly* in 1817, Coleridge supported him, feeling a vehement 'Hatred' 'toward the Jeffrieses, Cobbetts, Hunts', as well as the 'the Foxites, who have fostered the vipers' (CL IV 714). The ensuing campaign of prosecutions for blasphemous and seditious libel constituted nothing less than an era of blatant ideological repression.

16

The Problem of Art: Public Repression and Private Re-enactment

Coleridge's statements concerning *Wat Tyler* show the degree to which the position of 'righteous apostasy' influenced the development of the arguments in the second volume of the *Biographia* in which he sought to sublimate poetic symbol from the civic or political realm, and offers an important key to his ambivalence regarding the social function of imagination after 1817. Art offered a special kind of knowledge absolutely essential to the continuity of tradition and harmony in the state; for some of the reasons we have considered it could not, however, be widely or promiscuously disseminated. An important source for this view (and one which Coleridge cited in the July 1817 letter to Lord Liverpool (CL IV 762)) was Plato's account of the relation of the poet to the *polis* in the *Republic*.

The context of Plato's account is Socrates' definition of the education of the 'guardians', the Republic's semi-military ruling élite. The political role of the guardians is characteristic of the *Republic*'s 'distinction of powers', quite different from the 'One Life' unity of the Harringtonian republic defined by Coleridge and Wordsworth in the 1790s. The guardians are forbidden from participating in the activities of other social castes, and especially from aesthetic pursuits.[1] The separation of functions which determines the efficiency of the state is clearly threatened by the integrative ideal, the will to break free of limitations and to identify with the whole. For Socrates, the poet's claims for his artefact, different in kind from others, is a delusion comparable with that of democratic government:

> We are therefore quite right to refuse to admit him to a properly run state, because he wakens and encourages and strengthens the lower elements in the mind to the detriment of

reason, which is like giving power and political control to the worst element in the state and ruining the better element.[2]

Running beneath Plato's strictures with regard to art (which he seeks to limit to 'hymns to the gods and paeans in praise of great men'[3]) can be discerned a great respect for the socially-constitutive powers of poetry, particularly the religious myths of Homer and Hesiod. In his bid to substantiate the belief that 'God is the cause, not of all things, but only of good', [4] Plato attacked that representation of gods as endowed with human weaknesses and vices. One such case is the Hesiodic account of Chronos' castration of his father Ouranos (the heavens) in order to separate him from Gaia (mother earth).[5] This separation figured the origin of the enabling authority of priesthood; and precisely for this reason, Plato considered that it gave away too much in its revelation of a primordial union of earth and heaven, sundered by the human will-to-power. Stories threatening to the authority of an absolute, self-originating deity are not fit to be 'lightly repeated to the young and fools':

> It would be best to say nothing of it, or if it must be told, tell it to a select few under oath of secrecy, at a rite which required, to restrict it still further, the sacrifice not of a mere pig but of something large and difficult to get.[6]

It is an oversimplification to say of Plato that he is an enemy of *Pseudos* (fiction or falsehood);[7] he rather wished, like Coleridge in the 1817 letter to Street, to *licence* the public function of poetry and myth lest the original conjunction between cultural and political authority be revealed to those with no stakes in the preservation of hegemony. Plato accordingly sought to limit the enactment of *Pseudos* (with its 'higher critical' knowledge of the original liaison between Ouranos and Gaia) to a cast of licensed practitioners:

> Surely we must value truthfulness highly. For if we were right when we said just now that falsehood is no use to the gods, and only useful to men as a kind of medicine, it's clearly a kind of medicine that should be entrusted to doctors and not to laymen. . . . It will be for the rulers of our city, then, if anyone, to use falsehood in dealing with citizen or enemy for the good of the state; no one else must do so.[8]

Coleridge's version of the Platonic ambivalence regarding *Pseudos* is expressed as a kind of parable in chapter twenty-one of the *Biographia*. Coleridge describes his 1806 visit to the tomb of Pope Julius II in Rome, in the company of a Prussian artist, to view the *Moses* of Michelangelo, a work elsewhere praised as 'the only work of truly modern sculpture' (LR I 69). The heightened description of the episode evokes the potency of, as well as the dangers attendant upon, the 'gnostic inclusiveness' of art in the modern era. The harmony of English and German intellects distil upon the significance of Moses' horns, upon the formal harmony they achieve in balancing the patriarch's long flowing beard; but more profoundly, upon their occult significance as 'emblem of power and sovereignty among the Eastern nations' (BL II 116), locating Moses the divine law-giver within the context of his cultural and historical milieu. Clearly these observers are no mere dilettanti, but rather 'higher critics', who discuss

> the Achelous of the ancient Greeks; and the probable ideas and feelings, that originally suggested the mixture of the human and the brute form in the figure, by which they realized the idea of their mysterious Pan, as representing intelligence blended with a darker power, deeper, mightier, and more universal than the conscious intellect of man; than intelligence.
>
> (BL II 117)

These erudite (and heterodox) reflections are interrupted by an exemplary modern 'reductio', an intrusion repeating the arrival of the 'person from Porlock' (PW I 296) or the 'profane' republicanism of *Wat Tyler*. Enter the officers of the Napoleonic army of occupation who, in line with the Prussian's prediction, immediately focus upon the statue's horns 'they will begin by instantly noticing the statue in parts, without one moment's pause of admiration impressed by the whole' – deducing from them the properties of 'a HE-GOAT and a CUCKOLD' (BL II 117).

Coleridge's anecdote prepares the way for his indictment of Jeffrey's review of Wordsworth's *Excursion*. Attempting to reveal the 'high in the humble' by placing his lofty metaphysics in the mouth of a common pedlar, Wordsworth has repeated Michelangelo's synthesis of Pan and Moses, revealing the natural and civic origins of the higher law. The Reviewer's lampoon of the pedlar's 'pin-papers and stay tapes' (BL II 118) repeats the 'priapic' interpretation of the French officers, figures for their countrymen Volney and Dupuis. Coleridge's task in the *Biographia* volume two was to establish a Wordsworth whose poetry was no longer subject to critical reduction of this kind. But in his account of the imagination in volume one, he had revealed the potency of art in integrating the conscious 'civilized' mind with a 'darker power, deeper, mightier and more universal' than rational intelligence. The *Wat Tyler* affair seemed to show how dangerous imagination could be in the wrong hands, how the radical challenge of the 'One Life' ideal could encourage the lower elements of the mind and give power to the cthonic forces of change. Coleridge's interest in the Mystery cults show his concern to safeguard the 'One Life' ideal from these forces; the gnosis afforded by art, the generation of the divine Idea from 'the suppressed Titans of natural desire and appetite' (the secret kinship of religion and politics); these must be preserved in the hands of the initiates, if the idea of transcendance was to retain its power of conviction. Prometheus himself had been chained to Mt Caucasus for disseminating the heavenly flame amongst men, 'arming fools with fire'. Coleridge's new interest in the Mysteries displays a sense of the incompatibility of 'One Life' idealism with the realities of civilization and an acceptance of Plato's strategy; the public suppression of imagination in tandem with its constant private enactment by an initiated élite, the minimum condition for preventing the demise of religion as a symbolic focus for the community.

In the next section we will consider the influence of Vico on Coleridge's later years; in 1825, the year of his first reading of the *New Science*, Coleridge must have been fascinated by the Italian's account of the simultaneous origins of belief in God, and human society. Without belief in God, men would live like beasts; if the critical consciousness destroyed the authority of transcendence, then men 'would have nothing left to enable them to live in society; no shield of defence, nor means of council, no basis of support, nor even a form by which they may exist in the world at all'.[9] The 'higher critical' knowledge which Coleridge derived from the Moses of Michelangelo, divine law-giver endowed with animal horns, revealed the cthonic origins of law and reason in the collective self-creation of the people, the birthplace of God in myth and poetry, a revelation by which the poet or artist arrogates to himself the divine power of creation. We saw the extent to which Coleridge's account of imagination in the *Biographia* was overscored by what might be described as an Oedipal guilt, the usurpation of one's origin, and the appropriation of the law. In the late poem *Constancy to an Ideal Object* the self-exposed poet safeguards his debilitating knowledge, replacing the joyful delusion of belief by the taxing moral duty of *constancy*. The pressure of fact is responsible for the inane cruelty of the question 'And art thou nothing? (PW I 456); but the poet, like an unrequited lover, is constant to the image which it has become his moral *duty* to safeguard:

> An image with a glory round its head;
> The enamoured rustic worships its fair hues,
> Nor knows he makes the shadow, he pursues!

> (ll. 30–2)

Kantian dualism and acquiescence in the moral postulate became increasingly the mould of Coleridge's public faith after 1817, as Schellingian idealism, and the desire to assimilate, rather than suppress, the affections in symbolic participation were qualified and rejected.[10] If the imagination had lost a religion, the moral being had gained one; and clearly the sense of poetic self-projection as a surrogate God had been a perennial source of unease, betokening the insight as elegantly described by Elinor Shaffer: when 'the triumph of humanity is shattered, the image of God cannot be recreated in man once he is aware of it as self-projection. The visionary must maintain the separateness of God; His presence depends on it'.[11]

17

History-Writing, Higher Criticism and the Mystery Cults

Coleridge's strictures on the possibility of writing for a homogeneous public in the wake of the *Wat Tyler* affair offer a clearer understanding of his motives for attacking Wordsworth's '*Janus*-head of Spinoza and Dr Watts', the poet's insistence on 'being all things to all men'. It is hard to accord with Coleridge's condemnation in this case, given the importance of community to any poet in search of the authority of a representative voice, a symbolic reconciliation of private and public experience which must be a criterion of any vital culture.

Coleridge's interest in the classical Mysteries was determined by his sense of the *absence* of public voice as a vehicle for the symbolic experience he considered to be the condition of social and cultural coherence. The most famous Mystery cults of the ancient world were those of Samothrace and Eleusinius, clandestine religious rites which supplemented the empty and perfunctory devotions of the sacerdotal religions. The functions of the Mysteries, as Coleridge mentioned in the 1817 letter to Street (CL IV 713), was to safeguard the providential monotheism at a time of secularization and social ferment. The Mysteries were a dominant paradigm for his notion of the social function of the *Clerisy*, as outlined in *Aids to Reflection* and the *Constitution of the Church and State*, offering the institutional equivalent of the 'semi-dualism' which Coleridge worked out in his later years, a synthesis between Schelling's expansive idealism and Kant's 'distinction of powers'. Coleridge described the 'fundamental position of the Mysteries' as 'affirming that the productive powers or laws of nature are essentially the same with the active powers of the mind'.[1] But the Mysteries enabled Coleridge to contain the potentially subversive connotations of the 'One Life' theory, now enacted as a metaphorical activity, a spiritual and cultural counterweight to the secular and political realm.

The importance of Coleridge's interest in the Mysteries has not been readily realized partly because of his efforts to disguise this strictly non-Christian paradigm, the historical and providential role of which assumed greater importance than the narrative of traditional Christian eschatology. This is not to say that they challenged the Christian world-view, as such; on the contrary, the Mystery paradigm provided a 'higher critical' apologetic for Christian culture, but one based on a historicism independent of scriptual authority and 'revealed religion'. The Mysteries figured in all Coleridge's major public writings and lectures between the *Biographia* and the lecture on the *Prometheus of Aeschylus*, a historical defence of Christianity and a panacea for contemporary uncertainties, but one standing in an antithetical relationship to the 'spiritualized politics' of the 1795 Lectures. Why, however, did Coleridge establish his theory of culture on this apparently heterodox, classical paradigm, rather than upon a more traditional form of Christian apologetic?

The highly-charged manner in which contemporary political events were being experienced in the 1820s is evident from the resurgence of millenarianism in the period, notably that of Henry Drummond and Edward Irving's 'Albury House' group.[2] Unlike the radical chiliasts of the 1790s and the immediate post-war period, Drummond and Irving used the language of Apocalypse to indict a 'liberal' establishment which was considering Catholic Emancipation and Parliamentary Reform. Drummond's doctrine of the 'Apostate Nation' and 'Church Militant' was an extreme expression of the role which Coleridge envisaged for his 'national church', leading the errant state through the wilderness of political liberalism. Coleridge was associated with the group through his friendship with Irving, whose influence is evident in the title of the section of *Church and State* attacking Catholicism 'On the Third Possible Church or the Church of Anti-Christ', and in other places (CS 129). But the millenarianist influence should not be overstated in a work which, after all, was dismissive of Irving's extremism and of the whole exegetical basis of millenarianism. More concerned with regenerating the Arminianism of the established church than with a radical break-away protestantism, Coleridge was scornful of Irving's fundamentalism and 'bibliolatory', adopting the well-worn Augustinian strategy of denying that the Bible could be a basis for detailed millennial predictions. The

Apocalypse of St John should be read rather as 'the most perfect specimen of symbolic poetry' (CS 139n).

Coleridge's idea of providential history sought to play down the apocalyptic belief in direct divine intervention in human time, a traditional recourse of militant and politicized Christianity, common in the radical sects of the 1790s, amongst them Unitarianism.[3] Partly in reaction to the scepticism of the 'mythological school', posing an ideological threat to the religious establishment, and partly as a result of the *historismus* of German Idealism which guided Coleridge's intellectual interests after about 1804, the exegetical battles once fought over scriptual texts had now been transferred to the domain of history and mythology. The theory of Providential history developed by Coleridge between 1817 and 1825 carried an emotional and ideological burden which had formerly been the prerogative of scriptural exegesis.

Robert Preyer, in his 'Bentham, Coleridge, and the Science of History',[4] has characterized Coleridge's historiography as a rejection of the rationalism of Hume, Gibbon and Robertson. If many eighteenth-century historians had charted a steady moral and intellectual progress towards enlightenment, in opposition to superstition and irrationalism, the Coleridgeans, influenced by the historical relativism of the Germans, sought to show, in the words of J. S. Mill, that 'different states of human progress not only *will* have, but *ought* to have, different institutions'.[5] Coleridge was anxious to show that paradoxically, the laws impelling historical change were in reality identical to the higher Ideas revered by men, rather than the inexorable motion of an abstract nature; deviance from, and return to, these higher Ideas was constitutive of human time, of history. We will see how this developed as a notion of perennial struggle between political and religious idealism, or *civilization* and *cultivation*, closely linked to Coleridge's theological ideas, notably his complex philosophy of the Trinity.

An important influence on Coleridge's Providential history in the 1820s was the *Scienza Nuova* of Giovambattista Vico, to which Coleridge was introduced by the Italian political exile Giacchino de' Prati in 1825.[6] Vico's argument, hitherto unknown in England, was based on the supposition that history could be the object of man's immediate knowledge in a way that natural science could not, simply because human institutions were themselves made by men. Coleridge read this argument at the time of composing *Aids to Reflection*, the *Prometheus of Aeschylus*, and parts of *Church and State* with the excited exclamation 'pereant qui ante nos nostra dixere' (CL V 454), no doubt recognizing Vico's anticipation of the 'intellectual intuition' of the German Idealists. Vico's 'storia eternale ideale' offered an a priori model of providential history as a recurring cycle (or *ricorso*) of three epochs of human institution, government by a divine monarch, by aristocracy and by democracy, respectively. Vico's euhemerist interpretation of myths revealed the socially-constitutive nature of poetry, and the necessary correlation of political institutions with religious reverence for the founding-myths of these institutions. To study the myth-culture of a people would afford insight into the condition and nature of their institutions, for 'the order of ideas must follow the nature of institutions',[7] in contrast to rationalist historians who evaluated historical societies in terms of their conformity to an 'ahistorical' standard of reason. Vico's 'social' theory of religious myths dispensed with the notion of divine intervention as well as (strategically) avoiding the sacred history of the Jews and limiting its scope to the 'profane' histories of the Gentiles.

Vico not only permitted Coleridge a better understanding of what E. P. Thompson has called 'the logic of process'[8] than the eighteenth-century historians – in 1832 he complained that Gibbon's history was a patchwork of mere biography and anecdote without a philosophical method (TT II 231–2) – but also provided a framework of intelligibility for contemporary political uncertainties. Transition from aristocratic to democratic government was part of the triadic schema of historical change which would be followed by a return to the first stage, monarchy. In 1833 Coleridge cited Vico (against Spinoza's hypothesis of 'democratization' in the *Tractatus Politicus*) in support of his contention that 'the European nations are more or less on their way, unconsciously indeed, to pure monarchy' (TT II 44; 148). Although Vico's idea of the 'self-creation' of humanity appeared to be a sceptical argument, it was balanced (and differentiated from the sociological 'conjectural history' of the Scottish Enlightenment) by its emphasis upon the necessity for religious belief, the *priority* of the divine idea, and by its notion of *ricorso*, denying that history could be the domain of purposive progress. *Homo Faber* was subordinate to God and subject to laws beyond his own determination, and it was this devotion which guided men in the creation of their cultures. Vico provided Coleridge with a defence of a providential deity as a counterweight to historical *ricorso* on grounds independent of contested scriptural authority.

Vico's *ricorso* in many ways resembles Polybius' idea of the *anakuklōsis politeiōn*, an inexorable cycle of the three forms of government, which, as J. G. A. Pocock has argued, it was an object of Harrington's agrarian republic or *Oceana* to overcome. The 'spiritualized republic' theorized by Coleridge in the 1790s shared this goal: 'if . . . conceived in a millennial form, as a transcendence of history occurring sequentially within it, the perfectly virtuous republic might be assimilated to the *regnum Christi*'.[9] Coleridge's interest in *ricorso*, and espousal of Polybius's idea (TT II 149) represented a total revision of the early republicanism and a new conception of history.

In a letter (16 June 1825) on the subject of 'comparative history', Coleridge correctly identified Vico's influence on the Swiss historian B. G. Niebuhr, and described the 'revolutionary impact' of *ricorso* in showing 'the connection of the *Heroic* History of Greece and Rome with the *Feudal* History of Modern Europe, after the disruption of the Western Empire' (CL V 470). Coleridge followed Vico in seeing the revolutions of the classical world repeated in the Christian era, an important key to his interest in the apparently 'remote' paradigm of the Mysteries. Providential monotheism, of which Christianity was the ultimate expression, had provided a reorientation for humanity at times of civic collapse or of tyranny. The classical mysteries had preserved a faith in providence during the decline of the Greek and Roman republics; the early church, emerging from the Mysteries, had redeemed the cosmopolitanism of the declining Roman empire, making it the condition for the spread of the first 'mundane religion' and giving the slave-caste a dignity denied them in the Roman civic order. The medieval bishops, establishing free-trade zones around the cathedrals, had eased the Feudal yoke and permitted the birth of the burgher class and the development of commerce.[10] Coleridge's focus on the historical decline of civic idealism, in his case centred on the providential agency of the Mysteries, was a symptom of the current crisis of tradition and cultural identity. The collapse of the classical world was a predominant theme in historiography of the period, in works such as Gibbon's *Decline and Fall of the Roman Empire* (1777), Adam Ferguson's *History of the Progress and Termination of the Roman Republic* (1783) and B. G. Niebuhr's *Römische Geschichte* (1811–12).[11]

Coleridge's attempt to found Christian apologetic on a historical rather than a scriptural basis was also doubtless a reaction to the intense focus upon both the Jewish Theocracy and the personality of Christ as a political and moral teacher in the early Unitarian period. Coleridge's indifference to factual proofs of Christ's incarnation and resurrection (as well as to the Eucharist) was based, as James Boulger has reminded us, upon the *a priori* basis of his Christianity; but this must have also involved a shying away from the humanity of Christ, the 'Despised Galilaean', and the young Coleridge's Socinian interpretation of John 14.9: 'He that hath seen me hath seen the Father' (PW I 109, l. 9 and note).[12] In the Mysteries, Coleridge found a vehicle for articulating the *a priori* nature of Christianity and the necessity for redemption in a historical period pre-dating the birth of Christ, and in a social and political context which held up a mirror to the present.

The influence upon Coleridge of the German Higher Criticism has been authoritatively studied by Elinor Shaffer in '*Kubla Khan' and the Fall of Jerusalem*, a critical movement closely linked with the epistemological concerns of the post-Kantian idealists and the new *Historismus*. Coleridge's apologetics developed in opposition to a critical Deism which had historicized religious myths; even an Anglican like William Paley sought to defend revelation on the ground of its historical rationality, veering towards Arian and Socinian interpretations. Following the Germans, Coleridge shifted the grounds of the defence, in the words of Basil Willey freeing Christianity 'from the millstone of fundamentalism' and 'in effect producing a blue-print for all possible future defences of the faith'.[13] By the 'subtle apologetic manoeuvre' of mythologizing history Coleridge recuperated the sceptical strategy of historicizing and revealing the mythological co-ordinates of Christianity.[14] Rather than claiming 'plenary inspiration' for the letter of scripture, its privileged authority as the immediate and infallible words of God, Coleridge argued that the Bible was but one episode in the unfolding drama of providence, in which all men and nations had participated. The fact that the Bible contained undeniable anomalies and contradictions (increasingly obvious to scientific philology), and that it had structural homologies with other religious myths need not be an obstacle to faith. By means of his 'providential history', Coleridge radically expanded the text of revelation in an exegetical version of the epistemological concerns of the idealists, 'seeking out what had hitherto been considered sources of heteronomy, and incorporating these sources into a larger autonomous framework'.[15] In *Aids to Reflection* Coleridge described the Christian doctrines of Original Sin and necessary Redemption as vestiges of 'the original Patriarchal religion, before the Polytheistic decline', a notion of great importance for his interpretation of the Prometheus myth (AR 276). Because the classical Mysteries expressed the purest form of paganism, they provided a convincing argument for the necessity of Christianity. In *Confessions of an Inquiring Spirit* Coleridge wrote that 'the history of all historical nations must in some sense be [the history of Christianity]; – in other words, all history must be providential, and this is a providence, a preparation, and a looking forward to Christ' (CIS 41).

Coleridge's providential history represented a systematic revision of the historical meliorism of the 1795 *Lectures* and the Apocalyptical poetry of the same period, although as early as May 1799 he had questioned the necessitarian position 'Is the march of the Human Race progressive, or in Cycles?' (CL I 518). It also significantly qualified Schelling's 'epigenetic' idea of history as the self-revelation of the Absolute (an attitude we saw underpinning the *Biographia*'s theory of imagination), the product of Coleridge's problematic relation to contemporary social and political changes. He now sought to combine the Vicchian idea of *ricorso* with a more traditional Christian scheme of redemption which (in contrast to Schellingian or Hegelian dialectic) was based upon the dualistic division between a transcendent 'Divine Idea' and the profane and empty flux of human time. History defined as 'God's epic poem' became, after 1817, history as *tragedy*, as imagination's role as mediator between value and experience was limited to resistance and transcendence, 'the struggle to idealize and unify'. If Schelling's 'world system' had found its archetype in the ascending triads of Dante's *Commedia*, Coleridge now preferred to view the relationship between the divine principle and the world as one of *tragic* opposition, set within a scheme of ultimate Christian redemption. The 'lofty Struggle between irresistible Fate & unconquerable Free Will' found 'it's equilibrium in the Providence & the Future Retribution of Christianity' (CL V 35).

The tension between organicism and Christian dualism in

Coleridge's later thought cannot be resolved in any easy way, despite the fact that he believed the task of the 'philosophic theologian' was to do just that (see page 155 above). Clearly tragic opposition was incompatible with the theocratic definition of the State in *Lay Sermons* or the Philosophical Poem projected in the *Biographia*; the civic community cannot be *both* the realm of the sacred and of the profane. In 'Revolution as Tragedy', John Farrell argues that, in the work of Scott, Carlyle, Arnold, and Coleridge: 'The device of tragedy answers the challenge of *Realpolitick* . . . [these writers] attributed to tragedy a luminous and ennobling orientation in the deep meanings of human action, that no merely partisan or polemical spirit could attain.'[16] Coleridge expanded the idea of tragedy beyond its dramatic context into a general style of thought – he had after all been lecturing on tragedy since 1808 and was well acquainted with A. W. Schlegel's theory of tragedy. He commended the 'tragic providential' manner of Herodotus' history:

> [He] attempts to describe human nature itself on a great scale as a portion of the drama of providence, the free will of man resisting the destiny of events, – for the individuals often succeeding against it – but for the race always yielding to it, and in the resistance itself invariably affording means towards the completion of the ultimate result.
>
> (LR I 153)

The Mysteries represented for Coleridge the triumph of the 'resistance' (significantly they were also the seed-bed of the Greek tragedy (Friend I 504)) anticipating the contemporary role of Christian 'cultivation' in an era of secularism and social atomism. They provided an apologetic which avoided the egalitarian ethics of the New Testament as well as the problematic basis of scriptural authority, anticipating the necessity of Christianity in the context of a collapsing civic order. They afforded a means of communicating truth by balancing concealment with revelation, so as to integrate different levels and classes of men within a nominally common culture.

Since the 1808 'Fable of the Madning Rain' (Friend II 11–13), Coleridge had been experimenting with means of communicating 'moral' rather than 'verbal' truth, including 'the intention of the speaker, that his words should correspond to his thoughts in the sense in which he expects them to be understood by others' (Friend II 42). The Fable had spelt out the disastrous consequences of the failure to do this in the context of a factional and warring community, and the exhaustion of traditional symbols of authority. But the Mysteries showed a way to place dangerous truths beyond the reach of those who might have motives to abuse them, an antidote to the Jacobin's arming 'fools with fire under the pretence of conveying truth' (Ph L 159). *Pseudos* might be maintained in the hands of a specialized cast whose will to intellectual power was tempered by allegiance to social order. We will see how Coleridge developed a pedagogic method based on the Mystery initiation, in which an 'exoteric' doctrine based upon the literal 'mystification' of authority, and a form of reverence defined in terms of moral conduct, ascended to an esoteric revelation of higher critical knowledge and the Schellingian 'One Life' theory, thereby secured from perilous misinterpretations. Whilst the layman literally worships and obeys the 'sovereign principle', the demystified initiate perceives authority as a metaphor preserving the conditions of belief. The power and vested interest accompanying initiation ensure that the mystagogue has no stakes in broadcasting a literal version of the 'One Life' or uncovering the 'natural' origins of the transcendent idea. Thus his loss of belief corresponds to a growing awareness of the *necessity* of belief, and a sense of his duty of constancy to that necessity. Religion and politics are preserved in safe separation, even antagonism, which hides their secret kinship from view.

The Mystery represented Coleridge's version of Wordsworth's *'Janus*-head of Spinoza and Dr Watts', a doctrine which avoided the palpable insincerity of 'pious fraud' by creating the level at which it was to be comprehended, thereby avoiding the worst kinds of cultural confusion. In the *Philosophical Lectures*, Coleridge admired Pythogoras's 'moral politics': 'To tell truth, but so at the same time to convey it as to prepare the mind for greater truths' (Ph L 102). Reversing his youthful conviction, Coleridge sought to subordinate Truth to Mystery at every level of social and intellectual intercourse. After all, was not mystification a more expedient exercise of power than the violence of censorship and intellectual repression: 'If Truth yelps and bites at the Heels of a Horse that cannot stop, why, Truth may think herself well off if she only gets her teeth knocked down her Throat' (CL IV 713)?

18

The Mystery Cults: Sources and Explanation

Coleridge's interest in the Mystery cults was by no means eccentric for his age. Among the most salient recent and contemporary treatises on the subject were William Warburton's long exposition in *The Divine Legation of Moses* (Book II, section four, 1738–41); Thomas Taylor's *Dissertation on the Eleusinian and Bacchic Mysteries* (1790, but reprinted in the *Pamphleteer* in 1816); the Reverend G. S. Faber's *Dissertation on the Cabiri* (1803); and Schelling's *Üeber die Gottheiten von Samothrace* (1815); all of which were well known to Coleridge.[1] Schelling's work seems to have been the immediate source of his interest in the subject in the period after 1817, however, providing the material on the Cabiri for the eleventh *Lecture on Literature* (3 March 1818). It is probable that Coleridge's attention was drawn to the work by Ludwig Tieck during their meeting in London on 13 June 1817; the following day he ordered a copy of Schelling's *Die Weltalter*, a work of which the treatise on the deities of Samothrace was the only part to be published (CL IV 738).[2] Schelling had given the subject a more cursory treatment in the 1803 lectures *Üeber die Methode des akademischen Studiums*, a copy of which Coleridge had requested from Crabb Robinson on 26 November 1813 (CL III 461).

The Mysteries had been a popular subject in both English and German intellectual circles for some time; as Elinor Shaffer points out, 'comparisons between the pagan mystery religions and either the initial, or a later phase of ancient Christianity had been common for 200 years'.[3] John Toland's attack on the Mysteries in *Christianity not Mysterious* (see Chapter 2) was typical of Deist and Socinian aversion to 'double doctrine' and religious mystification; the equation of pagan priestcraft with the Roman Catholic hierarchy (amongst Anglicans like Warburton), and with the Anglican establishment (amongst dissenters like Priestley and Coleridge) was a common tactic. Coleridge had attacked 'double doctrine' in his 1795 lectures:

. . . though there had existed in the heathen world men of power and wise in their generation, yet their Doctrines never spread among the People, but were industriously concealed from them – most of the public Teachers had two sets of Opinions the first were called exoteric, or such as all were allowed to hear, the second which [were their] real opinions esoteric and communicated to a few favoured Disciples.

(Lects 1795 159)

The egalitarianism, rationality and unitarianism of early Christian doctrine had been corrupted by the admixture of Greek 'double doctrine' – especially the platonism of the Gnostics, ultimately responsible for 'all the Mysteries, Impostures and Persecutions, that have disgraced the Christian Community' (Lects 1795 199). The Gnostics had been responsible for importing the platonic notion of the Trinity into Christianity, 'a mysterious way of telling a plain Truth' (Lects 1795 208), an argument derived from Priestley's *History of the Corruptions of Christianity* and, ironically, from Bishop Warburton's *Divine Legation*.[4] The weakness of Warburton's apologetic strategy (like Paley's) is evident from the fact that Coleridge was able to recuperate its anti-Catholicism into an anti-Anglican argument.[5]

Warburton's strongly rationalist temper opposed mystification in the Christian church whilst at the same time admitting the necessity of the Mysteries in the ancient world. In his 1736 *Alliance between Church and State* (anticipating in title and theme Coleridge's 1829 work[6]) and the first section of the *Divine Legation*, Warburton argued that the doctrine of a future state of rewards and punishments was necessary to the functioning of civil society; civil authority had no power to promulgate such a doctrine, so that is was up to the church to encourage 'imperfect obligations' (such as gratitude, hospitality, charity) motivated by a belief in a future state, rather than deference to civil law.[7] The necessity of such a belief to the state was the crux of Warburton's litigious and paradoxical argument: because of the evident absence of the doctrine amongst the Jews (who abandoned the false priestcraft of their Egyptian masters), the Divine Legation of Moses represented an 'extraordinary providence', a miraculous Divine intervention to conserve the Jewish state. The coming of Christ obviated the need for the divine supplement, as well as the necessity for 'double doctrine' amongst the pagan priesthood; because the true doctrine of future rewards and punishments was now available, there was no longer cause for deceit.[8]

The function of the Mysteries in the gentile states was thus a deception practised for the public benefit, given the necessity (for the temporal power) of a supernatural sanction of future rewards and punishments. Whilst the 'exoteric' religion of the state was polytheism, 'Jupiter, Mercury, Venus, Mars and the whole Rabble of licentious Deities',[9] the esoteric doctrine of the Mysteries was a de-mystificatory intiation concerning the falsehood of polytheism, its factitious nature. Originating in the Egyptian cults of Isis and Osiris, the Mysteries were only revealed to those 'who were to succeed to the administration of the state', as well as to priests of the sacerdotal religion approved by their 'education, learning and quality';[10] slaves and foreigners were excluded from initiation, emphasizing the civic rather than 'otherwordly' function of the Mysteries. Their dual function was to reveal the truth about polytheism to initiates, whilst mystifying and concealing it from the people; their secrecy was conspicuous in order to excite curiosity and devotion, their rituals 'celebrated in the Night to impress Veneration and religious Horror'.[11] Initiation provided the rationale of the polytheistic deities whilst destroying belief in them: the gods were only civic heroes deified by a grateful posterity, a pantheon of national saints endowed with supernatural powers 'to keep the People in awe, under a greater Veneration for their Laws'.[12]

Warburton offered a civic exegesis of the classical myths not dissimilar to Vico's, for whom, in opposition to Bacon's hypothesis in *De Sapientia Veteram*, 'the wisdom of the ancients was the vulgar wisdom of the lawgivers who founded the human race, not the esoteric wisdom of great and rare philosophers'.[13] Book six of Virgil's *Aeneid*, for example, was read as an account of Aeneas' initiation into the Eleusinian Mysteries rather than an allegory of the soul's migration after death, although as Warburton was aware, Virgil's narrative could be read on both the esoteric and exoteric levels. The mythic cosmology figuratively represented the various transgressions of the civil laws, notably the geography of the underworld, inculcating 'respect for person and property'. The three realms of the underworld, Purgatory, Tartarus, and Elysium served a practical purpose: 'the Virtues and vices, which the Poet repapitulates as stocking these three Divisions with Inhabitants, are those which must more immediately effect

Society'.[14] The presence of infants in Purgatory (which Pierre Bayle had considered so repugnant) was a means of preventing the habit of child-exposure, common amongst the Romans.[15] This was Virgil's equivalent of the non-burial of debtors in the Egyptian polity (in which funeral-rites were of great importance): 'by artfully turning it as a Punishment on insolvent Debtors, grounded on it an institution of great Advantage to Society'.[16]

The poets of the ancient world like Virgil and later Apuleius upheld the true doctrines of the Mysteries after they had been tainted by a form of 'Spinozism' or corrupted by superstition or sexual licence, delivering 'the principle, with great caution, and pure and free of the abuse'.[17] The poets believed, unlike the corrupt priesthood or the sceptical philosophers, that social community was contingent upon the credibility of, and respect for, its religious myths. This point was of great importance for Coleridge's insistence that, in a period of scepticism and civic decline, the Mysteries offered the most highly-educated and politically 'responsible' citizens both an awareness of the metaphorical status of its deities (*de*-mystification) and of the *necessity* of belief in a carefully safeguarded distinction between literal and metaphorical modes of truth. The Mysteries had the unique power of containing as well as practically overcome scepticism. And yet, in Warburton's case, admiration for 'double-doctrine' in the ancient world was tempered by a fundamentalist faith in direct divine intervention, an 'extraordinary providence' not so readily available to Coleridge. The initiates' demystification, which in a negative sense showed up the bogus nature of the polytheistic pantheon, in a positive sense anticipated the revelation of the 'true' monotheism in Christ.

If Warburton seemed to advance to a perilous proximity to demystification in his account of the social and political origin and rationale of religious belief, it was because of his attempt to follow through the most 'advanced' sceptical arguments of his day and still discover the plausibility of revealed Christianity at the end of the road. Warburtonian rationalism approached the brink of a secular theory of religion, but could exempt Christianity on the grounds of its 'extraordinary providence', an apologetic which 'higher critics' like Coleridge found inconsistant and even offensive. For already implicit in Warburton was the secularizing insight expressed by Marx in his 'de-sublimation' of Feuerbach: 'all mysteries which lead theory into mysticism find their rational solution in human practice, and in the comprehension of this practice'.[18] In Schelling's philosophy of religion, Coleridge found a more adequate strategy for averting the full secularization of Christianity which Warburton and the rationalists had stood so close to articulating. Schelling's 'mythologization of history' found in the Mysteries a new relevance as providential guardians of the evolving religious experience of humanity, upholders of 'cultivation' as opposed to 'civilization' (Friend I 494).

In his *Methode des akademischen Studiums*, Schelling had cast the Mysteries as the germ of historical and cultural change, mediating the dialectical development of the 'ideal' and 'real' poles (Christianity and Classicism respectively); the goal of the Absolute in history, and of Schelling's philosophy, is the synthesis of these poles, 'not to construct the state as such, but an absolute organism in the form of the state'.[19] The Greek state was based on an external, civic religion 'a self-contained world of symbols for the ideas',[20] the natural gods of polytheism. During the classical period, the ascendency of the 'real' pole, the antinomy (ideality or infinity) was 'wrapped in a cocoon', only expressed in Greek poetry and veiled in the Mysteries; it only awaited the breaking of Christ's body to typify the 'sacrifice of finitude' and the apotheosis of the political religions of the ancient world.[21]

Schelling's account of the suppression of infinity in the classical state, the subordination of 'private' to 'public' values was similar to a point Coleridge made in a 1799 letter to Josiah Wedgwood: 'In Christian Countries an excellent Private Character totally devoid of all public Spirit is the most common of characters', whereas the Greeks and Romans had made 'sorry Fathers, bad Husbands & cruel Masters; but glowing & generous Patriots' (CL I 465). Schelling considered that the Mysteries had flourished as a result of dissatisfaction with this state of affairs; in Rome, centuries before Constantine,

> widespread dissatisfaction with material things was producing a longing for the spiritual and invisible; an empire in its decadence, whose power was purely temporal, failure of nerve in the face of the situation, a feeling of unhappiness . . . – brought about a collective readiness to embrace a religion which guides men to the ideal world, rendering happiness through renunciation.[22]

The Mysteries had a modern, as well as historical, significance for Schelling, given an antithetical imbalance in modernity 'since the Mysteries have become exoteric, the state has become esoteric; for although the individual lives in the whole, the whole does not live in the individual'.[23] In the post-Christian era a multiplicity of individuals have lost their formative principle of civic unity, so the modern *gnosis* of the Mysteries must accordingly infuse in them the aesthetic spirit of the Greeks, 'to effect a gospel of reconciliation between God and the world'.[24] The new idealism, notably the *Naturphilosophie* had sought to reclaim nature from its exile in an epoch of Christian dualism, and the modern poetry was envisaged as paving 'the way for a rebirth of esoteric Christianity and the Gospel of the Absolute'.[25] Schelling regarded the domain of history as the dialectical self-revelation of the Absolute, the new basis for a 'higher' mythology of Christianity freed from the limits of revealed religion, itself merely a fleeting intervention of God in the world symbolizing a transcendence of the Classical deities.[26]

Schelling's most developed analysis of the Mysteries was the 1815 oration to the Royal Academy of Bavaria, *Über die Gottheiten von Samothrace*, an account of the 'Eigentliches Ursystem' of mankind, 'key to an original system of belief antedating and underlying the varied mythologies and revelations of human history'.[27] Seeking to discover in the Cabiri (the pantheon of Samothracian deities) a mythic expression of the self-revelation of the Absolute, Schelling was able to complete the mythologization of Christianity which the sceptics had instigated, but without challenging or allegorizing the mythic authority of revealed religion. Revelation is a continuous process occurring in history, only to be comprehended by examining the developing mythological systems of mankind. Each new myth grows out of all the others, subsuming and transcending its precursors: Christianity is the most advanced of these levels, a view which permitted, in the words of Elinor Shaffer, 'a gnostic inclusiveness and a Christian orthodoxy as to the supremacy, finality and clarity of the revelation of Jesus Christ'.[28] Schelling's providential history differed from Coleridge's in its denial of an 'original' creation and a primordial revealed patriarchal monotheism, as well as from the 'Hindu' emanation theory of his contemporary, G. F. Creuzer.[29] It also denied Warburton's 'double doctrine', preferring to regard the Mysteries as standing in a complementary, rather than

contradictory, relationship to the sacerdotal mythology. Greek
polytheism (the theogony of Homer and Hesiod) was defended
against the charges of the 'dualists'; if Homeric epic 'breaks the
bond by which the many dieties are one god . . . [it] breaks it
only tentatively, in play, and with the proviso of restoring
it'.[30] Anticipating Coleridge's distinction between literal and
metaphorical truth, Schelling preferred to view the relationship
between the Cabiri and the sacerdotal gods as similar to that
between the popularizing and the scholarly (akroamatic) discourse
of the philosophers.[31] The truth-value of myth lies in its
representation of community, and cannot be withheld from the
people without forfeiting its authenticity as symbol. Thus
Warburton's 'double doctrine' would only have the effect of
'overturning the altars, and shaking the peace of civil society':

> To create with one hand and overthrow with the other, to
> deceive openly and enlighten in secret, to buttress the cult of
> the gods by laws and earnestly punish desecration while
> secretly nourishing and encouraging unbelief: what a way to
> make laws![32]

Schelling's indictment of 'pious fraud', his affirmation that truth
may be held *for* the people but not *from* them, may well have
influenced Coleridge's antipathy to the 'worldly prudence' of
Wordsworth's '*Janus*-head of Spinoza and Dr Watts'. Coleridge's
'semi-dualistic' interpretation of 'double doctrine' sought at once
to mystify *and* enlighten within the ascending levels of a hierarchy
of initiation, combining the Warburtonian and Schellingian
theories.

It is fortunate that we possess a record of Coleridge's
interpretation of the *Gottheiten von Samothrace*, not only in the
eleventh *Lecture on Literature* and the eleventh *Philosophical Lecture*
(Ph L 321–3), but also in his marginalia to G. S. Faber's *Dissertation
on the Cabiri* probably written in the years 1817–19 (M II 573–85).
Faber's hypothesis, that the Mysteries were the cults of a 'helio-
arkite' myth deriving from the worship of the patriarch Noah and
his seven sons (who had rescued the race from extinction in the
flood), was treated with scorn by Coleridge. He considered Faber's
pseudo-etymological method utterly bogus; using the same
technique, Coleridge offered to show that Thucydides' history of
the Peloponnesian war was merely a medley of mythic

representation of the story of Cain and Abel (M II 574n).[33] But his scrutiny of Faber in this period shows not only his interest in the Mysteries; it also shows the hold which Schelling's treatise had on him (evident in the marginal notes), as well as his reservations concerning its pantheism.

Schelling described the hierarchy of the Cabiric deities as being composed of two triads, the lower of which were named Axeiros, Axiotersis and Axiokersa. These were suppressed Titans, figuring the 'natural' origin of religions, or in Coleridge's 1818 description, 'different modifications of animal desire or material action, such as hunger, thirst and fire, without consciousness' (LR I 186). In the Faber marginalia, he described the lower Triad as 'the infernal Trinity – or dim Personëities of the Chaos in the throes of self-organization – corresponding according to Varro, to Pluto, Vulcan and Proserpina' (M II 583). Ascending to the higher Triad, the variously named deities were Jupiter (Jove), Cadmilos (Mercury, Hermes, Bacchus, Apollo, Helius, Minerva or Pallas in other accounts), and Venus, representing the 'higher' properties of Reason, of the Word (or communicative power) and Love, respectively (LR I 186).[34] The key to the whole pantheon was Cadmilos, mediator between the two triads, who also re-appeared as an additional eighth deity (his mediation between the higher and lower triads being counted as a separate manifestation). Cadmilos fulfilled the mediatory agency of Schelling's imagination, reconciling the 'higher' realm of civilization and intellect with the cthonic power of 'natura naturans', and also prefigured Christ, the Logos. In his copy of Faber, Coleridge described Cadmilos as 'the Mediator or Restorer of the fallen Souls – as the Conductor from Chaos to the $Ko\ \mu\zeta$ World of Law, Order, Beauty, so hereafter to be the reconductor from the Disorder or second Hades, the Redeemer – and in this function he is Bacchus, to be born on earth and worshipped . . . as the infant Bacchus' (M II 583–4). Coleridge went on to explain how this fitted the patristic notion of 'thrice-begotten Christ' who, like Cadmilos, has already been manifest twice before the incarnation. Coleridge's identification of Bacchus and Christ is as advanced as anything in the pages of Volney or Dupuis, but within the framework of a 'mythologized' providential history and the Mystery initiation it substantiated rather than challenged the authority of Christian revelation (Ph L 322–3).

Cadmilos represented a synecdoche for the Mystery rites as a

whole, both insofar as he mediated between the conscious powers
of Reason and the natural appetites, and as the historical link
between the 'Asiatic and Greek popular schemes of mythology'
(LR I 185) and the 'mundane' religion of Christianity. For Schelling
the higher Cabiri were only intimated in the Samothracian
pantheon because they prefigured revelation, the bridge between
the various national myths and the 'syncretic' cosmopolitanism of
Christianity. Clearly the Mystery initiate became a participant in a
historical community linking Christianity with the earliest
manifestation of mythic consciousness, 'the initiate himself became
a link of that magical chain, himself a Cabir, taken up into the
unbreakable relation and *joined* to the army of the higher gods'.[35]
Schelling emphasized the continuity of the magic chain in praising
the royal patron of the Bavarian Academy who had in 1813 joined
the Holy Alliance against Napoleon 'the Cabir-like alliance,
through which the power of a truly Typhonian realm was first
broken'; the Mysteries were laden with contemporary cultural
relevance, for they too 'once united people inwardly', and through
(their) rituals thousands of people, the best of their age, 'came to
know the highest dedication of life'.[36]

In his *Lay Sermons*, Coleridge had mentioned the power of
social regeneration traditionally attributed to the Mysteries, healing
the wounds of civilization (LS 188). In an unusually frank avowal
of the 'Dionysian' element of the Mysteries, he suggested in 1818
that the very survival of civilization was contingent upon its
continuing ability to commune with its origins in the cthonic
energies of nature, the 'suppressed Titans':

> The lower or Titanic powers being subdued, chaos ceased, and
> creation began in the reign of the divinities of mind and love;
> but the chaotic gods still existed in the abyss, and the notion of
> evoking them was the origin, the idea, of the Greek necromancy.
>   (LR I 186–7)

Like Vico's account of the origin of religious myths, the 'higher
ideas', in political institution, Coleridge discovered in the Mysteries
a means of safely inculcating the true meaning of power as it
emerged from community. Wordsworth himself had realized the
spiritual value of a harmonious civic order; as Coleridge wrote in
Blackwood's Magazine in October 1821, it was to the poet's 'habit of
tracing the presence of the high in the humble, the mysterious Dii

Cabiri, in the form of the dwarf miner, with hammer and spade, and week-day apron, we must attribute Wordsworth's *peculiar* power, his *leavening* influence on the opinions, feelings, and pursuits of his admirers . . . his works are a *religion*'.[37] But we have seen why Coleridge considered that the poet's peculiarly literal representation of the esoteric doctrine of the Mysteries, starting 'from the bottom up', too nearly risked arming fools with fire. Christian culture must rather fulfil the function of Tragedy in the Greek world, taking the mysterious reconciliation or *Katharsis* before the *polis*, 'a sort of Bible or Biblical instruction of the people' (SC I 186). The perilous knowledge of the kinship of art and power must be safely institutionalized within the ascending structure of the Mystery initiation. Coleridge's anxiety concerning the pantheism of Schelling's account of the 'epigenesis' of culture is evident in one of his comments on the Cabiric chain in the margins of Faber:

> The ancient Mystae were so far Pantheists, that they made the lowest first, the highest posterior – primi quia inferiores, ultimi quia supremi.

(M II 575)

This 'natural' priority, present in Wordsworth and Schelling alike, Coleridge found safely reorientated by Varro:

> Janus controls first things, Jupiter the highest things. Jupiter is rightly therefore called King of all. For first things are inferior to highest, because though the first things precede in time, the highest surpass them in dignity.

(M II 575n)

The priority of the 'suppressed Titans, the infernal Trinity', is chronological rather than symbolical; origin, with all its power of legitimation, is a necessary fiction before it is a literal fact. The necessity of the transcendent idea overrides the question of its empirical existence, status or interests. The truth of symbolic priority is only vouchsafed to the initiate for whom 'dignity' has assumed more significance than history, belief a greater power than fact.

19

'Cultivation' versus 'Civilization' in Coleridge's Providential History

> The Church is the last relic of our nationality . . . I think the fate of the Reform Bill, in itself, of comparatively minor importance; the fate of the national church occupies my mind with greater intensity.
>
> (TT II 23)

Behind Coleridge's 1832 judgement lay a life-long struggle to articulate a satisfactory relationship between religion and politics. In 1796, a Priest had been defined as 'a man . . . holding the scourge of power in his right hand and a bible (translated by authority) in his left' (PW I 117n); by 1817, however, the 'national church' was upheld as a *political* example to the landed class, it being the sole remaining proprietor of land 'essentially moving and circulative' (BL I 227). By 1832, the church was the 'last relic of our nationality', a complete revision of the 1796 idea of the social function of religious symbol and the 'mystery' of faith. The following pages will examine how this revision was worked out in terms of a philosophical history of civilization, a drama in which the Mysteries played the leading role.

From the scattered and fragmentary sources in the Philosophical and Literary lectures of 1818–19, the *Essays on Method* (1818) and the *Lecture on Prometheus* (together with the appended essay *On the Mysteries in relation to Greek Tragedy*[1]), we can piece together an original and consistent treatment of the historical relations between culture (art, mythology and religion) and the political and economic conditions of society. The interest of Coleridge's 'polar' history of the interplay of 'cultivation' and 'civilization' lies in its inclusiveness, in refusing to separate discrete discursive domains, an approach which earned the disapprobation of one of Crabb Robinson's friends who regretted that Coleridge 'makes a sad confusion of mythology, metaphysics, etc. etc.' (SC II 244). The contemporary ideological importance of Coleridge's providential history as a framework of intelligibility should be considered as a methodological 'given' in the light of the notion of *ricorso* discussed above.

In the *Literary Lectures*, Coleridge specified the relationship between 'civilization' and 'cultivation' in terms of that between republican political idealism (and its religious corollary, pantheism or polytheism) and the cosmopolitan 'mundane' religion evolving from the Patriarchal monotheism through Platonism to Christianity. The civic order of the republics had dissolved into democratic atomism, the result of commercial and imperialist expansion which undermined the role of the agrarian freeholder as exponent of 'the Spirit of the State'. But this perennial collapse of civic values is shown to be a 'fortunate fall', insofar as it revealed a transcendent and providential order behind the hubris of civilization, and permitted the re-emergence of spiritual devotion. The laws of God were revealed in the natural demise of the political order.

The distinction between 'civilization' and 'cultivation' was evident in the poetic myths of different societies, or of any one society at different stages of development, as Coleridge indicated in his comparison between Homeric and Miltonic epic in Lecture Ten. Whereas the *Iliad* was a *national* epic based on 'a single chapter from the volume of history', *Paradise Lost* was remarkable for an interest which transcended 'the limits of a nation' (LR I 172). In accordance with the Schellingian notion of Christianity as a synthesis and transcendence of all the world's myths, Milton's epic treated man as man rather than as a citizen of a particular state or time. Its subject-matter was metaphysical in the most literal sense, 'the origin of evil and the combat of evil and good', comprehending the Jewish and Mohammedan as well as the Christian worlds. Milton was the exemplary Christian poet, repeating the 'sacrifice of finitude', the Christian hero building the *Civitas Dei* upon the defeat of political idealism:

He was, as every truly great poet has ever been, a good man; but finding it impossible to realize his own aspiration, either in religion, or politics, or society, he gave up his heart to the living spirit and light within him, and avenged himself on the world by enriching it with this record of his own transcendent ideal.

(LR I 178)

Like the Mysteries, Milton's epic thus represented a triumph of the transcendent Idea over fallen man's tendency to polytheism, a 'confounding of God with Nature, and an incapacity of finding unity in the manifold and infinity in the individual' (LR I 184). 'Civilization', by implication is a function of man's fallenness, connected to Coleridge's complex theology of radical evil. Although properly beyond the scope of the present study, we may briefly follow James Boulger's lucid exposition to show the relevance of Coleridge's theological investigations for his theory of culture.[2]

In a late notebook (NB 26), Coleridge represented the origin of man as a pre-lapsarian identity with the Divine Will, in Boulger's words, 'a positive potency of willing itself always in the Absolute Will'.[3] Positive potency is, in a sense, of a non-being; everything being possible, nothing is actualized. From a 'wilful' desire to emulate the autonomy of the Absolute Will (*causa sui et effectus*) man falls into actuality, desiring to create rather than to obey. This finite individuation contradicts the Absolute, however, figured in Trinitarian theology as the paradoxical relationship between *Ipseity* and *Alterity*. Man is redeemed from this condition by the mediation of Christ, the Logos, at once god and Man, ipseity and alterity, embodying the God-like power to deliver and the man-like power to *choose* deliverance. In the terms of Coleridge's philosophy of history, the Satanic will-to-actuality is equated with civilization, the self-creation of man as a political being. In the *Essays on Method*, Coleridge described this apostasy as product of 'image or imagination', men's determination to 'shape their convictions and deduce their knowledge from without' (Friend I 501), whereby they 'receded from all true cultivation, as they hurried towards civilization' (Friend I 502). Accordingly, 'they built cities, invented musical instruments, were artificers in brass and iron, and refined on the means of sensual gratification, and the conveniences of courtly intercourse' (Friend I 501).

The Greeks represented civilization as the Promethean fire in their great myth of origin, a theft from heaven but a gift to mankind; in 1824, Coleridge described Prometheus as 'the Redeemer and the Devil jumbled together' (TT I 49). Adopting a material faith, the apostates built a 'temple consecrated to the material heavens' or the tower of Babel, a figure for both Milton's 'goodly tower of commonwealth' and Coleridge's 'old ruined tower' discussed in Part Two. Political idealism, as the biblical story confirms, is always self-defeating, as the 'confusion of lip' takes its toll on the builders of the tower: distinction of languages gave birth to the nations, each of which took its particular deity, 'kept aloof from each other by their ambitious leaders' (Friend I 502–3).

In the *Lecture on Prometheus*, Coleridge privileged the Jews as upholders of providential monotheism and 'cultivation' against the hubris of the 'civilizers', represented scripturally by Moses' extraction of the chosen people from the Egyptian yoke, a preparation for the redemptive 'mundane religion' of Christianity. The Jewish exodus was a return to a more primitive civic state in the wilderness, the result of their refusal to obey the Egyptian ban on sacrificing the sacred cow (LR II 326). Following Vico's euhemerist style of exegesis, Coleridge suggested that the sanctity of the cow had the sound political purpose of preventing a relapse from agricultural civilization to nomadic barbarism (LR II 327). Prohibiting the slaughter of cattle enforced the cultivation of the soil for a cereal diet, whereas pastoralism required regular slaughter of livestock. Polytheism (cow-worship, in this case) is thus closely linked with the 'progress' of civilization, and the Jewish insistence upon sacrificing represents a renunciation of such progress, as well as figuring (according to a familiar typology) the 'sacrifice of finitude' in Christ's crucifixion.

The significance of the Jewish renunciation lay at the heart of the esoteric doctrine of the Mysteries. Adapting Warburton's 'double doctrine', Coleridge demonstrated the co-existence, in the Greek world, of a true 'Orphism' in the Mysteries, with the sacerdotal polytheism of 'civilization'. The increasing importance of Tragedy to Coleridge's later thought is evident in his changing account of its origin: whereas in 1808 Tragedy was seen to have emerged from the Bacchanal, or polytheistic hero-worship of the Greek states, in 1818 it had originated rather in the Mystery cults (SC I 184, Friend I 504). In a reversal of Shaftesbury's anti-semiticism, Coleridge recognized everything of value in Greek culture as deriving from a Jewish source.[4] Thus the Greek Mysteries were linked with a patriarchal and Mosaic origin through an Asian channel, a defence of Christian orthodoxy against deists who located the birth-place of religious myths in Egypt, or the followers of Creuzer who preferred India. Although Coleridge's linkage between Jewish and Greek culture was tenuous, it was of considerable importance for one so enthusiastic about the Platonic strain in St. John's gospel. The Greeks 'took up the religious and lyrical poetry of the Hebrews; and the schools of the Prophets were, however partially and imperfectly, represented by the Mysteries, derived through the corrupt channel of the Phoenicians' (Friend I 503–4).

Coleridge's 'revisionist' theory of the origin of Greek culture derived from his interpretation of a passage in the second book of Herodotus' *Histories*, which described the diverse origins of the polytheistic Greek pantheon (of Egyptian derivation, only later systematized by Homer and Hesiod) and the Cabiric deities.[5] The Cabiri were derived from the un-named *Theoi* of the Pelasgian invaders, generally depicted in the form of the phallic Hermes, a fact which Coleridge rather gingerly drew attention to in an 1825 letter to John Taylor Coleridge (CL V 423). We touched upon the sexual and priapic associations of the Mysteries, the cult of natural desires and instincts, in connection with the Moses of Michelangelo and the invocation of the 'suppressed Titans'.

Coleridge described the Mysteries as 'secret schools of physiological theology', the source for the higher arts, sustaining the providential monotheism through the decadence of the popular religion and the philosophy of the learned classes:

> The Mysteries and the Mythical Hymns and Paeans shaped themselves gradually into epic Poetry and History on the one hand, and into the ethical Tragedy and Philosophy on the other.
>
> (Friend I 504)

As the civic state crumbled, the Mysteries and the Tragic poetry acted as an 'internal Theocracy' (Friend I 504) to 'counteract the demoralizing influence of the state religion, without . . . bringing into contempt the ancestral and local usages and traditions on which the patriotism of the citizens mainly rested . . . little less than essential in the constitution of a Greek republic'.[6] As this passage makes clear, the relation of the Mysteries to the civic state was a sensitive one, a point which anticipated the relationship of Coleridge's 'clerisy' to the civic ideal of the state in the *Constitution of the Church and State*. We will see how Coleridge payed lip-service to the Harringtonian 'balance' of the unreformed British constitution in that work, whilst making it clear that the National Church, and *not* the political state, was the 'last relic of our Nationality', a species of 'internal Theocracy'.

Coleridge continued his account of the providential agency of 'cultivation' in the 1818–19 *Philosophical Lectures*, translating his polar opposition into the epistemological terms of Reason versus Understanding. In a sense the lectures traced Coleridge's own philosophical genealogy, part of a 'cabiric chain' of philosophers and mystagogues from Pythagoras through Plato and Neo-Platonists to Paracelsus, Jacob Boehme and the German Naturphilosophers, although Schelling was himself given dismissive treatment (Ph L 391). The focus of the Lectures was Plato, a dominant figure of Coleridgean self-projection, representing a synthesis of Pythagorean hermeticism and Socratic 'common sense', and of course the providential anticipator of Christianity. Coleridge carefully discriminated Plato's philosophy from that of Socrates; critical of the latter's eudaemonism and pantheism, he feared that the 'Socratic method' (based on a display of iridescent intelligence) was too influenced by the dialectic of the philosopher's sophistic adversaries (Ph L 151, 220, 137). We mentioned above the civic impulse of Socrates' dying offering to Asclepius, typifying the philosopher's faith in 'the UNCOMMON excellence of common sense' (Ph L 136). Coleridge regretted that Socrates was 'too favourable to the prejudices and customs of those around him', notably the Greek philosphers' 'toleration of idolatry' (Ph L 154).

In contrast, Plato combined the social mission of Socrates with the esoteric doctrine of Pythagoras, the 'good sense' of the one with the 'moral objects' of the other (Ph L 158). Coleridge also declared his concern to 'combine & harmonize Philosophy and Common Sense' (CN II 2382), a purpose in line with the 'dual face' of the Mysteries. Plato represented the philosophical analogy of the Mysteries; his doctrine was also a distorted reflection of the original monotheism, a 'plank from the wreck of paradise thrown on the shores of idolatrous Greece, to this Divine Philosopher' (AR 27n). Plato's philosophy was closely associated with the decline of Greek republicanism, a political form now given low credence by Coleridge. Whilst agreeing with Polybius' assertion that the republics collapsed as a result of perjury and public corruption, the Sophistic influence which sundered *property* from political *propriety*, he considered this no loss to humanity. The republics were ruled by the mob, 'Prejudice was their judge, jury and executioner' and they arose out of a state of society which nothing but that fullness of genius (and) that paucity of life which is . . . insensible to deformity and to pain, could have rendered tolerable.

(Ph L 157)

The Platonic forms or Ideas maintained Pythagoras' separation of mind from the 'accidental' realm of phenomena, and a time of crisis in the state taught men that the sum of their humanity was greater than any of its particular manifestations.

Coleridge distinguished Plato's esoteric doctrines, nowhere expressed in his written works, from the exoteric philosophy of the Dialogues, the purpose of which was 'preparative, pre-disciplinary, tending to kindle the desire for the philosophy itself in the few minds thereto called' (Ph L 176). The purpose of these propaedeutic doctrines appear remarkably like that of Kant in the *Critique of Pure Reason*, no doubt partly as a result of the Kantianism of Coleridge's source, G. G. Tennemann's *Geschichte der Philosophie*. In a marginal note to Tennemann (cited by Kathleen Coburn in her edition of the *Philosophical Lectures*), Coleridge described Plato's 'exoteric' object as being:

to insinuate on every opportunity the insufficiency and alien nature of Conceptions formed by the Reflection (= Verstand, Understanding . . . [as opposed] to Vernunft, Reason, Nous) in relation to the proper objects of Philosophy (as opp. to Philology) viz. The Soul, Moral Freedom, God) – and this he effected by deducing contradictory results or absurdities from premises . . . logically undeniably.

(Ph L 426n)

Because neither sense-data nor reflection were adequate to the Ideas of Pure Reason, Plato simply *assumed* their existence as a given 'but gave them little more than their *negative* character', a tactic reminiscent of the Kantian antinomies of Pure Reason and the limitation of the Ideas to regulative status only (Ph L 426n).

At this point, however, Plato's 'Kantianism' ceased, just as the philosopher of Koenigsburg's *own* 'Kantianism' had been queried by Coleridge in the *Biographia*: 'I could never believe, it was possible for him to have meant no more by his *Noumenon*, or THING IN ITSELF, than his mere words express' (BL I 155).

Tennemann's account of the merely regulative status of Plato's forms seemed to Coleridge typical of one of the 'mechanistic' interpreters of Kant, completely counter to his own view of Kant as a cautious and discrete idealist. Kant's dualism preserved metaphysics from the forays of the understanding, but by no means denied their role as of paramount importance for philosophy. Tennemann's 'Kantianism' (determining his 'literalist' interpretation of Plato) was 'the *Rote* of a Parrot caged in the study of that great Modern' (Ph L 427n). Tennemann's limitation of the Ideas to regulative status was comparable to Aristotle's misunderstanding of his philosophical master, blind to the metaphorical 'semi-dualism' and the idealism of the Platonic esoteric doctrine, concealed by his propaedeutic structure. Coleridge showed no quarter to Tennemann's positivism; surely he

> must have understood that Plato had meant *something* higher and other than *regulative*. Of this something he could make nothing out to his own mind but a sort of Gods and Goddesses. This he naturally rejected as mere fancy-work and substituted the regulative.
>
> (Ph L 413n)

The structure of knowledge which Coleridge discerned in Plato's propaedeutic closely resembles the Mystery initiation, beginning with a dualistic separation of the Divine Ideas from the phenomenal world, or in philosophical terms, the regulative status of Pure Reason mitigated only by the constitutive efficacy of the moral postulate. This ascends by means of a rigorous ethical and spiritual discipline to the *gnosis* or esoteric doctrine whereby 'the productive powers or laws of Nature are essentially the same with the active powers of the mind'.[7] David Simpson has described the social and political bearing of this heuristic structure, with reference to Coleridgean symbol as

> the ideal principle of cohesion within a society necessarily made up of persons committed to different levels of understanding of that cohesion; what contains the seeds of freedom must appear as authority until such time as those seeds can develop.[8]

Coleridge was critical of metaphysical systems which began with, rather than culminated in *gnosis*, the immediate intuition of

the all-in-one in god, characteristic of Platonism and Neo-Platonism
(Ph L 241). The overscoring of Schellingian imagination in
Biographia chapter thirteen represented just such a critique of
'intellectual intuition' made objective; Schelling's philosophy was,
after all, dismissed as 'Plotinized Spinozism' (CL IV 883). Coleridge
was indignant at the availability of illumination in these systems,
which in his own was subordinated to the moral postulate 'what
by the efforts of reason we were to acquire painfully, arriving at
truth by possession and all the power and force of reasoning, this
was to appear in a blessed vision all at once' (Ph L 241). This
criticism motivated his dismissal of Schellingianism as a compound
of Hylozoick atheism and Plotinism/Proclism (CL IV 874) and a
translation of Behminism 'from visions into Logic' (CL IV 883).
Rather than sacrifice the moral efficacy of knowledge for immediate
intellectual gratification, ideas initially received as edicts, regulative
principles, should unveil their constitutive character in the *practice*
of those submitting to the pedagogic structure which they initiate.
Spiritual insight is a revelation showing the heuristic agency of
symbol, a covert metaphor which presents its rhetorical status as an
absolute truth.

This 'institution' of knowledge is at the heart of Coleridge's
later thought and represents an original synthesis of Kant and
Schelling, traditional Christian doctrine with the 'de-mystificatory'
insights of German idealism: it revealed a concern with preserving
knowledge as authority, in the style of Pythagoras' 'moral politics'
(Ph L 102). Plato had also realized the necessity of apportioning
the degree of knowledge to the level and class of the communicant,
in contrast to the indiscriminate broadcasting of the 'enlighteners'.
We saw how both Warburton and Schelling theorized the Mystery
initiation as a demystificatory process, culminating in a knowledge
of the origin and connection of the higher Gods with 'natural' or
political desires and passions. Coleridge represented this
metaphorical self-consciousness as an invocation of the 'suppressed
Titans' or Gods of Chaos (LR I 187), clearly the result of a 'higher
critical' knowledge which discerned the civic and political origins
of religious myth. God as man's central symbol was not a literal
person or event, 'the popping in . . . of the old man with a beard'
but a self-authenticating metaphor, an enabling fiction upon
which depended the possibility of human community. The
overwhelming vision of god's 'natural' origin must reveal itself
only to the initiate whose insight will support the necessity of

belief, a subordination of 'first things' to 'highest things'. Revelation of the metaphorical 'duplicity' of the transcendent idea is strictly forbidden outside the Mystery initiation, an evident concern of Coleridge's 1817 strictures on Schelling's identification of the Absolute with the Polar principle:

> Our first point therefore is – steadily to deny and clearly to expose, the Polarity as existing or capable of existing in the unity of a perfect Will or in the Godhead as *ens realissmum*.
>
> (CL IV 874)

Plato also took pains to disguise the copula between spirit and matter, the 'natural' origin of the higher ideas which the *naturphilosophers* so indiscretely broadcast. Coleridge was insistent that this concealment did not mean, as Tennemann would have it, that he was in reality a dualist:

> Matter in Plato is = Finiteness by Negation, the organ of which was ὑῤῥητον – not to be disclosed save in the inmost recesses of Academus – to the elect & prepared few.
>
> (Ph L 426n)

To a 'parrot' like Tennemann, Plato remains a dualist, the authority of his 'ideas' conserved in their regulative status, whereas to the initiates of the Cabiric chain, truth reveals itself as constitutive in the identity of mind and nature, the all-encompassing vision of the 'One Life' theory. Ideas are at once literal and metaphorical, depending upon the development of the communicant, commanding either belief or the moral necessity of belief, but in both cases representing the informing and enabling principle of humanity.

This 'semi-dualistic' structure of initiation permits us a better understanding of Coleridge's *Reason*, which has caused his critics so much confusion. In the section entitled 'On the difference in kind between the Reason and Understanding' in *Aids to Reflection*, Coleridge presented a characteristically difficult set of definitions. Understanding, coherently enough, is 'binding only in relation to the objects of our Senses, which we *reflect* under the forms of the Understanding' (AR 209). In conformity with the Kantian analysis, Reason is then subdivided into Speculative and Practical categories. The former is regulative only in relation to formal and abstract truths; in relation to Ideas of Reason (God, Freewill, Immortality, etc.) it can disprove false judgements but not *prove* their existence in an apodictic manner. Practical Reason, in contrast, is constitutive with regard to moral truths; according to Coleridge's 'Christianized' reading of Kant, to obey the moral imperative is to participate in the will of the Absolute (AR 209). The emphasis on the moral, rather than ontological, proof of God is consistent with the ascending structure of *Aids* and the 'moral politics' of the Mysteries. The 'organ of wisdom' is safely defined in Kantian terms as 'the Practical Reason of Man, comprehending the Will, the conscience, the Moral Being' (AR 168).

But Coleridge goes beyond this Kantian argument to postulate *another* organ of higher knowledge, recognizable from the Schellingian sections of the *Biographia* as a form of 'intellectual intuition' (BL I 289n). This organon of *'immediate* Beholding' is 'accompanied by a conviction of the necessity and universality of the truth so beheld' (AR 226n). Earlier Coleridge had defined it as 'a direct Aspect of Truth, an inward Beholding, having a similar relation to the Intelligible or Spiritual, as SENSE has to the Material or Phenomenal' (AR 216). James Boulger has commented on the 'unKantian' nature of this organon, a confusion of head and heart which presents insurmountable difficulties to scholars attempting to establish the consistency of Coleridgean theology. 'No honour could be done to either faith or reason by tampering with the distinction between the pure and practical reason so as to include in the latter the intuitive "eye of reason" of some Platonists and mystics'.[9]

Paul Hamilton has described this 'eye of reason' as an instance of the 'spiritual positivism' of Coleridge's later theology which vitiated the earlier notion of an ascending, experiential spiritual morality.[10] If, in the latter case, 'our growing body of knowledge is stirred to progress by the symbolic example of poetry', spiritual positivism, based on an immediate, extra-linguistic apprehension of truth, is an outgrowth of his political distrust for 'shared, public language' and a resort to an *ex cathedra* principle, an 'isolated realm of spiritual certainty'.[11] In the context of our hypothesis of the ascending hierarchy of the Mystery initiation, however, it is important to consider that 'intellectual intuition' (which unquestionably does represent such an *ex cathedra* principle in *Aids*) is intrinsically no different from the insight afforded by imagination in Schelling's aesthetic. What *has* changed is the quality of this *gnosis*, in giving access to a transcendent principle defined in opposition to the experiential or temporal realm, rather than the power, which in Lukács' words revealed 'the real forward movement and development of the universe'.[12] The mediating function of poetic symbol has become more and more restricted by its placement within the hierarchic structure of a 'moral politics'. Coleridge's 'intuitive' eye of reason was not a confusion of metaphysical or theological systems but rather an attempt to define the efficacy of the transcendent idea within the institution of culture.

By proposing *both* a moral programme and a 'mystical beholding' in his account of Reason, Coleridge sought to establish an ethical base for religious belief whilst avoiding the arid intellectualism of Kant, as classically defined in the 1793 treatise, *Die Religion innerhalb der Grenzen der blossen Vernunft*. For Coleridge the Will needed supernatural 'aids' in order to lay hold of the maximum of practical reason. As Elinor Shaffer has emphasized in her article 'Metaphysics of Culture',[13] Coleridge was more willing than Kant to accept the traditional (and strictly speaking counter-rational) 'aids' of Christian devotion:

> Behind Christianity lies only one transcendental idea, very similar to that offered by Kant in the *Metaphysics of Morals* as the foundation of morality: the desire to belong to a rational sphere. By Coleridge this is redrawn as the necessity, in order to lead a human existence, to project a superhuman existence.[14]

Coleridge accordingly tried to accommodate both Spinoza and Dr Watts within a single symbolic structure combining the most advanced form of apologetic with the simplest devotion to a personal God, whereby 'every doctrine is to be interpreted in reference to those, to whom it has been revealed, or who have or have had the means of knowing or hearing the same' (AR 168). The notion of an 'eye of wisdom', an immediate beholding, is adequate to the simple believer as a literal truth; he who obeys God will be vouchsafed a vision of the shining light. To the initiate, whose faith has been transformed into 'constancy to an ideal object', the validity of the supernatural projection is assured on the grounds of its heuristic efficacy. 'Belief' in an 'immediate beholding' is thus maintained, but at a metaphorical level.

This 'initiatory structure' based on the Mystery religion is the informing structure of *Aids to Reflection*: the apparent contradiction between practical reason and intellectual intuition, so awkwardly juxtaposed in that work, assumes full intelligibility if we read it in terms of 'moral politics'. At an early stage of *Aids*, Coleridge distinguished positive and negative proofs for the conformity of reason and religion; choosing the latter, 'fledged from morality', he mentioned that the positive one belonged to a more advanced stage of spiritual illumination, for 'spiritual truths can only spiritually be discerned' (AR 70). In the 'Aphorisms of Spiritual Religion' he excused himself from pontificating upon the Trinity or 'the still profounder Mystery of the Origin of Moral Evil':

> These Doctrines are not (strictly speaking) subjects of *Reflection*, in the proper sense of this word: and both of them demand a power and persistancy of Abstraction, and a previous discipline in the highest forms of human thought, which it would be unwise, if not presumptuous, to expect from any, who require '*Aids* to Reflection'.
>
> (AR 151)

Statements of this sort are, of course, themselves deliberately mystificatory, displaying all the ostentatious secrecy of rhetorical supernaturalism. The adequacy of the Christian symbols (the traditional function of the symbol is both to conceal and reveal) is maintained by means of a demonstration of their metaphorical veracity; Coleridge defined 'spirit' as an entity the property of which 'is to improve, enliven, actuate some other thing, not to be or constitute a thing in its own name' (AR 148).

The central metaphysical question as to whether ideas are regulative or constitutive, around which the foregoing argument has weaved, was not answered by Coleridge, to the perplexity of his subsequent interpreters (LS 114; CL V 14–15). As our treatment of Plato's 'moral politics' has shown, the question was suspended in the ascending hierarchy of initiation and the providential agency of the Mysteries, perennially breaking the limits of dogmatic systems to show the moral and cultural ('mythological'), rather than merely 'positivistic' application of ideas (BL I 152). Platonic 'moral politics' reconciled the historical antagonism between the great rival systems of Idealism and Materialism: Zeno and Democritus, Plato and Aristotle, scholastic Realists and

Nominalists, to the Schellingian idealists and the 'mechanistic' disciples of Kant.

The significance of the Platonic Mysteries in Coleridge's providential history lay in their realization in Christianity, a replacement of the various national religions by the Mysteries writ large, the first cosmopolitan monotheism. In a drastic reversal of his 1795 account of Platonism as the corrupter of primitive 'rational' Christianity, Coleridge now presented it as an essential element of the new doctrine. Christ the commoner, friend to his disciples, provided the 'exoteric' foundation for a personal religion which appealed to those disqualified or disillusioned with the spiritual vacuity of the civic deities. At the same time, the Platonism of St. John, the 'philosophical gospel' articulated the metaphysical significance of Christ's 'sacrifice of finitude' for the benefit of the intelligentsia. Christianity offered a pluralism of communication, without resorting to 'pious fraud', Socratic cajolement or Greek 'double doctrine':

Christianity presented the same thing to the wise and to the simple, to all mankind in the very mode which was fitted to them all; it presented it to the common people, to whom the Gospel was preached by the evidence of their senses. . . . while to the learned it presented the same truths authoritatively, and upon that authority upon which their own great philosopher had himself rested it finally.

(Ph L 233)

The civic religion of Rome collapsed because of commercial and imperial expansion, a huge influx of foreign slaves precipitating a collapse of reverence for the local and tutelary deities, and the class-partisanship of the Roman priesthood, 'an evident stronghold of the Patricians against the increasing power of the Plebeians' (Ph L 231; TT II 168). Parrying Gibbon's charges against the Christian's 'indolent or even criminal disregard to the public welfare',[15] Coleridge argued that Christianity existed independently of citizenship. Because it had inherited the initiatory structure of the Mysteries and Platonic 'moral politics', Christianity emerged from its chrysalis, the decaying empire, as a fully-fledged 'counter-ideology' which disassociated spiritual value from the civil realm. Otherwise (and here the argument implicitly counters the radical and unitarian interpretation of the early church):

> the consequence would be that from an inner religion, which was to soften all evils for the time and gradually by the means of persuasion to do away with them, it would have become a vulgar rights-of-man [fanaticism] and in its consequences would have brought disgrace on the sublime truths which it taught, and which are so sublime as to render even the supposition painful to a good man that it could have been so.
>
> (Ph L 236)

Although it made no attempt to construct a secular or political ideology, the spread of Christianity had important consequences for the temporal world. Both in its respect for individuals, independent of their status as citizens or slaves, and in its cosmopolitanism, it eased the unwieldy power of the patricians and aided and abetted commerce and trade between nations. This anticipated (according to the logic of the *ricorso*) the providential role of the mediaeval church in providing havens for runaway serfs in the cathedral cities, the seed-bed of a burgher class which might develop unfettered by Feudalism (Ph L 259). The relations between Christianity and the commercial order will be more fully developed below, notably in its role of providing a new ideal of 'cultivation' to balance commercial 'civilization', not with an alternative 'civic' model (as Jacobinism sought to do) but with a reorientation of values in the direction of transcendence. After Christ's crucifixion, the revolutions of the political world continued, but without the allegiance of the supreme values of humanity: sublimation guaranteed value, not because of, but despite, man's existence in time. The inexorable cycles of growth and decline, the pattern of *ricorso*, continued with the Emperor Constantine's bid to make 'the spiritual power . . . a complete reflex of the temporal' (TT II 169).

The significance of Coleridge's version of the Augustinian *Civitas Dei* lay in its status as an intervention in the contemporary ideological impasse, and this is the point to which we must return in concluding our account of the providential history and the Mystery paradigm. Coleridge's Christian humanism had effectively dismissed the 'Neo-Harringtonian' defence of civic virtue which in its various interpretations dominated eighteenth century thinking about society and culture. Lip-service to the ideal remained in the *Church and State*, but of greater importance now was the bid to moralize and cultivate the newly ascendent commercial order. Coleridge's 'distinction of powers' sought to wrest a viable moral rhetoric from the hands of an evanescent Toryism (and the growing threat of plebeian radicalism) in order to construct an ideology for commercial man based not on civic *virtue* but Christian *righteousness*: 'I dislike the frequent use of the word virtue, instead of righteousness, in the pulpit . . . it sounds too much like *Pagan* philosophy' (AR 7n).[16]

The case proposed in the foregoing pages is that the sublimation which the modern era knows familiarly as 'Culture' had its roots in the failure of the capitalist worldview to construct a viable moral and political defence for what J. G. A. Pocock has called 'capitalist man as a zōon politikon'.[17] The apologists of the new order had found the task 'immensely frustrated and blocked by the moral domination of Aristotelian and civic humanist values', which had already defined rentiers, stock-jobbers and all the bulls and bears of the credit economy as intrinsically corrupt.[18] In this light, Coleridge's decision also to propose the privatization of the individual and his public virtue, was a result of 'failing to discover an appropriate way of presenting him as a citizen'.[19] This is close to Coleridge's strategy of abandoning the 'One Life' ideal, which, I suggested, could not be sustained after the *Lay Sermons* and the bifurcation of secondary imagination in the *Biographia*, replacing it by the 'moral politics' of a Christian culture now defined in opposition to the civic realm, a species of 'internal theocracy'. This subordination of virtue by righteousness was a subtle defensive move; the narrative of providential history and the demonstration of the *a priori necessity* of Christianity, in terms of a Gnostic tradition perennially resisting the hubris of civilizers, turned the scepticism of the Enlightenment into an apologetic weapon. Coleridge's Christian humanism discovered in the cultural exhaustion and ideological impasse of the old society, the nutriments of a transcendent value-system sustaining traditional structures of authority in the new.

20

Coleridge's Lecture 'On the Prometheus of Aeschylus'

Coleridge's lecture on Prometheus, delivered to the Royal Society of Literature in March 1825, has been described by George Whalley (in the only exclusive critical treatment to date) as both 'a subtle figure of the Coleridgean philosophy' and 'a portentous and forbidding monument – opaque, intransigent, unlovely.[1] Even its author, for whom obscurity was often a stylistic strategy, felt a 'most remorseful Sympathy with the Audience, who could not possibly understand the 10th part' (CL V 461). This judgement should be taken as a challenge rather than as a prohibition, however, for the interest of the lecture as an uninhibited treatment of Coleridge's 'higher critical' interests is contingent upon its obscurity, its scholarly exegetical pretext and the intellectual élite – the highest level of initiate – which composed its audience.

The Prometheus myth, traditionally the most ancient in the Greek canon, as well as the most famous 'non-revealed' account of Fall and Redemption, had by Coleridge's time become a major focus for enquiries into the mythic origins of culture and religion. In his philosophical dialogue, *The Moralists*, Shaftesbury had read it as the creation of priestly mountebanks 'our modern Prometheuses' for whom it supplied a solution to the problem of evil – in the misdemeanors of the Titans – without implicating Jove himself. In line with the Deist's attack on priestcraft, Shaftesbury connected the myth with fraudulent motives: 'they could create diseases and make mischief in order to heal and to restore. But should we assign such a practice as this to heaven?'[2]

Vico, whom Coleridge was reading carefully at the time of composing the lecture, interpreted the myth as an explanation of the simultaneous origins of society and religion, human community as an outbirth of the fear of God. This fear, involved with a sense of original sin and the necessity of free will, was represented in the myth by the iron chain which bound the Titan to his mountain: savage man, wandering in the forests, had been surprised and terrified by a bolt of thunder which he took to be the wrath of God, and from which he sought refuge in a cave; forced to settle down with one woman and adopt agricultural habits, he achieved the transition from nomadic to agricultural economy, the condition of civilized society.[3]

But the myth had also invited more contemporary commentators. A. W. Schlegel, concerned like Coleridge with Aeschylus's tragic working of the Prometheus story, described it as 'a triumph of subjection', but nevertheless one which reflected (according to Schlegel's subscription to Kant's 'Stoic principle') the hard reality of man's moral and metaphysical predicament, 'with nothing to oppose to the combined and inexorable power of nature, but an unshaken will and the consciousness of elevated claims'.[4] That Coleridge sought a more complex interpretation of the agonistic relationship of Prometheus to Jove than Schlegel's harsh dualism is evident from an undated lecture note, in which dualism is shown to be of interest only when Fate is 'a higher and intelligent will' and the heroic resistance springs from some moral defect (SC I 138). Warburton's account of Prometheus as a Cabiri, appointed by Ceres to guard 'the sacred deposit of the Mysteries', a 'forbidden knowledge' stolen from heaven, may well have aroused Coleridge's interest in the relationship between the Greek Tragedy and the Mysteries;[5] both upheld the providential monotheism and the doctrines of original sin and the necessity of redemption at a time of polytheism and republicanism.

The influence of Coleridge's exegesis is evident in his son Hartley's 1821 treatment of 'the noblest Subject that perhaps a Poet has ever worked on' (CL V 142). Echoing his father's modification of Schlegel's dualism, Hartley presented Jupiter and Prometheus as figures for Law (nomos) and Reason (nous), 'contrasted and yet akin to each other'. Jupiter represented Natura naturans, necessity and the political realm (Nomos) and his wife Juno the 'sacerdotal Cultus', the 'wedded servant of the state', jealous of her husband's intrigues, notably with Io, the 'mundane religion, migrating from land to land'.[6] Prometheus figured 'the super-sensual light in man, free, though in bonds, and struggling against the despot with a prospect of ultimate emancipation'.[7] The interest of Hartley's fragment is in Prometheus' refusal to compromise with Jupiter's emissaries, notably the sylphs of natural beauty who offer to mediate between the two Titans, perhaps reflecting the mediatory power of imagination to effect symbolic reconciliation between the freedom of the finite will and the eternal necessity. Prometheus stubbornly refuses their offer; once 'poeticized', reason and will lose the energy of resistance and are condemned to endless participation in the cycles of the fallen world. Freedom from the 'metaphorical' chains binding the Titan's limbs would be submission to another enchainment, the endless series of causes and effects constituting the Stoic fate: the refusal to poeticize figured a rejection of compromise with profane modernity in the illusion of recovering the innocence of a lost Titanic age.

Hartley's failure with regard to his poem (there is some evidence that he cryptically wrote Prometheus' capitulation into the work as he failed to complete it, whereby the Titan chooses to become one with the Ocean and the endless process of Nature) may have been the result of what his father cruelly described as his son's 'moral *Idiocy* . . . the absence of a Self, it is the want or torpor of Will' (CL V 232). But in his introduction to the fragment, Derwent Coleridge suggested a more pertinent cause for his brother's capitulation, notably the disheartening competition of Shelley's *Prometheus Unbound* (1820), a work of 'splendid genius'. According to Shelley's bold reinterpretation, Prometheus' forgiveness of his tormentor was a saving insight which brought about the downfall of tyrannical institutions and religious establishments, a triumph of mutual cooperation and egalitarianism over man's self-captivating will-to-subjection. At the stylistic level Shelley's mythopoeia challenged the cultural hegemony of Christianity, whilst the downfall of Jove represented a 'twilight of the idols' whereby a transcendent deity was replaced by divine immanence, a self-evolving natural process. Derwent, truly his father's son, lamented the 'false and obvious' vulgarity of Shelley's interpretation: 'Jupiter is the oppression of the world, secular and religious, "the powers that be" as they appeared to his diseased vision; and Prometheus is relucting, upsurging humanity'.[8] In *Aids to Reflection*, betraying a *mea culpa* tone, Coleridge regretted the sort of pantheism celebrated by Shelley in *Mont Blanc* or *Prometheus Unbound*, 'an inward withdrawing from the Life and Personal Being of God . . . to the Omnipresence, in the counterfeit form of Ubiquity, to the Immensity, the Infinity, the Immutability! . . . a FATE, in short, not a Moral Creator and Governer!' (AR 396–7). His own interpretation of the Prometheus myth sought to define the necessary orientation of the divine principle, the spark of Reason, Will and religion, in relation to the world of natural and political process. In his re-binding of Prometheus, Coleridge emphasized that Titanic resistance and separation was the only condition of ultimate reconciliation.[9]

The 'esoteric' doctrine of Coleridge's lecture revealed the secret kinship of the tragic antagonists, a kinship which could only be manifest (paradoxically) on the condition of Prometheus' stern resistance to his tormentor. Prometheus had been chained to Mt Caucasus because of his theft of fire from heaven, and his dissemination of the divine spark amongst men. The gift was a threat to the absolute dominion of Jupiter insofar as it represented a principle different in kind from the evolved, animal base of human understanding. That the Fire was *stolen*, according to Coleridge, represented its diversity from 'the faculties which are common to man with the nobler animals'; it was a *spark* because it 'multiples itself by conversion, without being alloyed by, or amalgamated with, that which it potentiates, ennobles and transmutes'; from *heaven*, to mark its 'superiority in kind' (LR II 336–7). The theft represented man's fall from natural grace and his access to the divine will-to-creation. If Prometheus' theft figured the birth of 'civilization' and political idealism in the 'spiritualization' of the material base, his *binding* represented a separation of the divine principle from the manifest world. But Prometheus is far from being a powerless slave of inexorable natural law. Himself the 'Titanic kinsman' of Jupiter (whom he had helped to the throne in the overthrowal of the Saturnian dynasty), he represents a transcendent knowledge which sees beyond the limits of the 'natural' world. Like the gnostic 'cultivation' revealing a providential order in the downfall of human civilizations, Prometheus possesses the secret of the collapse of Jupiter's tyranny and the triumph and redemption of 'Alcides Liberator' (LR II 358). The eventual triumph of Alcides is contingent upon Prometheus' resistance to the exhortations and torments of Jupiter, whose continuing dominion depends upon his successful elicitation of the secret. Alcides the redeemer will be the bastard progeny of Jupiter himself, the offspring of his infidelity with Io, the 'mundane' religion, rather than his wife Juno, the 'sacerdotal cultus' (LR II 358).

The historical realization of Prometheus' secret in the birth of Christianity from the Mysteries (figured by Io) rather than the 'civic' idealism of polytheism is fairly evident; the relevance of this to the modern *ricorso*, the bearing of Coleridgean 'gnosis' upon the Anglican establishment, is more problematic, and will be returned to below. The focus of Coleridge's interpretation is present antagonism rather than future reconciliation, however, notably the primordial combat between the Titanic kinsmen, who represent the cultural and political domains respectively. Aeschylus' tragic scenario allowed Coleridge to develop the complex relationship between *Idea* and *Law* which was a central theme of his philosophy. This is based on an identity dependent upon separateness; clearly a dialectical antagonism deriving from the constitutive 'polar powers' of Schellingian idealism.[10] Jupiter and Prometheus represent a primordial conflict between *Nomos* and *Nous*, between an ever-expanding mass and an ordering principle of light which resists expansion. As Coleridge expressed it in the *Biographia*:

> grant me a nature having two contrary forces, the one of which tends to expand infinitely, while the other strives to apprehend or *find* itself in this infinity, and I will cause the world of intelligences with the whole system of their representation to rise up before you.
>
> (BL I 297)

This is expressed in the rather gnomic statement of the differential relation of the two powers 'the *nomos* is not idea, only because the idea has not become *nomos*' (LR II 343). By *realizing* itself (and this is consistent with Coleridge's account of the Fall, on page 186 above), Law has forfeited its ideality and become a blind force, constantly curbed by the Idea; idea maintains the power to check by withholding itself from manifestation, renouncing its will-to-actuality. This is the constitutive structure of Coleridgean 'semi-dualism', the *agon* of cultivation and civilization, the redemption of actuality by the ethic of resistance:

> [Idea and Law are] correlatives that mutually interpret each the other; – an idea, with the adequate power of realizing itself being a law, and a law considered abstractly from, or in the absence of, the power of manifesting itself in its appropriate product being an idea.
>
> (LR II 348)

Prometheus and Jupiter, their kinship notwithstanding, exemplify a primordial distinction of powers which is the condition for the ultimate reconciliation of man's tragic predicament with the ideal of his humanity.

Coleridge described this struggle between the 'presenting ideas' as the 'key to the Aeschylan mythology'; one might add that it is also the key to Coleridge's 'inner doctrine' in 1825, the esoteric supplement to *Aids to Reflection*. The qualities and actions of the tragic protagonists elucidate the relation between revealed and 'natural' truth, the domain of 'higher things' and of 'first things'. If the 'natural' knowledge of the understanding (or civilization) strives perpetually towards a higher, unconditioned status, its ambitions are always thwarted. For Coleridge after 1817, the 'Titans of natural desire and appetite' were decisively sundered from a higher realm of ideas; in the animal being,

> – the productive and self-realizing idea – strives, with partial success to re-emancipate itself from its product, and seeks once more to become *idea*: vainly indeed, for in order to this, it must be retrogressive, and it hath subjected itself to the fates, the evolvers of the endless thread, – to the stern necessity of progression.
>
> (LR II 345)

Like the cyclical, self-thwarting nature of civilization, natural or political man always falls short of the ideal: only by a proper subordination to the transcendent Idea, the redeeming gift of 'cultivation' can he rise above the stupendous meaninglessness of natural law. The discipline of the understanding in Logic is the highest achievement of the unaided mind, described in the *Philosophical Lectures* as the crowning glory of the Greek republics, 5, and a 'contemplation of unity in the balance of indifference the resolution of differences into unity by the establishment of a common object' (Ph L 73).

But the Prometheus myth portrays the higher reason as a captive of the tyrannical natural law, the historical expression, in Coleridge's opinion, of 'the forced amalgamation of the Patriarchal tradition with the incongruous Scheme of Pantheism' (AR 277). Prometheus is a figure of ambivalence, at once master and slave, the mythic exponent of what Elinor Shaffer has called 'an heroic sin: the self-creation of the human race. Moreover, it is necessary for Jove himself for eventually it will free him from his own natural law. . . . Creation necessitates rebellion and the consequent feeling of sinfulness'.[11] The Absolute is manifest in the indifference of the two powers (which is not to say their identity), the moral bearing of which is Prometheus' *constancy* to his secret, his refusal to yield to solicitation, one of the finest expressions of Coleridgean 'cultivation':

> Introduce but the least of real as opposed to *ideal*, the least speck of positive existence . . . into the sciential *contemplamen* or theorem, and it ceases to be science. . . . The *Nous* is bound to a rock, the immoveable firmness of which is indissolubly connected with its barrenness, its non-productivity. Were it productive it would be *Nomos*; but it is *Nous*, because it is not *Nomos*.

> (LR II 355)

The resistance of *Nous* has as its antithesis the anxiety of *Nomos* to elicit the secret of its fate, employing seduction as well as torture in its interrogation of the transcendent principle, 'to wrest the secret, the hateful secret . . . namely the transitoriness adherent to all antithesis; for the identity or the absolute is alone eternal' (L II 354). Prometheus is beguiled by the gnawing vulture; the solicitations of the 'Titanes Pacati' who, in Wordsworthian fashion, urge the prisoner to forsake his high calling – 'Forget the glories he hath known/And that imperial palace whence he came' (LR II 356); the sinister Hermes, figure for the rhetorical, the 'irrational in language' (in his role as 'false redeemer' it is tempting to interpret him as a symbol for the demagogues of the *Second Lay Sermon*); all demonstrate the propriety of the title 'Prometheus Bound'.

Like Kant's 'distinction of powers' or Coleridge's sublimation of secondary imagination, Promethean resistance maintains the possibility of the transcendent Idea in the face of the exhortations of the 'natural' intellect. Only by the separateness of mystification can the enabling idea be constitutive of human destiny, like Prometheus' secret withheld. The heuristic efficacy of symbol lies in its transcendence, its power to be desired, to command respect, to induce moral behaviour directed towards a supernatural goal.

Much of Coleridge's caution with regard to his 1825 lecture derived from its 'demystification' of the secret kinship of Prometheus and Jupiter, between nature and the divine Idea. The

reconciliation of the antagonists is the heart of the Mystery
initiation; it is a perilous moment in which belief explodes into
self-consciousness, in which the materiality of the presiding
metaphor reveals itself. Coleridge figured the horizon of such a
reconciliation, the invisible interface between spirit and matter, as
a distant event in the mythic chronology of the *Prometheus*; the
future deliverance of Alcides Liberator is remote, and contingent
upon present endurance. Sacrifice permits the possibility of 'the
power of potentiality, ennobling and prescribing to the substance',
a power which in the temporal realm is quite in excess of any
acquiescence or contract. Man's social existence depends on
supernatural sanctions: belief in a providential rather than a
'natural' destiny, marshalled by the cultural authority of 'prophecy
and foresight' is a metaphor for the power of conviction to *create*
the future. The licensed 'pseudos' of the Idea is an enabling
fiction which literally 'gets things done', on condition that its
status as metaphor remains mysterious, secret and separate.

Earlier in his lecture, Coleridge compared the Greek and Jewish
accounts of origin, the Prometheus and Adamite myths. Whereas
the Mosaic account of creation and the origin of evil was *allegorical*,
a mixture of history and fantasy based on a notion of a personal
God accommodated 'to the childhood of the human race' (LR II 335),
the Greek was *Tautegorical* or Symbolic, a synthesis of poetic form
and philosophical content (LR II 336). Different epochs of
providential history evolved different vehicles for the primal myth,
vehicles which represent not only philogenetic evolution, but also
ascending levels of spiritual self-consciousness in the individual
initiate. The stark dualism of the Jewish myth, for example, matches
the 'exoteric' doctrine of the Mysteries, for Coleridge based on
Kant's moral proof:

> [The Jews] imperatively assert an unbeginning creative One
> who neither became the world; nor is the world eternally; nor
> made the world out of himself by emanation, or evolution; –
> but who willed it, and it was!
>
> (LR II 340)

But the more intellectually developed symbol of the Greek
Mysteries, product of man domesticated in his worldly
environment, accepted deity as a super-sensuous ground of
creation, 'not so properly the cause of the latter' (i.e. of creation)

'as the occasion and the still continuing substance' (LR II 340–1). Rather than having temporal precedence over the world He has willed into being, God is considered the necessary condition for its productivity and continuing existence. The Greek notion of deity is clearly subject to the sceptical question 'And art thou nothing?', identification with the realm of natural process. But Prometheus, traditionally associated with Chronos the castrator, the separator of Ouranos the heavens and Gaia the earth, figures the Mystery rite, suppressing (and yet covertly invoking) the chaotic Titans so that the reign of the higher Gods may proceed. The separation of God was the cultural function of the Mysteries and the Greek tragedy, to 'counteract the demoralizing effects of the state religion, without compromising the tranquillity of the state itself' (LR II 331). In 1825 Coleridge feared that the vehicle on this instruction, the *Tautegory* of the Greek 'philosophical poem' was no longer available to the 'disassociated' modern sensibility; the Schellingian modern epic envisaged in the *Biographia* was dismissed in favour of the complex Coleridgean figure of semi-dualism, breaking the Hellenic continuity between Reason and sense in order to preserve the possibility of transcendence. Coleridge's admiration for the *Prometheus* as a myth of origin is strictly esoteric, not projecting it as an article of public doctrine: 'Not that I regard the foregoing as articles of faith, or as all true; – I have implied the contrary by contrasting it with, at least, by shewing its disparateness from, the Mosaic, which, *bona fide*, I do regard as the truth' (LR II 349). Revealed religion takes precedence over Hellenic aestheticism; the Jewish dispensation with its notion of a personal God, willing the Law, is the only one 'true for the meditative sage, yet intelligible, or at least apprehensible, for all but the fools in heart' (LR II 340).[12]

Coleridge, no less than Shelley, avoided the resolution of Aeschylus' *Prometheus* (so far as it can be reconstructed), whereby the prisoner divulged his secret to Jupiter, Io was wed to Peleus and the Titan released, 'a catastrophe', in the younger poet's words, 'so feeble as that of reconciling the Champion with the Oppressor of mankind'.[13] Coleridge's interest lay rather in the binding of Prometheus, the continuous resistance he so admired in the *Histories* of Herodotus:

the free will of man resisting the destiny of events, – for the individuals often succeeding against it, but for the race always yielding to it, and in the resistance itself invariably affording means towards the completion of the ultimate result.

(LR I 153)

The birth of Alcides Liberator is not really the sequel in narrative or temporal terms, at least in the way that Aeschylus' reconciliation of the protagonists was the resolution of the *Prometheus Bound*; it is rather a means of figuring a victory over necessity won by the very act of resisting and enduring. The spirit is not a literal being or event, not even the historical birth of Christ, although this is the most powerful 'exoteric' representation available to the modern consciousness. The spirit neither precedes human time (as the Greek myth makes clear) nor signals its culmination in the unveilings of Apocalypse. Rather it represents the transcendence which enables the temporal to continue without exhausting itself, a communal belief which presents an ideal of his humanity to man in the conviction of a uniform origin and destiny. But Coleridge can endorse the subtle Greek idea of the deity only within the circumscribed terms of a cultural élite and the language of the mystagogue: the divine idea as neither an old man with a beard nor a pantheistic Juggernaut, not so much the *cause* of being as its occasion and the still continuing substance' (LR II 341).

21

Conclusion: the Constitution of the Church and State

Four months after his lecture to the Royal Society of Literature, Coleridge wrote to his friend J. Blanco White that he was on 'the point of putting to the Press a small Work on the Church in it's two fold sense – viz. as an Institution of Christ, and as a State Institution' (CL V 485). Because he regarded the Church, rather than the unreformed Constitution, as 'the last relic of our nationality', it was incumbent upon Coleridge to define the 'twofold' nature of *enclesia* and *ecclesia*, the national and spiritual churches, as an 'internal theocracy' which might moralize and cultivate the new social and political order. Fearing that even the 'last relic' was in danger of disestablishment, as a result of pressure from the more extreme advocates of Catholic Emancipation (TT II 123), Coleridge was driven to a more specific and publicly accessible account of the agonistic relationship between Prometheus and Jupiter, between cultivation and civilization, than his 1825 lecture. *Church and State* is more significant as a work of cultural, rather than High Tory, politics, exerting little energy in attacking the Reformers, at least in comparison with the denunciation of demagogues in the *Second Lay Sermon*. Coleridge's private fulminations against Reform are, however, recorded in *Table Talk*.

In the sub-plot of the *Lecture on Prometheus*, Coleridge represented the difference, in an ancient Greek setting, between a national and a 'spiritual' church, in the story of the jealousy of Juno (the 'ever-quarrelsome' church of republican paganism) for her husband's (the state) love for Io, the providential monotheism. Juno represents the *enclesia* or 'national church', 'a church by law established for the mere purposes of the particular state, unennobled by the consciousness of instrumentality to higher purposes' (LR II 351), whilst Io is the *ecclesia*, linking up the

210

classical Mysteries to Christianity and 'revealed religion'. Although Coleridge denied a historical parallel between Juno and the contemporary Anglican establishment, both the logic of *ricorso* and the fact that his public subscription to contemporary Anglicanism was elsewhere often in inverse proportion to his private scruples, would seem to warrant such a surmise. As J. S. Mill pointed out, Coleridge's 'idea' of a national church in this work 'pronounced the severest satire on what in fact it is'.[1] Coleridge had attacked the Roman clergy for being 'a stronghold of the Patricians against the increasing powers of the Plebians' (TT II 168); his indictment of the erastian Anglican establishment was no less severe. The 'fatal error' of the church was

> its clinging to court and state, instead of cultivating the people. The Church ought to be a mediator between the people and the government, between the poor and the rich. As it is I fear the church has let the hearts of the common people be stolen from it.
>
> (TT I 199)

In the mythic narrative, Jupiter as the political state had reacted against Junonian jealousy by craving for a religion which embodied the authority of true spiritual community, rather than the partiality of class interests. It was in this sense that he was depicted as a 'general lover', intriguing successively with Europa and Io (LR II 352). Io's wandering and the persecution which Juno brought down upon her, is, according to Coleridge, unique (with the *Prometheus* story) in the Greek mythology, 'in which elsewhere both Gods and men are mere Powers and Products of Nature' (AR 277). Io figures the cabiric chain of gnostics and mystics beloved of Coleridge, 'all, who had dared draw living waters from the *fountain*'; her suffering, persecution by the 'haughty priests of learning' (BL I 149).

The 'national church' is shown to partake more of the civic character of the state than of the 'transcendent' cosmopolitanism of the 'mundane' religion: it is however dependent upon the disinterestedness of the latter for its spiritual authority. As in Jupiter's love for Io, the state, bound by the stern law of natural necessity, craves the transcendence of the Divine Idea as much as it resents the troublesome matrimony of the established Church. Coleridge's argument is clearly levelled against the erastianism of

Warburton's *Alliance between Church and State*, in its projection of
an Anglicanism regenerated by the Gnostic Mysteries. The
condition of the state must be subordinate to its national church
rather than vice-versa; and the authority of the latter must derive
from the 'ecclesia', the historical community of Christianity.
Coleridge's idea of culture derives from the traditional spiritual
authority of the Anglican church, but gives it a new priority, and
a higher sanction:

> The phrase, 'Church and State' has a sense and a propriety in
> reference to the *National* Church alone. The Church of Christ
> cannot be placed in this conjunction and antitheses without
> forfeiting the very name of Christian. The true and only contra-
> position of the Christian Church is to the world.

(CS 117)

Coleridge was concerned to show the historical genealogy of the
Nationality or national church in terms of its *a priori* necessity and
ideality; Christianity added to the authority of this counter-weight
to the civic state, but was not essential to it. Thus the civic
religions of Greece and Rome were 'but brilliant exceptions of
history generally' (CS 32) whereas a 'national reserve' had been a
feature of all the 'cultivated nations' – the Hebrews (the Levites
now singled out, in contrast to the 'unitarian' interpretation of the
Mosaic theocracy in the 1795 *Lectures*), and the Gothic,
Scandinavian and Celtic Tribes (CS 33). The subjectivism and
spiritual 'other-worldliness' of the Goths, praised in the *Philosophical
Lectures* for their role in overthrowing the civic 'bigotry' of classical
republicanism (Ph L 257), had contributed, in tandem with
Christianity, to laying the foundation of a new burgher class
which was now entering its historical majority. This was evidently
the providential role of the 'nationality':

> The church alone relaxed the iron fate by which feudal
> dependency, primogeniture, and entail would otherwise have
> predestined every native of the realm to be lord or vassal . . .
> under the fostering wing of the church, the class of free citizens
> and burghers were reared.

(CS 72)

Coleridge's account of the emergence of the commercial order
from the 'nationality' or Christian cultivation was, as already

intimated, of the utmost importance in countering a secular Enlightenment historiography which regarded the development of 'manners' as dependent upon economic progress.[2] Coleridge reversed the priority of Adam Smith or Adam Ferguson's 'materialism' by demonstrating the origin and dependency of the commercial order on the national church.[3] Coleridge was not, however, demonstrating hostility to the principle of commerce as he had done in 1795, least of all as the champion of an exclusive Tory landed interest; rather he was proposing a 'Titanic kinship' between the commercial order and the national church whereby the apparent antagonism of the two protagonists might be seen as a form of symbiosis. The importance of this axis is evident in the somewhat vestigial role awarded to the civic idealization of landed property in *Church and State*.

In his transposition of the 'One Life' ideal from a 'Harringtonian' civic idealism to the 'internal theocracy' of spiritual cultivation, Coleridge clearly felt that evacuation of value from the political realm should not compromise 'the tranquillity of the state itself' or weaken 'that paramount reverence, without which a republic . . . could not exist', a principal concern of the Greek Mysteries (LR II 331). Coleridge eulogized the virtues of the unreformed constitution in *Church and State*; indeed his praise for the 'harmonious balance of the two great correspondent, at once supporting and counterpoising, interests of the state, its permanence and its progression' seemed rather blindly to project an ideal on to a real situation (CS 29). This was of course the 'Neo-Harringtonian' balance of conflicting interests within the state, the ballast of which was the supremacy of landed property: the 'vascular' structure of the agrarian interest would check the 'permeative' nature of the progressive commerical order (CS 86–6).

No doubt partly as a result of a *practical* imbalance between the relative representation of the two interests in the unreformed House, partly because of Coleridge's increasing indifference to the civic realm as such, the presentation of the Neo-Harringtonian 'homeostasis' has a distinctly palsied appearance in 1829. Apparently overlooking the fact of the imminence of the biggest constitutional crisis since 1688, Coleridge argued for the realization of the ideal in the current state of the constitution:

The line of evolution, however sinuous, has still tended to this point, sometimes with, sometimes without, not seldom,

perhaps, against, the intention of the individual actors, but
always as if a power, greater, and better, than the men
themselves, had intended it for them.

(CS 30)

The halting progress of this tortuous sentence betrays Coleridge's
difficulty in discerning the 'cunning of reason' in the contemporary
political situation. Given the subordinate role in which he had
cast 'civilization' in his 'providential history' it is hardly surprising
that the certainty with which Coleridge had acclaimed the 'Divine
Humanity' as pilot of the state (in the *Stateman's Manual*) should
now be rendered in the agnostic terms of 'as if . . .' The
appropriation of the civil ideal by partial interest increasingly
defined in the language of class has clearly nullified the potential
of 'spiritualized politics', precipitating a return to a cyclical model
of history. The inexorable repetition of mutually antagonistic
forms of government (Polybius' *anakuklosis* or Vico's *ricorso*) stands
as the profane counterpart to the 'withheld' power of cultural
idealism (TT II 149).

A philosophy of politics or of the secular realm is abandoned to
the hands of the political economists and their self-seeking
pragmatism: 'Certain things being actually so and so; the question
is, *how* to *do* so and so with them' (TT II 129–30). The question of
political, as opposed to spiritual, idealism has become merely a
quixotic posture: 'if you desert the conditions of reality, or of
common probability, you may show forth your eloquence or your
fancy, but the utmost you can produce will be a *Utopia* or *Oceana*'
(TT II 129–30). Idealism is cast in the Promethean role, chained to
a barren rock, the only means of wielding the energetic mass, the
chaotic flux of spiritless history. Cultural authority, the privilege
of an unconditioned vantage-point, has become possible only on
condition of a separation from social, economic and political
reality: the very attempt to project a political solution to the
deadlock in the unbinding of Prometheus immediately forfeits the
basis of unconditioned power, and therefore the validity of the
solution.

It is perhaps ironic that to the emergent liberal establishment of
nineteenth-century England, Coleridge's reorientation of social
authority became part of the machinery of reform, the new
morality of the commercial order. This is evident in the importance
of the idea of 'cultivation' in the work of writers as diverse as J. S.

Mill, George Eliot and Matthew Arnold, and is captured by Mill's words 'How much better a Parliamentary Reformer, then, is Coleridge, than Lord John Russell, or any Whig who stickles for maintaining this unconstitutional omnipotence of the landed interest.'[4] The vestigial 'Neo-Harringtonian' balance of commerce by land for which Coleridge's 1829 work has become unjustifiably celebrated is perhaps no less of an ideological facade than the role of the landed aristocracy in Victorian England: in Harold Perkin's words,

> The capitalist middle-class were the "real" rulers of mid-Victorian England, in the sense that the laws which were passed and executed by landed Parliaments and Governments were increasingly those demanded by the business-men, and which is not necessarily the same people, their ideological mentors.[5]

The innovation and real importance of *Church and State* lay in its account of the relationship between commerce and cultivation: landed property, despite its rhetorical importance, was relegated to a secondary role of converting financial fortunes into more concrete and inheritable form (CS 24–5). For all his 'reactionary' denunciation of Reform in *Table Talk*, Coleridge's later works were of lasting importance in the formation of a liberal idea of culture, rather than as High Tory apologetics for the traditional political order.

If in chapter eleven of the *Biographia* Coleridge had upheld the exemplary proprietorship of the Church against the spectre of a 'capitalized' landed gentry, the example of the 'National Church' was here directed rather at the business-men. The clandestine kinship of Prometheus and Jupiter, the latter now representing the blind, morally-untethered force of capital, underlay their overt antagonism: after all the tyrant's origin and the secret of his destiny lay in the hands of his recalcitrant captive. In 1818, Coleridge had defined Trade and Literature (*not* land) as the constitutive forces of history: 'without trade and literature, mutually commingled, there can be no nation; without commerce and science, no bond of nations' (Friend I 507). *Church and State* was a reminder to the new order that it owed ethical and historical priority to the National Church, and that without the maintenance

of this endowment and reverence no form of civilization would be
for long possible. Prometheus, as founder as well as redeemer of
Jupiter's dynasty holds the key to the latter's conscience, forfeited
by the tyrant to the expansive demands of material empire. Like
Kubla Khan in his temporal paradise, haunted by 'ancestral voices
prophecying war', Jupiter is aware that in Prometheus' resistance
lies the limit of his power, the secret of his fate. The knowledge
which he desires reverses the relations of mastery, placing his
dominion in the hands of his barren and tormented slave. This
perverse, agonistic relationship is the secret kinship between
culture and capitalism, and the last condition of authority in a
society which has abandoned the participatory virtue of civic
humanism for the professional ethic and the 'distinction of
powers'.

The continuing tenability of the moral vantage-point in a liberal
democracy, driven only by the lure of the commodity and the
caprice of market forces, is contingent upon Promethean guile,
the desire for a secret withheld. Such was the guile which
Coleridge employed in his prescription of limits to the ever-
expanding mass of human desires, his assertion of a transcendent
Idea and a myth of origins which reversed the power relations of
master and slave. The Coleridgean metalepsis functioned by
deriving commerce from Christian cultivation, showing the
dependence of man's 'natural' existence upon a supernatural
origin and destiny. In the power of this enabling fiction the
principle of authority found a point to place its fulcrum and wield
the lawless mass.

Because Capitalism failed to engender an intrinsic paradigm for
'civic' behaviour (as agrarian freehold had done for the 'old
society'), it was incumbent on the guardians of the bourgeois
order to preserve the idea of culture by separating it from material
and social practice. Abandoned to the pursuit of self-interest, the
speculative realm, commercial man must save his conscience in
the endowment of a 'national reserve' as the condition for his
abiding humanity, righteousness and self-respect. The relationship
of Coleridge's endowed class, the 'Clerisy', to the material realm
stood somewhere between that of the eighteenth-century clergy-
man (whom the title invoked, and yet stood at variance from),
and that Promethean figure whom the twentieth century came to
call the 'critical intellectual'. If the former, like the Reverend
Augustus Debarry in George Eliot's *Felix Holt*, represented a

religious order which fulfilled the 'imperfect obligations' of the civil, comprising the younger sons of the gentry whose parishes overlapped their families' estates, the latter fulfils a far more ambivalent socio-political role. He stands, in the words of Edward Said, 'between culture and system', 'a counter-ideological stance' which paradoxically embodies an important function of 'the heterogeneous plurality of the modern state'.[6] Coleridge's 'guardian' is considerably *more* pluralistic, detached from the political base of his society than the former, but more simply hegemonic and considerably less alienated than the latter. Despite the torture endured on his barren rock, he is confident of the desirability of the secret he withholds.

It has been one of the presuppositions of the foregoing study of Coleridge that the transcendent 'evasion' of the Promethean stance manifested a power more properly termed *Ideological* than political or theological. Coleridge's thought, especially in the earlier 'One Life' period, showed an understanding of what is today called ideology, where that concept is defined as a category 'in which the practico-social predominates . . . over the theoretical, over knowledge',[7] notwithstanding his theological rather than 'scientific' expression of its tenor. I have argued that such an insight was constitutive of the 'One Life' theory but was increasingly suppressed in the later thought, in terms of a separation of the Idea from social practice. Ideology is a powerful critical tool (as Coleridge knew) in its reaffirmation of the hidden kinship between Jupiter and Prometheus, between politics and imagination.

The Coleridge of Carlyle's portraiture, sitting 'on the brow of Highgate Hill . . . looking down on London and its smoke-tumult, like a sage escaped from the inanity of life's battle',[8] implemented this separation in order to preserve a unifying culture at a time when the possibility of a moral overview was threatened as never before by the hazard and exigency of human relations defined by the cash nexus. In Coleridge's defence it must be said that the preservation of an unconditioned Idea and an existential freedom overriding necessity and a manipulative reverence for facts has been historically liberating; it has taught us amongst other things that politics need not necessarily be subordinated to the historical Juggernaut of economic forces beyond all human control. Rhetorical sublimation may still be used for liberating, as well as for totalitarian ends; behind

Coleridge's transcendent Idea was the supposition that what men
have made, men may know and control:

> By an *idea*, I mean . . . that conception of a thing, which is not
> abstracted from any particular state, form, or mode, in which
> the thing may happen to exist at this or that time; nor yet
> generalized from any number or succession of such forms or
> modes; but which is given by the knowledge of *its ultimate aim*.
>
> (CS 12)

Yet it is ironic that the problems attendant upon this liberating
idealism become evident when we examine it in its historical
context and specificity. The continuing power of Coleridge's
unconditioned Idea depended upon its mystification and its
professional separation from democratic consensus. A cultural
élite enacts in private the desire of the many, an ostentatious
secrecy which attracts whilst it excludes. The function of cultivation
becomes to instil reverence rather than enlightenment; discernable
in Coleridge's account of the clerisy in *Aids* and *Church and State* is
a concern, that in relation to the education of the lower class, they
'should let sleeping dogs lie' by inculcating devotion and habits of
social discipline rather than knowledge and critical inquiry (AR
290–2).

The mystification of knowledge and its attendant authority
which we have been examining was an expedient measure which
arose from fear of 'arming fools with fire'; *because* they lack
education in social responsibility, the people must revere a
mystified authority until such time as they are ready for
knowledge. But the sense we get in charting the progress of
Coleridge's thought of a cultural élite holding knowledge in trust
at a time of transitionary uncertainty, was sustained as a historical
norm. No educational programme appeared to distribute the trust
amongst those for whom it was held, or to ease the social tension
which has resulted from the withholding. The 'Promethean idea'
existed as foreclosed; self-absorbed, class-specific, incapable by its
very nature of representing political needs or social change. Born
of a need to conserve a spiritualized politics from the fragmentation
of the secular, the doctrine of 'cultivation' came ironically to
participate in the separation against which it had been projected.
Unable to sustain the positive and fruitful social ideal of its
inauguration, the intention to prevent further deterioration ended

by merely sanctifying existing abuses. Coleridge's thought finally collapsed back into the dualism which it had sought to challenge. Blinded by the vision of a static order of freedom, the transcendent idea lost the power of mediation, stumbling through the realm of social change and human potential as if through a wasteland. It is characteristic of Shelley, the unbinder of Prometheus, that he perceived this profound ambivalence in the features of the man he never saw:

> You will see Coleridge – he who sits obscure
> In the exceeding lustre and the pure
> Intense irradiation of a mind,
> Which, with its own internal lightning blind,
> Flags wearily through darkness and despair –
> A cloud-encircling meteor of the air,
> A hooded eagle among blinking owls – [9]

Notes

INTRODUCTION

1. Jurgen Habermas, *Theory and Practice*, trans. by John Viertal (London: Heinemann 1974) p. 4.
2. Ibid., p. 4.
3. *The Works of Edmund Burke*, 8 vols (London: George Bell, 1899) II, 297.

CHAPTER 1

1. W. J. B. Owen and J. W. Smyser have carefully detailed these allusions and influences in their edition of Wordsworth's *Prose Works* (I, 166–89).
2. E. P. Thompson distinguishes two dominant strains of radicalism based on what might be described as 'Whiggish' and Paineite ideologies respectively. The first criticized 'the eighteenth century in the light of its own theory, the second, more delayed, reaction, was to bring the theory itself into disrepute. And it was at this point that Paine entered with the *Rights of Man'*, *The Making of the English Working Class* (London: Gollancz, 1964; rpt Pelican Books 1968) p. 97.
3. E. P. Thompson, 'Disenchantment or Default? A Lay Sermon' in *Power and Consciousness*, eds C. Cruise O'Brien and W. D. Vanech (New York and London: New York University Press and London University Press, 1969) pp. 149–81. James Chandler, *Wordsworth's Second Nature: a Study of the Poetry and Politics* (Chicago University Press, 1984).
4. 'Disenchantment or Default?', pp. 149–50.
5. Ibid., p. 152.
6. Ibid., p. 152.
7. See also BL I 189.
8. M. H. Abrams, 'English Romanticism – the Spirit of the Age' in *Romanticism Reconsidered*, ed. Northrop Frye (New York: Columbia University Press, 1963) pp. 26–72.
9. Chandler, p. 185.
10. Quoted by Chandler, p. 65.
11. Coleridge later described radical political clubs and associations (in a letter to the Beaumonts) as 'Ascarides in the Bowels of the State . . . wicked Conspiracies' (CL II 1001). For a more detailed account of this topic see Kelvin Everest's *Coleridge's Secret Ministry: the Context of the Conversation Poems 1795–8* (Sussex: Harvester Press, 1979) pp. 115–18; E. P. Thompson, *English Working Class*, p. 105 and the introduction to *Lectures 1795*, 'Coleridge and Political Associations', p. xlix.

12. Caroline Robbins, *The Eighteenth Century Commonwealthmen: Studies in the Transmission, Development and Circumstance of English Liberal Thought from the Restoration of Charles II until the War with the Thirteen Colonies* (Cambridge, Mass.: Harvard University Press, 1959) pp. 347–8.

13. Coleridge regretted an 'apparent versatility of the Principle with the Occasion' in Burke's political conduct (Friend II 124, 12 Oct. 1809). But see BL I 191–2 and Friend I 448–9 for his later unqualified praise of Burke.

14. In 1804, Wordsworth wrote to George Beaumont that Burke, even more than Joshua Reynolds, had 'lived too much for the age in which he lived' (EY 491).

15. In the notes of his edition of the *Prelude* of 1805, De Selincourt dates Wordsworth's 'change from faith in the practical issues of the revolution' to abstract Godwinianism, to Spring 1795, 'when he gave up his belief in the "general will" and became for the first time a pure individualist' (Prelude 1805 306–7n).

16. See Lects 1795 lxvii–lxxx for a good account of Coleridge's relations to Godwinism. Compare with his remarks on *Political Justice* in *The Watchman*, p. 98 and his dialogue with 'Caius Gracchus', p. 194.

17. Bernard Bailyn in his *Ideological Origins of the American Revolution* (Cambridge, Mass.: Harvard University Press, 1967), has described this 'old' form of eighteenth-century radicalism as concerned not so much with democracy as 'the need to purify a corrupt constitution and fight off the growth of prerogative power' (p. 283).

CHAPTER 2

1. *Disquisitions relating to Matter and Spirit* (London, 1777) pp. 106, 108. See bibliography for other works by Joseph Priestley which were an important influence on Coleridge.

2. See John Yolton, *Thinking Matter: Materialism in Eighteenth Century Britain* (Oxford: Basil Blackwell, 1984).

3. Trevor Levere, *Poetry Realized in Nature: S. T. Coleridge and early Nineteenth Century Science* (Cambridge University Press, 1981) pp. 121; 123; 128; 248n6. See also Rom Harré, 'Knowledge' in *The Ferment of Knowledge*, eds Roy Porter and George Rousseau (Cambridge University Press, 1980) p. 51.

4. John Prior Estlin, *Evidences of Revealed Religion, with reference to a pamphlet called 'The Age of Reason'* (Bristol, 1796).

5. Richard Price's *Observations on Civil Liberty* (London, 1776) was ideologically close to Priestley's *Essay on the First Principles of Government* (1768).

6. For Gilbert Wakefield, see 'Disenchantment or Default?', p. 164; Kelvin Everest, p. 29; Norman Fruman, *Coleridge: the Damaged Archangel* (London: Allen & Unwin, 1971) pp. 243–5.

7. For Coleridge's essay on Cartwright, see Friend II 130–40.

8. For further details see George Whalley, 'Coleridge and Southey in Bristol, 1795', *Review of English Studies* (Oct. 1950) 324–40.

9. Levere, p. 20. See also Roger Sharrock, 'The Chemist and the Poet', *Notes and Records of the Royal Society of London*, 17 (1962) 57–76; and J. Z. Fullmer, 'The Poetry of Humphry Davy', *Chymia*, 6 (1960) 102–6.

10. 'Disenchantment or Default?, p. 162.

11. Alexander Monro (1733–1817), *Observations on the Structure and Functions of the Nervous System* (Edinburgh, 1783). See *Doctors Monro: a Medical Saga* by R. E. Wright-St. Clair (London: Wellcome Medical History Library, 1964).

12. George Whalley, 'The Bristol Library Borrowings of Southey and Coleridge 1793–8', *The Library*, 5th series, 4 (1949–50) 114–32.

13. *The Oceana of James Harrington and his other Works*, ed. John Toland (London 1700). Harrington described nature as 'the very word of God . . . that same spirit of God which in the beginning mov'd upon the waters . . . his plastic virtue?. See also W. Craig Diamond, 'Natural Philosophy in Harrington's Political Thought', *Journal of the History of Philosophy*, 16 (1978) 387–98; 387. The editors of Lects 1795 290n2 suggest that Coleridge may have owned Toland's edition in 1795, although of course he read many more books than he owned. M. H. Abrams argues for Cudworth's influence here, in 'Coleridge's "A light in sound"', *Proceedings of the American Philosophical Society*, 116, 6 (1972) 458–76; 459. For an account of the origin of the concept, see W. B. Hunter, Jnr, 'The Seventeenth Century Doctrine of Plastic Nature', *Harvard Theological Review*, 43 (1950) 197–213.

14. W. K. Wimsatt, 'The Structure of Romantic Nature Imagery' in *The Verbal Icon* (Kentucky University Press, 1954). See CL II 864–6 for Coleridge's criticism of Bowle's nature poems, highly revealing in this context.

15. *Disquisitions*, p. xxxviii.

16. Ibid., p. 84.

17. Levere, p. 22.

18. Sharrock, 'The Chemist and the Poet', 60.

19. Ibid., p. 69.

20. J. E. MacEvoy and J. E. McGuire, 'Priestley's Way of Rational Dissent', *Historical Studies in the Physical Sciences*, 5 (1975) 325–404; 384.

21. *Experiments and Observations on Different Kinds of Air*, abridged edition, 3 vols (Birmingham, 1790) I xxiii.

22. *Disquisitions*, p. 31, 49–50.

23. Harold Perkin, *The Origins of Modern English Society, 1780–1880* (London: Routledge & Kegan Paul, 1969) pp. 33–4. For historical accounts of the Unitarian and Dissenting interest, see Caroline Robbins, pp. 223–370; Anthony Lincoln, *Social and Political Ideas of English Dissent 1763–1830* (Cambridge University Press, 1938); R. V. Holt, *The Unitarian Contribution to Social Progress in England* (London: Allen & Unwin, 1938); Donald Davie, *A Gathered Church: Literature of the English Dissenting Interest 1700–1930* (London: Routledge & Kegan Paul, 1978); E. P. Thompson, *English Working Class*, pp. 26–54.

24. Caroline Robbins, op. cit.
25. See Margaret C. Jacob, *The Newtonians and the English Revolution, 1689–1720* (Sussex: Harvester Press, 1976) p. 238.
26. Thomas McFarland, *Coleridge and the Pantheist Tradition* (Oxford: Clarendon Press, 1969) p. 75 and Excursus notes iii, pp. 266–7.
27. Margaret Jacob, *Newtonians*, pp. 201–50, for Bruno's influence on Toland. Also Frances Yates, *Giordano Bruno and the Hermetic Tradition* (London: Routledge & Kegan Paul, 1964), and Alice Snyder, 'Coleridge on Bruno', *MLN*, xlii (Nov. 1927) 427–36. See also CN I 927 and Friend I 94 115–18.
28. John Toland, *Letters to Serena* (1704; rpt Facsimile, Frommen Verlag Stuttgart Bad-Cannstatt, 1964), Letter Four (pp. 131–62) and Letter Five (pp. 163–239).
29. Snyder, p. 435.
30. Coleridge may have read Harrington by 1795 – he certainly possessed the Toland edition of the *Works* by 1800. His articles on the French Constitution in the *Morning Post* (1799–1800) show the influence of *Oceana*, as Thomas Poole pointed out to him at the time. *Thomas Poole and his Friends*, by M. E. Sandford, 2 vols (London 1888) II, 4. See also CN I 639–41 and 934n and EOT I 48 for further details.
31. Norwich 1796.
32. J. G. A. Pocock, *Harrington's Political Works* (Cambridge University Press, 1977) 141.

   For the historical background to eighteenth-century classical republicanism see also Pocock's *Politics, Language and Time: Essays on Political Thought and History* (London: Methuen, 1972), and *The Machiavellian Moment: Florentine Political Thought and the Atlantic Republican Tradition* (Princeton University Press, 1975). See also Franco Venturi, *Utopia and Reform in the Enlightenment* (Cambridge University Press, 1971); Zera Fink, *The Classical Republicans: an Essay in the Recovery of Thought in Seventeenth Century England* (Evanston: Northwestern University Press, 1945); Caroline Robbins, op. cit.; Margaret C. Jacob, *The Radical Enlightenment: Pantheists, Freemasons and Republicans* (London: Allen & Unwin, 1981).

   In his introduction to *Harrington's Pol. W.*, Pocock argues that the post-1688 interpretation of Harrington was a more significant tradition in the formation of the constitutionalist ideologies of various political factions than that of Locke's *Two Treatises on Government* (1690) p. 145. In the 1790s, Burke, Priestley, Price, Paine, Cartwright, Wordsworth and Coleridge all drew on various themes in Harrington. Pocock's tentative remarks with regard to this influence of this tradition on Coleridge's 'new theory of the relations between land, commerce and culture' will be borne out in the present study (*Harrington's Pol. W.*, p. 152). But caution should be exercised in stressing the differences as well as the common points between these differing interpretations. The error of identifying Wordsworth's thought in the 1796–1805 period with Burke's ideological position results from lack of circumspection in this matter.
33. Margaret Jacob, *Newtonians*, pp. 64–5.
34. Ibid., p. 65.

35. Friend II 279. Coleridge distinguished the 'pious deists' from the followers of Hobbes, but by 1809 was critical of their pelagian Free-thought.
36. Christopher Hill, *The World Turned Upside Down: Radical Ideas during the English Revolution* (London: Temple Smith 1972; rpt Pelican Books 1975) pp. 107–50.
37. A. A. Cooper, Third Earl of Shaftesbury, *Characteristics* (1711), 2 vols (London: Grant Richards, 1900; rpt Gloucester Mass.: Peter Smith 1963) II, 3–153.

    For the influence of Shaftesbury on Goethe and Schiller, see L. M. Price, *The Reception of English Literature in Germany* (Berkeley: University of California Press, 1932).
38. Margaret Jacob, *Newtonians*, pp. 208–9.
39. See for example Priestley's sermon on the eve of his departure for America. *The Present State of Europe compared with Antient Prophecies* (London, 1794).
40. See note 32 above.

CHAPTER 3

1. Caroline Robbins, op. cit., p. 242.
2. Pages 383–427 in Toland's 1700 edition.
3. Zera Fink makes this point in her article 'Wordsworth and the English Republican Tradition', *Journal of English and German Philology*, 4 (1948) 107–26; 111–12. See also E. P. Thompson, *English Working Class*, p. 164 and Thelwall's notes on the Agrarian Law in his republication of Moyle's *Constitution and Government of the Roman State*, p. 21n.
4. Pocock, *Harrington's Political Writings* (henceforth HPW) p. 778.
5. Ibid., p. 625 and Coleridge's Lects 1795 119; 125.
6. Pocock, ibid., p. 634 and Coleridge, ibid., pp. 126–8.
7. Lects 1795 129.
8. Pocock, HPW, p. 633.
9. Ibid., p. 649.
10. Ibid., p. 42.
11. Ibid., p. 838.
12. Wordsworth and Coleridge adopted Hartley's rather than Godwin's versions of the 'system of necessity'. See Lects 1795, pp. lviii–lxxx for a concise account of Coleridge's relations with the necessitarians. See also Kelvin Everest, op. cit., pp. 69–96.
13. Marilyn Butler, *Romantics, Rebels and Reactionaries* (Oxford University Press, 1981) p. 85.
14. See Pocock's *The Machiavellian Moment*, ch. 14, 'Virtue, Passion and Commerce'.
15. J. R. MacGillivray, 'The Pantisocracy Scheme and its immediate background', *Studies in English by Members of University College, Toronto, Collected by Principal Wallace* (Toronto University Press, 1931) p. 141.

Brissot de Warville, the future Girondist leader, published an account of his American travels, *Nouveau Voyage dans les Etats-Unis* (1791). Coleridge quoted Joel Barlow's 1792 English translation of this work in the *Conciones ad Populem* (Lects 1795 47). Zera Fink has drawn attention both to Wordsworth's connection with Brissot and the latter's keen interest in Harrington and Algernon Sidney in 'Wordsworth and the English Republican Tradition', 108–9. Priestley's son-in-law, Thomas Cooper, had also written a handbook for dissenters planning to emigrate to America, entitled *Some Information Respecting America* (1794). It was eagerly devoured by the Pantisocrats, alongside the many other travel books that constitute much of the early reading of Southey and Coleridge.

16. Wordsworth to Tom Poole, 9 Apr. 1801.
17. Kelvin Everest, p. 91.
18. Frances Ferguson, *Wordsworth: Language as Counter-Spirit* (New Haven, Conn.: Yale University Press, 1977) p. 18.
19. Pocock, HPW, p. 778.
20. John Milton, *Paradise Lost*, Book 4, ll. 208–87. *The Poems of John Milton*, eds J. Carey and A. Fowler (London: Longmans, 1968) pp. 622–30.
21. See David Simpson, *Wordsworth and the Figurings of the Real* (London: Macmillan, 1982) pp. 156–69.
22. See W Prose II 207 for Wordsworth's approving citation of Dr Brown, author of *An Estimate of the Manners and Principles of the Times*, 2 vols (London, 1758–59), an exponent of moral and economic 'Spartanism', a recurrent feature of the 'commonwealth tradition'. Priestley's 'laissez-faire' argument in *Principles of Government* attacked Brown on this score (pp. 64–104). Wordsworth also cites Thomas Gray's description of Grasmere: 'Not a single red tile, no flaring gentleman's house or garden-wall, breaks in upon the repose of this little unsuspected paradise; but all is peace, rusticity, and happy poverty, in its neatest and most becoming attire' (W Prose II 208).
23. For a different treatment of this motif, see Geoffrey Hartman's 'Reflections on the Evening Star.' in *New Perspectives on Wordsworth and Coleridge*, ed. by G. Hartman (New York and Columbia: Columbia University Press, 1972) pp. 85–132.
24. Toland, *Letters to Serena*, III 75. Leclerc's epigram on an extract of Eratosthenes. Wordsworth echoes this passage in the *Prelude* 1805, V, ll. 44–8.
25. P. B. Shelley, *Poetical Works*, ed. Thomas Hutchinson (Oxford University Press, 1934) p. 526, 'To Wordsworth'.
26. E. P. Thompson, 'The Peculiarities of the English', in *The Poverty of Theory and other Essays* (London: Merlin Press, 1978) p. 49.

CHAPTER 4

1. See Nathaniel Teich, 'Coleridge's BIOGRAPHIA and the Contemporary Controversy about Style', *The Wordsworth Circle*, 32

(1972) 61–70. The political connotation of Wordsworth's stylistic innovation is summed up in the following passage by Francis Jeffrey, commenting on Maria Edgeworth's *Popular Tales*: 'an attempt . . . somewhat superior in genius, as well as utility, to the laudable exertions of Mr Thomas Paine to bring disaffection and infidelity within the comprehension of the common people, or the charitable endeavours of Messrs Wirdsworth & Co. to accommodate them with an appropriate vein of poetry', *Edinburgh Review*, iv (1804) 329–30.

2. *The Diary, Reminiscences and Correspondence of Henry Crabb Robinson*, ed. T. Sadler, 3 vols (London: Macmillan, 1869) I 304–5.

3. See Don Bialotostosky, 'Coleridge's Interpretation of Wordsworth's Preface to Lyrical Ballads', *PMLA*, 93 (1978) 912–24. Bialotostosky argues that 'more interesting reasons' motivated Coleridge's criticism than the 'internal' aesthetic objections canvassed in the *Biographia*: 'the issues we discover when we match these two arguments at their fullest strength will, I suspect, be momentous for Anglo-American Criticism', p. 923. Gene W. Ruoff takes an 'essentialist' view of Wordsworth's poetics in 'Wordsworth on Language: towards a Radical Poetics for English Romanticism', *The Wordsworth Circle*, 3, 4 (1972) 204–11. Ruoff rather wildly discovers an anticipation of Roland Barthes' 'Writing Degree Zero' in the Wordsworthian 'real language of men in a state of vivid sensation'.

4. Pocock, HPW, p. 164.

5. W. J. B. Owen, *Wordsworth as Critic* (London: Toronto University Press and Oxford University Press, 1969) p. 73.

6. See CN I 1044. In late 1801 and early 1802, Coleridge was reading J. R. Reche's *Versuch über die Humane Sympathie* (Düsseldorf, 1794), with its references to Kant's *Critique of Judgement*, a work which Coleridge had undoubtedly come across during his stay at Göttingen. Coleridge quoted from Schiller's *Über Naive und Sentimentalische Dictung* (1795) in a notebook entry of 1803 (CN I 1705 and *n*).

7. 'Simple and Sentimental Poetry' in *Schiller's Works: Essays Aesthetical and Philosophical* (London: George Bell, 1884) p. 325.

8. See J. O. Hayden, *Romantic Bards and British Reviewers* (London: Routledge & Kegan Paul, 1971), sections 1 and 2, pp. 3–176.

9. *Edinburgh Review*, I (Oct. 1802) 68.

10. *The Complete works of William Hazlitt in Twenty-one Volumes*, Centenary edition, ed. P. P. Howe (London and Toronto: J. M. Dent 1930–34) V 163.

11. Ibid., p. 164.

12. *British Critic*, 17 (Feb. 1801) 126n.

13. *European Magazine* (1791) 135. Coleridge copied down Smith's point in a notebook entry of August 1801: CN I 775 and n.

14. Kenneth Maclean, *Agrarian Age: a Background to Wordsworth* (Connecticut: Archon Books, 1970) p. 100.

15. G. R. Sanders, *Coleridge and the Broad Church Movement* (Durham, N.C.: Duke University Publications, 1942).

CHAPTER 5

1. *Edinburgh Review*, I (Oct. 1802) 66.
2. Roger Sharrock, 'Coleridge's Revolt Against Liturature', *Essays in Criticism*, 3 (1953) 396–412.
3. Hazlitt, *Complete Works*, IV, 124.

CHAPTER 6

1. Paul Hamilton, *Coleridge's Poetics* (Oxford: Basil Blackwell, 1983) p. 39.
2. James Beattie, *An Essay on the Nature and Immutability of Truth in Opposition to Sophistry and Scepticism* (1770; 4th edition, London 1773) p. 43.
3. MacEvoy and MacGuire, op. cit. 377.
4. 'Imperatives determine either the conditions of causality of a rational being as an efficient cause only in respect to its effect and its sufficiency to bring this effect about, or they determine only the will, whether it be adequate to the effect or not. In the former case, imperatives would be hypothetical and would contain only precepts of skill; in the latter, on the contrary, they would be categorical and would alone be practical laws', Kant, *Critique of Practical Reason*, trans. with intro. by Lewis White Beck (New York: Liberal Arts Press, 1956) Part One, Book I, sect. i, p. 18.
5. Kant, *Critique of Judgement*, trans. J. Creed Meredith (Oxford University Press, 1952) pp. 82–3.
6. Peter Uwe Hohendahl, *The Institution of Criticism* (Ithaca: Cornell University Press, 1982).
7. Ibid., p. 52.
8. Samuel Johnson, *The Rambler*, 93 (5 Feb. 1751), ed. with intro. by D. D. Eddy, 2 vols (New York and London: Garland Publishing, 1978) I, 555.
9. Hohendahl, p. 49.
10. Adam Ferguson, *An Essay on the History of Civil Society* (1767), ed. Duncan Forbes (Edinburgh University Press, 1966) p. 218.
11. Hamilton, p. 6.

CHAPTER 7

1. Thomas McFarland, *Coleridge and the Pantheist Tradition* (Oxford: Clarendon Press, 1969); Gian Orsini, *Coleridge and German Idealism* (Carbondale & Edwardsville: S. Illinois University Press, 1969); Rene Wellek, *Immanuel Kant in England 1793–1838* (Princeton University Press, 1931), *A History of Modern Criticism, 1750–1955*, 6 vols (New Haven: Yale University Press, 1955–   ); *Confrontations: Studies in the Intellectual and Literary Relations between Germany, England and the*

United States during the 19th Century (Princeton University Press, 1965), K. M. Wheeler, *Sources, Processes and Methods in Coleridge's "Biographia Literaria"* (Cambridge University Press, 1980); Elinor Shaffer, *'Kubla Khan' and the Fall of Jerusalem: the Mythological School in Bible Criticism 1770–1880* (Cambridge University Press, 1975); Robert Preyer, 'Bentham, Coleridge and the Science of History' in *Leipziger Beiträge zur Englischen Philologie*, 41 (Verlag Poppinghaus, 1958); Trevor Levere, 'Coleridge, Chemistry and the Philosophy of Nature' in *Studies in Romanticism*, 16, 3 (1977) 349–80, and *Poetry Realized in Nature: S. T. Coleridge and early 19th Century Science* (Cambridge University Press, 1981); Raimonda Modiano, *Coleridge and the Concept of Nature* (London: Macmillan, 1985). Rosemary Ashton, *The German Idea: Four English Writers and the Reception of German Thought 1800–1860* (Cambridge University Press, 1980).

2. Hamilton, op. cit., p. 21; Marilyn Butler, op. cit., ch. 3, 'The Rise of the Man of Letters: Coleridge'.
3. I. A. Richards, *Coleridge on Imagination* (London: Kegan Paul, 1934); Norman Fruman, *Coleridge: The Damaged Archangel* (London: Allen & Unwin, 1971).
4. Marilyn Butler, op. cit., p. 146.
5. See Chapter 6.
6. Hamilton, op. cit. The 'contractual' criterion of *desynonymization* is one, like the radical theory of poetry, 'whose obvious political implications he tries to keep undifferentiated' (p. 21n).
7. As well as Peacock's 'Mr Flosky', see Hazlitt's 1817 review of the *Biographia, Edinburgh Review*, XXVIII (Aug. 1817) pp. 488–515.
8. Both Wellek and Orsini recognize this debt; McFarland does not.
9. In *Confrontations*, pp. 6–7, Wellek cites an 1806 letter from Sophie Bernhardi, the sister of Ludwig Tieck, to A. W. Schlegel, praising 'a wonderful Englishman who had studied Kant, Fichte and Schelling and the old German poets and admires Schlegel's translation of Shakespeare unbelievably'. Sophie had unfortunately forgotten his name, but there can be little doubt as to whom she referred.
10. SC II 214 (24 Nov. 1811). Entries in *Crabb Robinson's Diary* for this period more often reveal Coleridge's 'Kantian' distrust of Schelling. See, for example, I 380–1.
11. *On University Studies*, trans. E. S. Morgan, ed. N. Guterman (Ohio University Press, 1966).
12. Dorothy Emmet, 'Coleridge on Powers in Mind and Nature' in *Coleridge's Variety*, ed. John Beer (London: Macmillan 1974) pp. 166–82, 178.
13. John Beer, 'Coleridge and Wordsworth: the Vital and the Organic' in *Rereading Coleridge: Approaches and Applications*, ed. W. B. Crawford (Ithaca: Cornell University Press, 1979) pp. 160–90, 169.
14. H. J. Jackson, 'Coleridge's Collaborator, J. H. Green', *Studies in Romanticism*, 21 (Summer 1982) 160–79.
15. See CL III 354–61 for Coleridge's denial of the plagiarism charge in relation to A. W. Schlegel.
16. Fruman, op. cit, p. 187.

17. Ibid., p. 182.
18. See McFarland, *Coleridge and the Pantheist Tradition*, 27, for the 'mosaic' organization; Shaffer, op. cit., p. 6.
19. Rosemary Ashton, *The German Idea*, pp. 1–2.
20. Ibid., pp. 30; 9.
21. Ibid., p. 11.
22. Ibid., pp. 30–3.
23. Baroness Staël Holstein, *Germany*, 3 vols (London: J. Murray, 1813); A. W. Schlegel, *Lectures on Dramatic Art and Literature*, trans. John Black (London, 1815). In 1826, J. G. Lockhart wrote, 'all the world is acquainted with these two works', Ashton, op. cit., p. 63.
24. Marilyn Butler, op. cit., p. 120, and ch. 5, 'The Cult of the South'.
25. Ashton, op. cit., p. 9 (Holcroft); 12 (W. Taylor and Crabb Robinson). Wellek, *Kant in England*, p. 287 (Crabb Robinson).
26. Wellek, *Kant in England*, pp. 11–16; 28–32 (Baader & Niebuhr); p. 7 (Nitsch).
27. CN I 249 and n, on John Thelwall and Thomas Beddoes early interest in Kant.
28. Abbé Barreul, *Memoires pour servir a l'Histoire du Jacobinism* (London, 1797–98), English trans. 1798.
29. Wellek, *Kant in England*, p. 140. Crabb Robinson to his brother Thomas, 4 Jan. 1801.
30. Ibid., p. 141, and ch. 2, 'The Scotch Philosophy and Kant'.
31. Harold Perkins, *The origin of Modern English Society 1780–1880* (London: Routledge & Kegan Paul, 1969) pp. 252–70.
32. Shaffer, op. cit., pp. 29–30.
33. Pierce C. Mullen, 'Romantic as Scientist: Lorenz Oken', *Studies in Romanticism*, 16, 3 (1977) 381–400. Mullen stresses the ideological vanguardism of the German scientific and intellectual renaissance.
34. Levere, 'Coleridge, Chemistry and the Philosophy of Nature', pp. 351, 376. See also G. De Beer, *The Sciences were never at War* (London: Nelson, 1960).
35. Levere, *Poetry Realized in Nature*, p. 13.
36. Ashton, op. cit., p. 24. For Coleridge's defences of Spinoza in 1815 see BL I 246–7 note and BL II 245. For his 1825 attack on the spirit of Spinoza's system, its substitution of power for a personal God, see AR 396–7.
37. Levere, *Poetry Realized in Nature*, p. 201.
38. Levere, 'Coleridge, Chemistry and the Philosophy of Nature', pp. 377–8. Coleridge found the medical profession especially congenial to his interests; in the *Biographia* he hailed the physiologist Richard Saumarez as the English heir to Giordano Bruno, 'the first instaurator of the dynamic philosophy in England', BL I 163.
39. See CL IV 757–63 for Coleridge's criticism of the 'philosophy' prevalent amongst the ruling classes.
40. E. P. Thompson, *The Poverty of Theory and other Essays* (London: Merlin Press, 1978) p. 63.
41. See Hamilton, op. cit., pp. 27–41.
42. Thomas McFarland, 'A Complex Dialogue: Coleridge's doctrine of

Polarity and its European Context', ch. 5 of *Romanticism and the Forms of Ruin* (Princeton University Press, 1981) p. 301.

43. M. H. Abrams, 'Coleridge's "a light in sound" ', *Proceedings of the American Philosophical Society*, 116, 6 (1972) 458–76; 473.

44. Joseph Esposito, *Schelling's Idealism and Philosophy of Nature* (London: Associated University Presses, 1977) p. 90, cited and trans. from Schelling's *Sammtliche Werke*, II, 395.

45. Rom Harré, 'Knowledge', *The Ferment of Knowledge*, eds Roy Porter and Georges Rousseau (Cambridge University Press, 1980) p. 27.

46. Cf. M. H. Abrams, op. cit., '[Coleridge] based his early formulations of the polar principle on the theory of his scientific friend Humphry Davy, that all substances are the product of elementary forces, even before he absorbed the views of Kant and the metaphysical system of Schelling', p. 473.

47. Kelvin Everest, op. cit., p. 197–8.

48. Esposito, op. cit., p. 35.

49. 'Untitled Verses' in John Davy, *Memoirs of Humphry Davy*, I, 110. Cited in Roger Sharrock, 'The Chemist and the Poet', p. 60.

50. Barry Gower, 'Speculations in Physics: the History and Practice "of Naturphilosophie"', *Studies in the History and Philosophy of Science*, 3, 4 (Feb. 1973) 301–56, 322.

51. Levere, 'Coleridge, Chemistry and the Philosophy of Nature' (henceforth, CCPN) p. 357.

52. *The Collected Works of Sir Humphry Davy*. ed. John Davy, 9 vols (London, 1840) VIII, 34.

53. Levere, CCPN, p. 357.

CHAPTER 8

1. Edward Said, *The Word, the Text and the Critic* (Cambridge, Mass.: Harvard University Press, 1983) pp. 241–2.

2. *Blackwoods Magazine*, XVIII (1825) p. 350. Cited by Perkins, op. cit., p. 265.

3. Ashton, op. cit., pp. 67, 92, for Carlyle's impressive misinterpretation of Kant.

4. In *German Aesthetic and Literary Criticism: Kant, Fichte, Schelling, Schopenhauer, Hegel*, ed. David Simpson (Cambridge University Press, 1984) p. 30.

5. Ibid., p. 31.

6. Peter Hohendahl, op. cit.

7. Simpson, op. cit., p. 33.

8. Matthew Arnold, 'The Function of Criticism at the Present Time' in *Lectures and Essays in Criticism*, ed. R. H. Super (Ann Arbor: University of Michigan Press, 1962) pp. 265–6.

9. Simpson, op. cit., p. 15.

10. Ibid., p. 33.

11. *Critique of Judgement*, trans. J. Creed Meredith (Oxford: Clarendon, 1952) pp. 53–7.
12. *Diary, Reminiscences and Correspondence of H. Crabb Robinson*, I, 305.
13. Marx and Engels, *The German Ideology* (Part One), ed. and with intro. by C. J. Arthur (London: Lawrence & Wishart, 1970) p. 65.
14. *Critique of Pure Reason*, trans. Norman Kemp Smith (London: Macmillan, 1929) p. 29.

CHAPTER 9

1. Ashton, op. cit., pp. 193–4.
2. Marilyn Butler, op. cit., p. 73.
3. Baroness Stael Holstein, *Germany*, I, p. 172.
4. Pierce C. Mullen, 'Romantic as Scientist', p. 382.
5. Ben Knights, *The Idea of the Clerisy in the 19th Century* (Cambridge University Press, 1978) p. 26.
6. Esposito, op. cit., p. 19.
7. Staël Holstein, op. cit., 111, 112.
8. See A. Harding, *Coleridge and the Idea of Love* (London: Cambridge University Press, 1974) pp. 169–94, for a useful discussion of Coleridge and Transcendental Self-Consciousness. See also Orsini, op. cit., pp. 118–19.
9. D. M. MacKinnon, 'Coleridge and Kant' in *Coleridge's Variety*, op. cit., p. 201.
10. McFarland, *Coleridge and the Pantheist Tradition*, pp. 95–7.
11. Esposito, op. cit., p. 45.
12. BL I lxxxii, and McFarland, *Coleridge and the Pantheist Tradition*, pp. xxxii–xxxv.
13. Margaret Jacob, *The Radical Enlightenment*, p. 224, for the connection between the spinozistic 'One Life' and the philosopher's republicanism.
14. E. Cassirer, *The Philosophy of Symbolic Forms*, trans. R. Mannheim, 3 vols (New Haven: Yale University Press, 1953–57) II, 4. See also p. 9: 'Precisely because the cosmos can be understood and interpreted only through the human spirit, hence through subjectivity, what would seem to be the purely subjective content of mythology has at the same time a cosmic significance.'
15. McFarland, *Coleridge and the Pantheist Tradition*, pp. 103–4.
16. *On University Studies*, p. xiii.
17. Ibid., p. xiii.
18. McFarland, '*A Complex Dialogue*', p. 292. McFarland follows Coleridge in recognizing the Bruno of the 'Coinzidenza de Contrarii' as the founder of the Dynamic System in the modern epoch. Cf. BL I 162–3.
19. Simpson, op. cit., p. 150.
20. Elinor Shaffer, op. cit., p. 86.
21. Hans-Georg Gadamer, *Truth and Method*, trans. G. Barden and J. Cumming (London: Sheed & Ward, 1975) p. xii.
22. Cited in Esposito, op. cit., p. 237.

CHAPTER 10

1. BL I lxxxvii and chapter 13, n.2.
2. Hamilton, op. cit., p. 48.
3. Barry Gower, 'Speculation in Physics'.
4. Cf. Hamilton, op. cit., p. 55.
5. CN 1705 and n (1803); CL IV 791–2 (Dec. 1817). But cf. CL V 140 (Jan. 1820), in which Coleridge endorses Kant's sole dependence on the moral postulate.
6. Jeffrey Barnouw, 'The Morality of the Sublime: Kant and Schiller' in *Studies in Romanticism*, 19 (Winter 1980) 498–515; 502–3.
7. *Critique of Judgement*, p. 127.
8. A. W. Schlegel, *Lectures on Dramatic Art and Literature, 1808–9*, trans. John Black, 2 vols, 2nd edn (London, 1840) I, p. 79.
9. F. W. Schelling, *System of Transcendental Idealism*, trans. Peter Heath, with introduction by Michael Vater (Charlottesville: University Press of Virginia, 1978) p. 226n. When quoting from this work I will refer first to the Peter Heath translation, giving also page references to Albert Hofstadter's translation of Part 6 included in Simpson, op. cit. All quotations are from the Heath translation (Simpson, op. cit., pp. 125 and 267n16).
10. See Part Three, p. 172.
11. Barnouw, op. cit., p. 497.
12. Simpson, op. cit., p. 144.
13. *Das älteste Systemprogramm des deutschen Idealismus*, 1796. Cited in *University Studies*, pp. xi–xiv.
14. Wordsworth, *Prelude*, vi, ll. 557–72. E. D. Hirsch, *Wordsworth and Schelling: a Typological Study of Romanticism* (New Haven: Yale University Press, 1960) p. 64. Hirsch compares Schelling's 'intellectual intuition' with the Wordsworthian 'Spots of time'.
15. Georg Lukács, *The Destruction of Reason*, trans. Peter Palmer (London: Merlin Press, 1980) p. 146–7.
16. *Trans. Idealism*, p. 230 (Simpson, p. 128).
17. Ibid., p. 229 (Simpson, p. 268n).
18. BL sh I lxxi.
19. *Trans. Idealism*, pp. 229–30 (Simpson, 128).
20. Ibid., pp. 233 (Simpson, p. 130).
21. Ibid., p. 223 (Simpson, p. 123).
22. Giovambattista Vico, *The New Science*, 3rd edn, 1744; rev. trans. T. G. Bergin and M. H. Fisch (Ithaca: Cornell University Press, 1968) p. 425.
23. *Trans. Idealism* (henceforth TI), p. 223 (Simpson, p. 123).
24. TI 232 (Simpson, p. 130).
25. *On Dante in Relation to Philosophy*, Simpson, p. 142.
26. TI 233 (Simpson, p. 130).
27. Ibid.
28. Vico, op. cit., pp. 301–21. Cf. also TI I 128–9, 12 May 1830: 'Of course there was *a* Homer, and twenty besides.'

29. Simpson, p. 269n25.
30. Gadamer, op. cit., p. 26.

CHAPTER 11

1. TI, pp. 223–4 (Simpson, p. 123). I will hereafter use *art* and *poesie* (retaining the German here to distinguish the term from 'poetry' in general, the literal English translation), to describe the conscious and unconscious elements at work in aesthetic activity. This should not, however, be confused with Coleridge's use of the term *Poesy* in the 1818 lecture *On Poesy or Art*, to signify *muta poesis*, i.e. the non-linguistic arts as opposed to *poetry* (BL sh II 255).
2. TI 224 (Simpson, p. 124).
3. *Plastic Arts in Relation to Nature*, Simpson, p. 149.
4. Ibid., p. 152.
5. Ibid., p. 150.
6. Ibid., p. 155.
7. TI 225 (Simpson, p. 124). See Wellek, *A History of Modern Criticism*, vol. 2, *The Later 18th Century*, pp. 236–7. Schiller in part 'shared the extravagant Hellenism' of Goethe, Humboldt and Holderin. Compare this with Wellek's remarks on Schelling's Hellenism in vol. 3, *The Romantic Age*, pp. 76–7.
8. Simpson, p. 136.
9. Schiller's Sixteenth Letter: 'The beau-ideal, though simple and indivisible, discloses, when viewed in two different aspects, on the one hand a property of gentleness and grace, and on the other an energetic property; in experience there is a gentle and graceful beauty, and there is an energetic beauty', *Schiller's Works* (London: G. Bell, 1882) pp. 73–4. In the text I have preferred E. M. Wilkinson and L. A. Willoughby's translation, *melting* and *bracing*. *On the Aesthetic Education of Man, in a Series of letters* (Oxford: Clarendon Press, 1967).
10. *On University Studies*, pp. 145–6.
11. E. D. Hirsch, op. cit., p. 118.
12. *Of Human Freedom*, trans. J. Gutmann (Chicago: Open Court, 1936) pp. 67–8.
13. Simpson, p. 151.
14. Cf. *On University Studies*, p. 144.

CHAPTER 12

1. D. M. Fogel, 'A Compositional History of the Biographia Literaria', *Studies in Bibliography*, XXX (1977) 219–94.
2. CL IV 757–63.

3. IN CL IV 973 (Nov. 1819) Coleridge distinguished between the *Stateman's Manual*, directed at a *Learned* readership, and the *Second Lay Sermon*, written for a more general public. See CL V 289 and p. 141 below.

4. The text which now stands as the 1818 Lecture *On Poesy or Art* may have been written at an earlier period. I see no justification for Shawcross's assertion that 1818 'is the earliest period to which the inward evidence would allow us to assign it' (Bl sh II 317n). His argument that in this period Schelling helped Coleridge to 'emancipate himself from the Kantian limitations' could hardly hold for long after the March 1818 lectures; by the time of the *Philosophical Lectures* (Dec. 1818–Mar. 1819) Coleridge was praising Kant and denouncing Schelling's 'catholicism'. Shawcross contradicts his own point that Coleridge was moving away from imagination and a Schellingian 'interpretation of the world of existence as a manifestation of a spiritual principle' towards an emphasis on Practical Reason and Will much closer to Kantian dualism, as exemplified in *Aids to Reflection*. See Shawcross's introduction, Bl sh I lxxix–lxxxix, and II 317n.

5. Fruman, op. cit., p. 196.

6. Hamilton, op. cit., p. 18.

7. See Levere, *Poetry Realized in Nature*, pp. 126–37 for a discussion of Coleridge's attempt to substitute an initiating act of Divine Will for the evolution of an inner necessity, an apologetic strategy more commonly known as 'Creationism'.

8. See Fruman, op. cit., pp. 103–4, and Shawcross's note, Bl sh I 268–9 (note to p. 176).

9. According to Fruman (p. 104), all ten theses derive directly from Schelling; the first six take their content (and sometimes language) directly form *Trans. Idealism*; the seventh and eighth 'may be found variatim in 3 pages of *Abhandlung über des Verhältniss des Idealen und Realen in der Natur* (1798), the ninth and tenth from *Trans. Idealism* again'. Engells and Jackson Bate revise this opinion in their contention that Theses 1–6 come from *vom Ich als Princip der Philosophie* (1795), 7 and 8 from the *Abhandlung*, 9 and 10 from *Trans. Idealism* (BL I 264–87n). The editors also note that Theses 1, 2, 3, 6, 7, 9, and 10 'have definite, though not strictly verbal parallels 'with Jacobi's *über Lehre des Spinoza*, pp. 398–434, a work which had a great influence on Schelling. Schelling is, however, still the immediate source (BL I 268n). CN III 4265 is also important for understanding the composition of chapter twelve and tracing the exact borrowings from Schelling.

10. Both Orsini (op. cit., pp. 214–15, 257) and James Boulger, *Coleridge as Religious Thinker* (New Haven, Conn.: Yale University Press, 1961, p. 118) imply that Schelling identified *knowing* and *being* in transcendental self-consciousness, according to Coleridge's understanding of the *Trans. Idealism*. This permits them to read chapter twelve as his theistic *critique* of German Idealism. The editors of the New Princeton edition correct this misconception (BL I 274n2): 'Schelling states that theoretical philosophy cannot, given its own criteria, successfully assert that God is the ground of *Our Knowledge*, nor can it identify God

with the *Ich*; god is an object determined by the *Ich*, whose *existence* cannot be proved ontologically. . . . Coleridge is not *disagreeing* with Schelling, but rather accepting points about God and the 'I' that Schelling himself outlines yet does not include in a rigorous and purely theoretical system.' In later years, Coleridge came to believe this 'distancing' of the Absolute was a sophistic means of preserving moral freedom, disguising the latent Spinozism of Schelling's system. In the late poem 'Self-Knowledge' (PW I 487), the exhortation 'Ignore Thyself, and strive to know thy God' (l. 10) demonstrates a subordination of the sort of self-consciousness objectified in aesthetic experience to the 'method of the Will', the Kantian imperative.

11. TI 229–30 (Simpson, p. 128).
12. Schiller, 'Aesthetic Letters', *Works*, p. 63: 'these two notions . . . exhaust the notion of humanity, and a third *fundamental impulsion*, holding a medium between them, is quite inconceivable. How then shall we re-establish the unity of human nature, a unity that appears completely destroyed by this primitive and radical opposition?'
13. In *The Collected Historical, Political and Miscellaneous Works of John Milton*, ed. John Toland (Amsterdam, 1698) 3 vols, II, 785. Milton continues 'the Foundation indeed they laid gallantly, but fell into a worse confusion, not of Tongues, but of Factions, than those at the Tower of Babel; and have left no Memorial of their Work behind them remaining, but the common laughter of Europe'.

CHAPTER 13

1. Orsini, op. cit., p. 223.
2. Some of the classic studies are: M. H. Abrams, *The Mirror and the Lamp* (Oxford University Press, 1953) pp. 161–2, 168–9, 175–6; J. Bullitt and W. Jackson Bate, 'The Distinction between Imagination and Fancy in 18th Century Criticism', *MLN*, lx (1945) 8–15; Earl Wassermann, 'Another 18th Century Distinction between Fancy and Imagination', *MLN*, lxiv (1949) 23–5; Wellek, *The Romantic Age*, 164–5. Fruman, op. cit., 177–83.
   BL I xcvii–civ offers a concise history of the distinction.
3. TI 230–1 (Simpson, p. 128).
4. McFarland, *Coleridge and the Pantheist Tradition*, pp. 33, 42.
5. Coleridge elided the phrase 'a repetition in the finite mind of the eternal act of creation in the infinite I AM', in his copy of the *Biographia* (BL sh I 272n).
6. Wellek, *Romantic Age*, p. 159; *Orsini*, op. cit., p. 222.
7. TI 232 (Simpson, p. 129).
8. Simpson, p. 149.
9. I use 'traditional' in Gramsci's sense, a category of intellectuals 'already in existence . . . which seemed indeed to represent an historical continuity uninterrupted even by the most complicated and radical changes in political and social forms'. Antonio Gramsci,

Selections from the Prison Notebooks, ed. and trans. by Quintin Hoare and Geoffrey Nowell Smith (London: Lawrence & Wishart, 1971) p. 7.

10. R. F. Storch, 'The Politics of Imagination', *Studies in Romanticism*, 21 (Autumn 1982) 448–56.
11. A. W. Schlegel, *Lectures*, I, p. 44.
12. Simpson, p. 151.
13. Ben Knights, *Idea of the Clerisy*, p. 20.
14. 'The Rhetoric of Temporality' in *Interpretations: Theory and Practice*, ed. Charles S. Singleton (Baltimore: Johns Hopkins Press, 1969) pp. 173–209, 177.
15. Levere, *Poetry Realized in Nature*, p. 193. As Levere indicates, Watt's definition, although later than Coleridge (1859–68), 'conforms to STC's usage' (p. 259n99).
16. De Man, op. cit., p. 177.
17. Ibid., p. 188.
18. Ibid., p. 189.
19. Harold Perkin, op. cit., p. 209. Perkin's account of the 'vertical relations' of 18th century society, 'the great functional interest – agriculture, and the various branches of trade, industry and the profession' serving as corporative political distinctions has been challenged by E. P. Thompson in 'Patrician Society, Plebeian Culture', *Journal of Social History* VII, 4 (Summer 1974) 382–405. Thompson argues that patronage and paternalism were facades which hid real but sublimated class conflicts (p. 387). The important point for my argument is that the development of class *consciousness* in the 1817 period had a tremendous effect on 'organic' social theories like Coleridge's; for example, the tripartite form of the *Lay Sermons* militates against the holistic and unifying form of the project, leading to the sublimatory 'separation from separation'. As E. J. Hobsbawm puts it, 'under capitalism, class is an immediate and in some sense a directly *experienced* historical reality, whereas in pre-capitalist epochs it may merely be an analytical construct which makes sense of a complex of facts otherwise inexplicable'. From 'Class Consciousness in History' in *Aspects of History & Class Consciousness*, ed. I. Meszaros (London: Routledge & Kegan Paul, 1971) p. 8.
20. Michael Fisher, 'Morality and History in Coleridge's Political Theory', *Studies in Romanticism*, 21 (Autumn 1982) 457–60, 458.

CHAPTER 14

1. 'On the Poetical Use of the Heathen Mythology', *London Magazine*, 26, 5 (Feb. 1822) pp. 113–24.
2. Marilyn Butler, op. cit., pp. 113–37.
3. *London Magazine*, p. 113.
4. Marilyn Butler, op. cit., p. 131.

5. *The Poems of Hartley Coleridge*, ed. Derwent Coleridge, 2 vols (London, 1851) II, 280.
6. *London Magazine*, p. 113.
7. Ibid., p. 113.
8. Ibid., p. 114.
9. Edward Gibbon, *History of the Decline and Fall of the Roman Empire*, ed. with intro. by J. B. Bury, 7 vols (London: Methuen, 1909) II, 16.
10. *London Magazine*, p. 115.
11. *Crabb Robinson's Diary*, II, 446. See Ph. L 464n36 for Kathleen Coburn's remarks on Schelling's imputed catholicism.
12. *London Magazine*, p. 116.
13. Ibid., p. 117.
14. Ibid., p. 116.
15. Ibid., p. 116.
16. James Boulger, *Coleridge as Religious Thinker*, p. 10.
17. See LR I 289 for another attack on Dupuis. Coleridge read Dupuis in Nov. 1796. See Marilyn Butler, op. cit., pp. 78–80.
18. *The Complete Poetical Works of Percy Bysshe Shelley*, ed. Thomas Hutchinson (London: Oxford University Press, 1934) pp. 800–35.
19. *London Magazine*, pp. 116–17.
20. Ibid., p. 116.
21. Ibid., p. 119.
22. Ibid., p. 119.
23. Richard Payne Knight, *The Progress of Civil Society: a Didactic Poem* (London, 1796) Book 3, ll. 306–7.
24. J. J. Rousseau, 'Essay on the Origin of Languages', *On the Origin of Languages: J. J. Rousseau, "Essay on the Origin of Languages", J. G. Herder, "Essay on the Origin of Language"*, trans. J. H. Moran and A. Gode (New York: Frederick Ungar, 1966) p. 27: 'All that is needed for quickly rendering a language cold and monotonous, is to establish Academies among the people who speak it'; Adam Ferguson, *An Essay on the History of Civil Society* (1767), ed. Duncan Forbes (Edinburgh University Press, 1966) pp. 173–4.
25. *Progress of Civil Society*, Book 3, ll. 479–84.
26. *London Magazine*, p. 119.
27. Ibid., p. 117.
28. *Crabb Robinson's Diary*, II, 395, 19 June 1828.
29. Ibid., p. 273.

CHAPTER 15

1. This is structurally similar to the Christian interpretation of Wordsworth's 'uniformitarianism' in BL II 130.
2. *The Examiner*, 5, Apr. 1817; *Hazlitt's Complete Works*, 19, 196–8.
3. Harold Perkin, *The Origins of Modern English Society*, p. 183.

CHAPTER 16

1. Plato, *The Republic*, trans. with intro. by Desmond Lee (Harmondsworth: Penguin, 1974) p. 153.
2. Ibid., p. 435.
3. Ibid., p. 437.
4. Ibid., p. 135.
5. Ibid., p. 132.
6. Ibid., p. 132.
7. Ibid., p. 130.
8. Ibid., p. 144.
9. Vico, op. cit., p. 426. See *Crabb Robinson's Diary*, II, 297–8, for Coleridge on Vico.
10. See CL V 14 (14 Jan. 1820) and compare with CL IV 791–2 (13 Dec. 1817).
11. Elinor Shaffer, *'Kubla Khan' and the Fall of Jerusalem*, p. 188.

CHAPTER 17

1. 'Summary of an Essay on the Fundamental Position of the Mysteries in Relation to Greek Tragedy', *Notes and Lectures on Shakespeare and some of the old Poets and Dramatists*, ed. Mrs H. N. Coleridge, 2 vols (London, 1849), II, 218–222; 221. This essay is *not* included in H. N. Coleridge's 1836–39 *Literary Remains*.
2. See W. H. Oliver, *Prophets and Millennialists: the uses of Biblical Prophecy in England from the 1790's to the 1840's* (Auckland, N.Z.: Auckland University Press and Oxford University Press, 1978) pp. 99–149.
3. See *Religious Musings* (1796) for Coleridgean 'Apocalytic'. His later thoughts on Miracles reveal an antipathy to doctrines of direct divine intervention: CIS pp. 70–3.
4. Robert Preyer, op. cit.
5. Ibid., p. 16.
6. M. H. Fisch, 'The Coleridges, Dr Prati and Vico', *Modern Philosophy*, 41–2 (1943–45), 111–22; 113–14. Coleridge quoted from Vico in the *Theory of Life*, which, as Fisch points out, is the first mention of Vico in English literature if we count date of composition rather than publication. But the source of this quotation was Jacobi's *Von den Gottlichen Dingen*; it is certain that Coleridge had not read *The New Science* or *Autobiography* before 1825. The copy of the NS borrowed from Dr Prati was the 6th edn (3 vols) published in Milan in 1816.
7. Vico, op. cit., p. 78.
8. E. P. Thompson, *The Poverty of Theory*, p. 278.
9. *The Political Works of James Harrington*, p. 17.
10. See LS 215n; PH L 232–3, 258–60.
11. See Thomas Arnold's review of Niebuhr's *Römische Geschichte* in the *Quarterly Review*, 32 (June 1825) pp. 67–92. Niebuhr noted that the

differentiation of classes and individuals from the totality of the community at the end of the 'childhood period' of Rome, and the rise of class antagonism, coincided with an end to the production of folk poetry and communal myths. Robert Preyer, p. 30.

12. Coleridge took the Eucharist in 1827 for the first time since Cambridge days. See Boulger's discussion, pp. 175–85.
13. Basil Willey, *Nineteenth-Century Studies* (London: Chatto & Windus, 1949) p. 40.
14. Shaffer, op. cit., p. 54.
15. Esposito, op. cit., p. 21.
16. John Farrell, *Revolution as Tragedy: the Dilemma of the Moderate from Scott to Arnold* (Ithaca: Cornell University Press, 1980) p. 35.

CHAPTER 18

1. William Warburton, *The Divine Legation of Moses Demonstrated on the Principles of a Religious Deist*, 2 vols (London 1738–41), and a rev. and extended edn, in 5 vols (London 1765). All references to 1738–41 unless stated otherwise.
   Thomas Taylor the Platonist: Selected Writings, ed. with intro. K. Raine and G. M. Harper (London: Routledge & Kegan Paul, 1969).
   Rev. G. S. Faber, *Dissertation on the Cabiri*, 2 vols (Oxford, 1803).
   Schelling's Treatise on 'The Deities of Samothrace', trans. with intro. by Robert F. Brown (Montana: Scholars Press, University of Montana, 1974, 1977).
   Cf. Richard Haven, 'Coleridge and the Greek Mysteries', *MLN*, 70 (June 1955) 405–7. Haven *under*estimates Schelling's importance.
2. See K. M. Wheeler, 'Coleridge's Friendship with Ludwig Tieck', *New Approaches to Coleridge: Biographical and Critical Essays*, ed. Donald Sultana (London: Vision, Barnes & Noble, 1981) pp. 96–112.
   William K. Pfeiler, 'Coleridge's and Schelling's Treatise on the Samothracian Deities', *Modern Language Notes*, 52 (Mar. 1937) 162–5.
3. Shaffer, op. cit., p. 148.
4. *Divine Legation*, I, 172. The Church Fathers had depraved the 'pure paganism' of the Mystery doctrine.
5. See Boulger, op. cit., pp. 20–2 on Paley's antipathy to internal evidences (mystical or spiritual interpretations) of Christianity. The young Coleridge had partaken of this: in Feb. 1798 he regarded Hume's critique of causality as 'the sole pillar of modern atheism', CL I 385–6.
6. William Warburton, *Alliance between Church and State, or The necessity and equity of an established religion and a test-law demonstrated* (London, 1736). See H. N. Coleridge's *Preface* to the 1839 edn of *Church and State* (CS 196–7, App. A) for a comparison between Warburton and Coleridge on this matter.
7. *Divine Legation*. I, 13.
8. Ibid., I, 303–24; 303–4.

9. Ibid., I, 149.
10. Added in 1765 edn of *Divine Legation*, I, 163. W. is quoting from Clemens Alexandrinus.
11. Ibid. (1738–41), p. 143–4.
12. Ibid., p. 150.
13. Vico, op. cit., p. 120.
14. *Divine Legation*, I, 204.
15. Ibid., pp. 207–8.
16. Ibid., p. 202.
17. Warburton added the strictures on Spinozism, a philosophy fatal to their efficacy inasmuch as it denied the doctrine of future rewards and punishments, in the 1765 edn, I, p. 278.
18. Marx, 'Theses on Feuerbach: Thesis viii', *The German Ideology* (London: Lawrence & Wishart, 1970) p. 122.
19. *University Studies*, p. 114.
20. Ibid., p. 84.
21. Ibid., pp. 85, 91.
22. Ibid., p. 93.
23. Ibid., p. 111.
24. From Schelling's 1804 memorial essay on Kant, cited in *University Studies*, p. 158n to p. 102.
25. Ibid., p. 102.
26. Ibid., p. 90.
27. Robert Brown's intro. to Schelling's *Deities of Samothrace*, p. 4.
28. Shaffer, op. cit., p. 186.
29. G. F. Creuzer, *Symbolik und Mythologie der alten Völker, besonders der Griechen (1810–12)*, 6 vols (Leipzig U. Darmstadt, 1819–23).
30. *Deities of Samothrace*, p. 26.
31. Ibid., p. 25.
32. Ibid., p. 25.
33. The editor cites n36 f.79 (CN V).
34. Schelling is less specific about the higher triad than he is about the lower, the divine analogy in the world to what in God is the pole of necessity as subordinate to the pole of freedom. See *Deities of Samothrace*, pp. 51–6.
35. Ibid., p. 29.
36. Ibid., p. 30.
37. *Blackwood's Magazine*, lvi, 10 (Oct. 1821) p. 259. Ph L 321–2 for Cabiri as miners.

CHAPTER 19

1. In *Notes and Lectures on Shakespeare*, ed. Mrs H. N. Coleridge (1849), cf. n43.
2. Boulger, op. cit., chs 4 and 5, esp. pp. 154–7.
3. Ibid., p. 158.
4. A. A. Cooper, Third Earl of Shaftesbury, *Characteristics* (1711), I,

22–4; 188–90, 'the strange adherence and servile dependency of the whole Hebrew race on the Egyptian nation'.

5. Herodotus, *The Histories*, trans. Aubrey De Selincourt, rev. with intro. by A. R. Burn (Harmondsworth: Penguin, 1972) p. 150 (Bk II, 53).
6. 'The Mysteries in relation to the Greek Tragedy', *Notes and Lects*, II 219.
7. Ibid., II, 221.
8. David Simpson, *Wordsworth and the Figurings of the Real* (London: Macmillan, 1982) p. 117.
9. Boulger, op. cit., p. 84.
10. Hamilton, op. cit., pp. 192–9.
11. Ibid., pp. 200–1.
12. Lukacs, *The Destruction of Reason*, p. 147.
13. Elinor Shaffer, 'Metaphysics of Culture: Kant and Coleridge's "Aids to Reflection" ', *Journal of the History of Ideas*, 31 (1970) 199–218.
14. Ibid., p. 217.
15. Gibbon, *Decline and Fall of the Roman Empire*, II, 41.
16. See also AR, p. 188 where Coleridge associates the term 'Virtue' with Shaftesbury and his disciples, who 'prefer a philosophic Paganism to the morality of the Gospel'. He sought to define a specifically Christian 'Virtue' based on its etymological sense of 'Manliness'.
17. J. G. A. Pocock, *The Machiavellian Moment*, p. 460–1.
18. Ibid. and generally, ch. 13, 'Land, Trade and Credit'.
19. Ibid., p. 461.

CHAPTER 20

1. George Whalley, 'Coleridge's Lecture on the Prometheus of Aeschylus', *Proceedings and Transactions of the Royal Society of Canada*, vol. 54, ser. 3 (June 1960) 13–24; 14.
2. Shaftesbury, 'The Moralists', *Characteristics*, II, 17. In the 1808 *Friend* II 279–80, Coleridge criticized Shaftesbury's denial of original sin, a 'splendid but delusory tenet' based on a misinterpretation of Plato.
3. Vico, op. cit., p. 9; 121: 'Authority . . . is the iron ring by which the giants, dispersed upon the mountains, were kept chained to the earth by fear of the sky and of Jove, wherever they happened to be when the sky first thundered. Such were Tityus and Prometheus . . .'.
4. Schlegel, *Lectures on Dramatic Art and Literature*, I, 117, 115.
5. Warburton added this in the 1765 edn of the *Divine Legation*, I, p. 174. CL IV 781 (Nov. 1817) shows Coleridge to have been reading the *Prometheus* of Aeschylus at around the same time as Schelling's *Gottheiten von Samothrace*.
6. *Poems of Hartley Coleridge*, II, 282. For STC's account of 'nomos politikos' see LR II 351.
7. Ibid., 282.

8. Ibid., 283.
9. See CL VI 850 (Dec. 1830) for Coleridge on Shelley; here he considered the poet's 'atheism' as 'the next best religion to Christianity'. Coleridge felt that he could have easily effected Shelley's conversion. Compare this with Crabb Robinson's high regard for Shelley's 'natural piety'. *Crabb Robinson's Diary*, II, 387.
10. In Coleridge's account of the Greek cosmogony, the Deity or Ground of Being is a synthesis of Light 'as the one pole or antagonistic power' and Darkness (or Gravity) as 'the principle of mass, a wholeness without distinction or parts', LR II 339. This was an adaptation of Schelling's polar powers of *Schwere* and *Lichtwesen* as defined in the 1799 *Naturphilosophie*.
11. Shaffer, op. cit., p. 156. See TT II 267 for Coleridge's interpretation of the Trinity as a representation of the 'mythic double-bind'.
12. Compare this with the 'religious deism' which determined Coleridge's rejection of an anthropomorphic God in Dec. 1802 (CL II 893). He increasingly sought, in Boulger's words, 'certain traditional notions about the Trinity which might strengthen the concept of personëity as the basis for a philosophical theism with its ultimate sanction in will and conscience', op. cit., p. 131.
13. *Shelley's Poetical Works*, p. 205.

CHAPTER 21

1. *J. S. Mill on Bentham and Coleridge*, intro. by F. R. Leavis (Cambridge University Press, 1980) p. 147.
2. J. G. A. Pocock, *The Machiavellian Moment*, p. 498. The Scots Conjectural Historians, and notably Adam Smith, 'initiated a theory of *Homo Faber*, of labour as the author of value. . . . Man could now be described as a cultural animal, and culture as a product of economics'. See also Pocock's 'The Political Economy of Burke's analysis of the French Revolution', *The Historial Journal*, vol. 25, 2 (1982) 331–50, which shows up the similarities in Burke's privileging of 'manners' and Coleridge's idea of Christian 'cultivation'.
3. See J. S. Mill, op. cit., p. 148. Coleridge 'vindicated against Bentham, Adam Smith, and the whole 18th century, the principle of an endowed class for the cultivation of learning, and for diffusing its results among the community'. See Ben Knights, *The Idea of the Clerisy in the 19th Century*.
4. J. S. Mill, op. cit., p. 151.
5. Harold Perkin, op. cit., p. 272.
6. Edward Said, *The World, the Text and the Critic*, p. 171 and chapter 9, 'Criticism between Culture and System'.
7. Ben Brewster's definition from the glossary to his translation of Louis Althusser, *For Marx* (London: Allen Lane, Penguin, 1969) p. 252. The relation between ideology and 'science' in Althusser's thought is a complex one, projecting the possibility of a transformation

of the former into the latter category. I have argued that Coleridge's thought is underpinned by an awareness of ideology as 'the *lived* relation betwen men and their world, or a reflected form of this unconscious relation'.

8. Thomas Carlyle, *The Life of John Sterling* (London: Chapman & Hall, 1851) p. 69.
9. 'A Letter to Maria Gisborne', *Shelley's Poetical Works*, p. 368, ll. 202–8.

Bibliography

Abrams, M. H., *The Mirror and the Lamp: Romantic Theory and the Critical Tradition* (Oxford University Press, 1953).

——, 'English Romanticism: the Spirit of the Age', *Romanticism Reconsidered*, ed. Northrop Frye (New York: Columbia Press, 1963) pp. 26–72.

——, 'Coleridge's "A light in sound": Science, Metascience, and Poetic Imagination', *Proceedings of the American Philosophical Society*, CXVI (1972) 458–76.

Althusser, L., *For Marx*, trans. Ben Brewster (London: Allen Lane, Penguin, 1969).

Arnold, M, 'The Function of Criticism at the Present Time', *Lectures and Essays in Criticism*, ed. R. H. Super (Ann Arbor: University of Michigan Press, 1962) pp. 258–85.

Arnold, T., Review of Niebuhr's *Römische Geschichte*, *Quarterly Review*, 32 (June 1825) 67–92.

Ashton, R., *The German Idea: Four English Writers and the Reception of German Thought 1800–1860* (Cambridge University Press, 1980).

Bailyn, B., *Ideological Origins of the American Revolution* (Cambridge, Mass.: Harvard University Press, 1967).

Barrell, J. (ed.), with intro. S. T. Coleridge, *The Constitution of Church and State* (London: J. M. Dent, 1972).

——, *English Literature in History 1730–80: an Equal, Wide Survey* (London: Hutchinson, 1983).

Barruel, Abbé, *Mémoires pour servir à l'Histoire de Jacobinism*, 4 vols (London, 1797–98, English trans. 1798).

Barnouw, J., 'The Morality of the Sublime: Kant and Schiller', *Studies in Romanticism*, 19 (Winter 1980) 498–515.

Barth, J. R., *The Symbolic Imagination* (Princeton University Press, 1977).

Beattie, J., *An Essay on the Nature and Immutability of Truth, in opposition to Sophistry and Scepticism* (1770; 4th edn, London, 1773).

Beer, G., *Darwin's Plots: Evolutionary Narrative in Darwin, George Eliot, and 19th Century Fiction* (London: Routledge & Kegan Paul, 1983).

Beer, J., *Coleridge the Visionary* (London: Chatto & Windus, 1959).

—— (ed.), *Coleridge Variety* (London: Macmillan, 1974).

——, *Coleridge's Poetic Intelligence* (London: Macmillan, 1977).

——, 'The Revolutionary Youth of Wordsworth and Coleridge: another view', *Critical Quarterly*, 19 (1977) 79–87.

——, 'Coleridge and Wordsworth: the Vital and the Organic', *Reading Coleridge: Approaches and Applications*, ed. W. B. Crawford (Ithaca: Cornell University Press, 1979) pp. 160–90.

Berlin, I., *Vico and Herder: Two Studies in the History of Ideas* (London: Hogarth Press, 1976).

Bialostosky, D. H., 'Coleridge Interpretation of Wordsworth's "Preface to Lyrical Ballads"', *PMLA*, 93 (1978) 912–24.

Boulger, J., *Coleridge as Religious Thinker* (New Haven, Conn.: Yale University Press, 1961).

Brinkley, R. F., *Coleridge on the Seventeenth Century* (Durham, N.C.: Duke University Press, 1955).

Brisman, L., 'Coleridge on the Supernatural', *Studies in Romanticism*, 21 (Summer 1982) 123–59.

Brown, J., *An Estimate of the Manners and the Principles of the Times*, 2 vols (London, 1757).

Brown, R. F., trans. with intro. and notes, *Schelling's Treatise on 'The Deities of Samothrace'* (Montana: Scholar's Press, University of Montana, 1974, 1977).

——, *The Later Philosophy of Schelling: the Influence of Boehme on the Works of 1809–15* (Lemsburg and London: Bucknell University Press and Associated University Press, 1977).

Bruno, G., *The Expulsion of the Triumphant Beast* (Lo Spaccio de la Bestia Trionfanta), trans. and ed. Arthur D. Imerti, with intro. and notes (New Brunswick, N.J.: Rutgers University Press, 1964).

Bullitt, J. and Bate, W. J., 'The Distinction between Fancy and Imagination in 18th Century English Criticism', *MLN*, lx (1945) 8–15.

Burke, E., *Works*. 8 vols (London: G. Bell & Sons, 1899).

Butler, M., *Peacock Displayed: a Satirist in his Context* (London: Routledge & Kegan Paul, 1979).

——, *Romantic, Rebels and Reactionaries: English Literature and Its Background 1760–1830* (Oxford University Press, 1981).

Calleo, D. P., *Coleridge and the Idea of the Modern State* (New Haven, Conn.: Yale University Press, 1966).

Carlyle, T., *The Life of John Sterling* (London: Chapman & Hall, 1851).

Caskey, J. D. and Strapper, M. M., *Samuel Taylor Coleridge: a Selective Bibliography of Criticism 1935–77* (Westport, Conn.: Greenwood Press, 1978).

Cassirer, E., *The Philosophy of Symbolic Forms*, trans. R. Mannheim, intro. C. Hendel, 3 vols (New Haven, Conn.: Yale University Press, 1953–57).

Chandler, J., 'Wordsworth and Burke', *ELH*, 44 (1980) 741–71.

——, *Wordsworth's Second Nature: a Study of the Poetry and Politics* (Chicago University Press, 1984).

Christensen, J. C., *Coleridge's Blessed Machine of Language* (Ithaca and London: Cornell University Press, 1981).

Cobban, A., *Edmund Burke and the Revolt against the Eighteenth Century: a Study of the Political and Social Thinking of Burke, Wordsworth, Coleridge and Southey* (New York: Barnes & Noble, 1960).

Coleridge, S. T., *Collected Letters of S. T. Coleridge*, Rd. E. L. Griggs. 6 vols (Oxford and New York: 1956–71).

——, *The Notebooks of S. T. Coleridge*, ed. K. Coburn, 5 vols (New York; Princeton N.J. and London, Routledge & Kegan Paul, 1957).

——, *The Complete Poetical Works of S. T. Coleridge*, ed. with textual and bibliographical notes by E. H. Coleridge, 2 vols (Oxford: Clarendon Press, 1912).

——, *Marginalia*, ed. G. Whalley, vol. 1, *Abbt to Byfield*, 1980; vol. 2,

Camden to Hutton, 1984 (London and Princeton, N.J.: Routledge & Kegan Paul and Princeton University Press, 1980–00: *The Collected Works of S. T. Coleridge XII.*

——, *Lectures 1795: on Politics and Religion*, ed. Lewis Patton and Peter Mann (London and Princeton N.J.: Routledge & Kegan Paul and Princeton University Press, 1971): *The Collected Works of S. T. Coleridge I.*

——, *The Watchman*, ed. Lewis Patton (London and Princeton, N.J.: Routledge & Kegan Paul and Princeton University Press, 1970): *The Collected Works of S. T. Coleridge II.*

——, *Essays on his Times*, ed. D. V. Erdman, 3 vols (London and Princeton, N.J.: Routledge & Kegan Paul and Princeton University Press, 1978): *The Collected Works of S. T. Coleridge III.*

——, *The Friend*, ed. B. Rooke, 2 vols (London and Princeton, N.J.: Routledge & Kegan Paul and Princeton University Press, 1969): *The Collected Works of S. T. Coleridge IV.*

—— (with R. Southey), *Omniana: or Horae Otiosiores*, ed. R. Gittings (Slough, Bucks: Centaur Press, 1969).

——, *Lay Sermons*, ed. R. J. White (London and Princeton, N.J.: Routledge & Kegan Paul and Princeton University Press, 1972): *The Collected Works of S. T. Coleridge VI.*

——, *Hints Towards the Formation of a More Comprehensive Theory of Life*, ed. Seth B. Watson (London, 1848).

——, *Biographia Literaria*, ed. with his Aesthetical Essays, by J. Shawcross, 2 vols (Oxford University Press, 1907).

——, *Biographia Literaria*, eds James Engell and W. Jackson Bate, 2 vols (London and Princeton, N.J.: Routledge & Kegan Paul and Princeton University Press, 1983): *The Collected Works of S. T. Coleridge VII.*

——, *Coleridge's Shakespeare Criticism*, ed. T. M. Raysor, 2 vols (London: Constable, 1930).

——, *The Literary Remains of S. T. Coleridge*, coll. and ed. by H. N. Coleridge, 4 vols (London: W. Pickering, 1836–39).

——, *Notes and Lectures on Shakespeare, and Some of the Old Poets and Dramatists, with Other Literary Remains of S. T. Coleridge*, ed. Mrs H. N. Coleridge, 2 vols (London: W. Pickering, 1849).

——, *Philosophical Lectures*, ed. K. Coburn (London: Pilot Press, 1949).

——, *Aids to Reflection, in the Formation of a Manly Character on the Several Grounds of Prudence, Morality and Religion* (London: Taylor & Hessey, 1825).

——, *Confessions of an Inquiring Spirit* (1840), ed. with intro. by H. St. J. Hart (London: A. & C. Black, 1956: rpt. of 3rd edn. 1853, with intro. by J. H. Green and notes by Sara Coleridge).

——, *On the Constitution of the Church and State*, ed. J. Colmer (London and Princeton, N.J.: Routledge & Kegan Paul and Princeton University Press, 1976): *The Collected Works of S. T. Coleridge X.*

——, *Specimens of the Table Talk of the late S. T. Coleridge*, ed. H. N. Coleridge, 2 vols (London: John Murray, 1835).

Coleridge, Hartley, 'On the Poetical Use of the Heathen Mythology', *The London Magazine*, 26, 5 (Feb. 1822) 113–24.

——, *The Poems of Hartley Coleridge*, ed. Derwent Coleridge, 2 vols (London, 1851).

Colmer, J. A., *Coleridge, Critic of Society* (Oxford: Clarendon Press, 1959).

Cooper, A. A. 3rd Earl of Shaftesbury, *Characteristics of Men, Manners, Opinions, Times* (1711), 2 vols (London: Grant Richards, 1900; rpt. Gloucester, Mass.: Peter Smith, 1963).

Cruezer, G. F., *Symbolik und Mythologie der alten Völker, besonders der Griechen (1810–12)*, 6 vols (Leipzig und Darmstadt, 1819–23).

Cudworth, R., *The True Intellectual System of the Universe* (London, 1678).

Darwin, E., *The Botanic Garden; or, The Loves of the Plants* (London, 1789).

Davie, D., *A Gathered Church: Literature of the English Dissenting Interest 1700–1930* (London: Routledge & Kegan Paul, 1978).

Davy, Humphry, *Collected Works*, ed. J. Davy, 9 vols (London, 1840).

Davy, J., *Memoirs of the Life of Sir Humphry Davy, Bart*, 2 vols (London, 1836).

De Beer, G., *The Sciences were never at War* (London: Nelson, 1960).

De Man, P., 'The Rhetoric of Temporality', *Interpretations; Theory and Practice*, ed. C. S. Singleton (Baltimore: Johns Hopkins Press, 1969) pp. 173–209.

——, *Blindness and Insight: Essays in the Rhetoric of Contemporary Criticism* (New York: Oxford University Press, 1971).

——, 'The Epistemology of Metaphor', *Critical Inquiry*, 5 (1978–79) 13–30.

Diamond, W. Craig, 'Natural Philosophy in Harrington's Political Thought', *Journal of the History of Philosophy*, 16 (1978) 387–98.

Drummond, W., *Academical Questions*, vol. 1 (London, 1805).

——, *Origines: or Remarks on the Origin of Several Empires, States, and Cities*, 3 vols (London, 1824).

Dupuis, C., *Origine de tous les cultes, ou religion universelle*, 7 vols in 12. Paris, an III (1794–95).

Eagleton, T., *Criticism and Ideology: a Study in Marxist Literary Theory* (London: NLB, 1976).

——, *Literary Theory: an Introduction* (Oxford: Basil Blackwell, 1983).

——, *The Function of Criticism: from the Spectator to Post-Structuralism* (London: Verso, 1984).

Engell, J., *The Creative Imagination: Enlightenment to Romanticism* (Cambridge, Mass. and London: Harvard University Press 1981).

Engels, F., See Marx and Engels.

Esposito, J. L., *Schelling's Idealism and Philosophy of Nature* (London: Associated University Presses, 1977).

Estlin, J. P., *Evidences of Revealed Religion, and Particularly Christianity, Stated, with Reference to a Pamphlet Called The Age of Reason (by T. Paine); in a Discourse Delivered at the Chapel in Lewin's Mead, Bristol, Dec 25th 1795* (Bristol, 1796).

Everest, K., *Coleridge's Secret Ministry: the Context of the Conversation Poems 1795–98* (Sussex: Harvester Press, 1979).

Faber, G. S., *A Dissertation on the Cabiri*, 2 vols (Oxford, 1803).

Farrell, J., *Revolution as Tragedy: the Dilemma of the Moderate from Scott to Arnold* (Ithaca: Cornell University Press, 1980).

Ferguson, A., *An Essay on the History of Civil Society* (1767) ed. Duncan Forbes (Edinburgh University Press, 1966).

——, *History of the Progress and Termination of the Roman Republic*, 3 vols (London, 1783).

Ferguson, F., *Wordsworth: Language as Counter-Spirit* (New Haven Conn.: Yale University Press, 1977).

Fichte, J. G., *Science of Knowledge* (*Wissenschaftslehre*) (1794), ed. and trans. Peter Heath and John Lachs (New York: Meredith Corporation, 1970; Cambridge University Press, 1982).

——, *On the Nature of the Scholar* (*Über das Wesen des Gelehrten und seine Erscheinnungen im Gebeite der Freiheit*) (1805), trans. W. Smith (London, 1845).

——, *Addresses to the German Nation* (1807–8), trans. R. F. Jones and G. H. Turnbull, ed. and rev. G. A. Kelly (New York and Evanston: Harper & Row, 1968).

Fink, Z. S., *The Classical Republicans: an Essay in the Recovery of a Pattern of Thought in 17th Century England* (Evanston: Northwestern University Press, 1945).

——, 'Wordsworth and the English Republican Tradition', *Journal of English and German Philosophy*, 4 (1948) 107–26.

Fisch, M. H., 'The Coleridges, Dr Prati and Vico', *Modern Philology*, 41–2 (1943–45) 111–22.

Fischer, M., 'Morality and History in Coleridge's Political Theory', *Studies in Romanticism*, 21 (Autumn 1982) 457–60.

Fogel, D. 'A Compositional History of the Biographia Literaria', *Studies in Bibliography*, 3 (1977) 219–34.

Foucault, M., *Madness and Civilization*, trans. R. Howard (London: Tavistock, 1967).

——, *The Order of Things*, trans. A. Sheridan (London: Tavistok, 1970).

——, *Language, Counter-Memory, Practice: Selected Essays and Interviews*, ed. with an intro. Donald F. Bouchard, trans. by D. F. Bouchard and Sherry Simon (Oxford: Basil Blackwell, 1977).

——, 'The Order of Discourse' in *Untying the Text; a Post-Structuralist Reader*, ed. with intro. Robert Young (London: Routledge & Kegan Paul, 1981) pp. 48–78.

Fruman, N., *Coleridge: the Damaged Archangel* (London: Allen & Unwin, 1971).

Fullmer, J. Z., 'The Poetry of Humphry Davy', *Chymia*, 6 (1966) 102–26.

Gabriel, M., *Coleridge et Schelling* (Paris: Editions Aubière-Montaignes, 1971).

Gadamer, H. G., *Truth and Method*, trans. and eds Garrett Barden and John Cummings (London: Sheed & Ward, 1975).

Gibbon, E., *History of the Decline and Fall of the Roman Empire*, ed. with intro. John B. Bury, 7 vols (London: Methuen, 1909).

Godwin, W., *An Enquiry Concerning Political Justice, and Its Influence on General Virtue and Happiness*, 2 vols (London, 1973).

Goethe, J. W., *Goethe on Art*, ed. John Gage (Berkeley and Los Angeles: University of California Press, 1980).

Gower, B., 'The History and Practice of Naturphilosophie', *Studies in the History and Philosophy of Science*, 3, 4 (Feb. 1973) 301–56.

Gramsci, A., *Selections from the Prison Notebooks*, ed. and trans. Quintin Hoare and G. Nowell Smith (London: Lawrence & Wishart, 1971).

Habermas, J., *Theory and Practice*, trans. by John Viertel (London: Heinemann, 1974).

——, *Knowledge and Human Interest*. trans. by J. T. Shapiro (Boston: Beacon Press, 1971).

Hamilton, P., *Coleridge's Poetics* (Oxford: Basil Blackwell, 1983).

Harding, A. J., *Coleridge and the Idea of Love: Aspects of Relationship in Coleridge's Thought and Writing* (London: Cambridge University Press, 1974).

——, 'Development and Symbol in the Thought of S. T. Coleridge, J. C. Hare, and John Sterling', *Studies in Romanticism*, 18 (1979) 29–48.

Harrington, J., *The Oceana of James Harrington and His Other Works*, ed. John Toland (London, 1700).

——, *The Political Works of James Harrington*, ed. with intro. J. G. A. Pocock (Cambridge University Press, 1977).

Hartley, D., *Observations on Man, his Frame, His Duty, and His Expectations*, 2 vols (London, 1749).

Hartmann, G., 'Reflections on the Evening Star', *New Perspectives on Wordsworth and Coleridge; Selected Papers from the English Institute*, ed. with foreword by G. Hartmann (New York and London: Columbia University Press, 1972) pp. 85–132.

Haven, R., 'Coleridge, Hartley and the Mystics', *JHI*, 29 (1959) 477–94.

——, 'Coleridge and the Greek Mysteries', *MLN*, 70 (June 1955) 405–7.

Havens, M. K., 'Coleridge on the Evolution of Language', *Studies in Romanticism*, 20 (1981) 163–83.

Hayden, J. O., *Romantic Bards and British Reviewers* (London: Routledge & Kegan Paul, 1971).

——, 'The Reviewers and Wordsworth', *Studies in Philology*, 68 (1971) 105–21.

Hazlitt, W., *The Complete Works of William Hazlitt, in 21 volumes*, ed. P. P. Howe (London and Toronto: J. M. Dent, 1930–34).

Hegel, G. W. F., *The Phenomenology of Spirit*, trans. A. V. Miller, intro. J. N. Findlay (Oxford: Clarendon Press, 1977).

——, *Lectures on the Philosophy of World History, Intro; Reason in History*, trans. H. B. Nisbet, intro. Duncan Forbes (Cambridge University Press, 1980).

——, *Hegel's Aesthetics* (intro. to the Berlin Aesthetic Lectures of the 1820s), trans. T. M. Knox, intro. by C. Karelis (Oxford University Press, 1979).

Herodotus. *The Histories*, trans. Aubrey De Selincourt, rev. with intro. A. R. Burn (Harmondsworth: Penguin, 1972).

Hill, C., 'Republicanism after the Revolution', *New Left Review*, 3 (May/June 1960), 46–51.

——, *The World Turned Upside Down: Radical Ideas during the English Revolution* (London: Temple Smith, 1972; rpt. Pelican, 1975).

Hirsch, E. D., *Wordsworth and Schelling: a Typological Study of Romanticism* (New Haven: Yale University Press, 1960).

Hobsbawm, E. J., *The Age of Revolution 1789–1848* (London: Weidenfeld & Nicholson, 1962).

——, 'Class Consciousness in History', *Aspects of History and Class Consciousness*, ed. Istvan Meszaros (London: Routledge & Kegan Paul, 1971) pp. 5–21.

Hohendahl, P. U., *The Institution of Criticism* (Ithaca: Cornell University Press, 1982).

Hunter, W. B., 'The 17th Century Doctrine of Plastic Nature', *Harvard Theological Review*, 43 (1950) 197–213.

Holt, R. V., *The Unitarian Contribution to Social Progress in England* (London: Allen & Unwin, 1938).

Jackson, H. J., 'Coleridge's Collaborator, J. H. Green', *Studies in Romanticism*, 21 (Summer 1982) 160–79.

Jackson, J. R. de J., *Method and Imagination in Coleridge's Criticism* (London: Routledge & Kegan Paul, 1969).

—— (ed.), *Coleridge, The Critical Heritage* (London: Routledge & Kegan Paul, 1970).

Jacob, M. C., 'John Toland and the Newtonian Ideology', *Journal of the Warburg and Cortauld Institutes*, xxxiii (1969) 307–31.

——, *The Newtonians and the English Revolution 1689–1720* (Sussex: Harvester Press, 1976).

——, *The Radical Enlightenment: Pantheists, Freemasons, and Republicans* (London: Allen & Unwin, 1981).

Johnson, S., *The Rambler*, ed. with intro. and notes by D. D. Eddy, 2 vols (New York and London: Garland Publications, 1978).

Kant, I., *The Critique of Pure Reason*, trans. N. Kemp Smith (London: Macmillan, 1929).

——, *The Critique of Practical Reason*, trans. with intro. Lewis White Beck (New York: Liberal Arts Press, 1956).

——, *The Critique of Judgement*, trans. J. C. Meredith (Oxford: Clarendon Press, 1952).

——, 'What is Enlightenment? (Was ist Aufklärung?)' (1784), *German Aesthetic and Literary Criticism; Kant, Fichte, Schelling, Schopenhauer, Hegel*, ed. D. Simpson (Cambridge University Press, 1984) pp. 29–34.

——, *Metaphysische Anfangsgründe der Naturwissenschaft* (Riga, 1786).

Kennedy, W. F., *Humanist versus Economist: the Economic Thought of S. T. Coleridge* (University of California Press, 1958).

Knights, B., *The Idea of the Clerisy in the 19th Century* (Cambridge University Press, 1978).

Leavis, F. R., 'Coleridge in Criticism', *Scrutiny*, IX (1940–41) 57–69.

Lentricchia, F., *Criticism and Social Change* (Chicago and London: University of Chicago Press, 1983).

Levere, T., 'Coleridge, Chemistry and the Philosophy of Nature', *Studies in Romanticism*, 16, 3 (Summer 1977) 349–80.

——, *Poetry Realized in Nature: S. T. Coleridge and Early Nineteenth Century Science* (Cambridge University Press, 1981).

Lincoln, A., *Some Political and Social Ideas of English Dissent 1763–1830* (Cambridge University Press, 1938).

Lovejoy, A. O., *The Great Chain of Being: a Study of the History of an Idea* (Cambridge, Mass.: Harvard University Press, 1936).

——, *Essays in the History of Ideas* (Baltimore: Johns Hopkins Press, 1948).

Lowman, M., *A Dissertation on the Civil Government of the Hebrews* (London, 1740).

Lukács, G., *History and Class Consciousness: Studies in Marxist Dialectics*, trans. Rodney Livingstone (Cambridge, Mass.: MIT Press, 1971).

——, *The Destruction of Reason*, trans. P. Palmer (London: Merlin Press, 1980).

MacEvoy, J. G. and McGuire, J. E., 'Priestley's Way of Rational Dissent', *Historical Studies in the Physical Sciences*, 6 (1975) 325–404.

McFarland, T., *Coleridge and the Pantheist Tradition* (Oxford: Clarendon Press, 1969).

——, *Romanticism and the Forms of Ruin* (Princeton University Press, 1981).

MacGillivray, J. R., 'The Pantisocracy Scheme and its immediate Background', *Studies in English by Members of University College, Toronto* collected by Principal M. Wallace (University of Toronto Press, 1931) pp. 131–69.

Macherey, P., *A Theory of Literary Production* trans. G. Wall (London: Routledge & Kegan Paul, 1978).

MacKinnon, D. M., 'Coleridge and Kant' in *Coleridge's Variety*, ed. J. Beer (London: Macmillan, 1974).

Maclean, K., *Agrarian Age: A Background for Wordsworth* (Connecticut: Archon Books, 1970).

Marks, E. R., *Coleridge on the Language of Verse* (Princeton University Press, 1981).

Marx, K. and Engels, F., *The German Ideology (Part One)* ed. with intro. C. J. Arthur (London: Lawrence & Wishart, 1970).

Metzger, L., 'Coleridge's Vindication of Spinoza: an Unpublished Note', *JHI*, xxi (1960) 279–93.

Mill, J. S., *On Bentham and Coleridge*, intro. by F. R. Leavis (Cambridge University Press, 1980).

Miller, C., 'Coleridge's Concept of Nature', *JHI*, xxv (1964) 77–96.

Milton, J., *The Collected Historical, Political and Miscellaneous Works of John Milton*, ed. John Toland, 3 vols (Amsterdam, 1698).

——, *The Poems of John Milton*, eds J. Carey and A. Fowler (London: Longmans, 1968).

Modiana, R., *Coleridge and the Concept of Nature* (London: Macmillan, 1985).

Monro, A., *Observations on the Structure and the Function of the Nervous System* (Edinburgh, 1783).

Monk, S. H., *The Sublime: a Study of Critical Theories in 18th Century England* (New York: Modern Language Association, 1935).

Moorman, M., *William Wordsworth, a Biography*, 2 vols (Oxford: Clarendon Press, 1957, 1965).

Moyle, W., *The Constitution and Government of the Roman State* (1699), ed. John Thelwall (Norwich, 1796).

Muirhead, J. H., *Coleridge as Philosopher* (London: Allen & Unwin; New York: Macmillan, 1930).

Mullen, P. C. 'Romantic as Scientist: Lorenz Oken', *Studies in Romanticism*, 16, 3 (1977) 381–400.

Nidecker, H., 'Notes Marginales de S. T. Coleridge', *Revue de littérature comparée*, vii (1927) 530–5, 736–46.

Niebuhr, B. G., *Römische Geschichte*, 2 vols (Berlin, 1811–12).

Nock, A. D., *Early Gentile Christianity and Its Hellenistic Background* (New York: Harper & Row, 1964).

Orsini, G., *Coleridge and German Idealism* (Carbondale and Edwardsville: Southern Illinois University Press, 1969).

Owen, W. J. B., *Wordsworth as Critic* (London: University of Toronto Press, Oxford University Press, 1969).

Paine, T., *The Age of Reason; Being an Investigation of True and Fabulous Theology* (London, 1794–95).

Park, R., 'Coleridge's Two Voices as a Critic of Wordsworth', *ELH*, xxxvi (1969), 361–81.

——, *Hazlitt and the Spirit of the Age* (Oxford University Press, 1971).

Parrinder, P., *Authors and Authority. A Study of English Literary Criticism and Its Relation to Culture, 1750–1900* (London: Routledge & Kegan Paul, 1977).

Payne Knight, R., *The Progress of Civil Society. A Didactic Poem* (London, 1796).

——, *An Inquiry into the Symbolical Language of ancient art and mythology* (London, 1818).

Peacock, T. L., *Nightmare Abbey* (London, 1818).

——, 'The Four Ages of Poetry' in *Memoirs, Essays and Reviews*, ed. by Howard Mills (London: Rupert Hart-Davis, 1970) pp. 117–34.

Perkin, H., *The Origins of Modern English Society 1780–1880* (London: Routledge & Kegan Paul, 1969).

Pfeiler, W. K., 'Coleridge's and Schelling's Treatise on the Samothracian Deities', *MLN*, 52 (Mar. 1937) 162–5.

Piper, H., 'The Pantheistic Sources of Coleridge's Early Poetry', *JHI*, xx (1959) 47–59.

——, *The Active Universe. Pantheism and the Concept of Imagination in the English Romantic Poets* (London: Athlone Press, 1962).

Plato, *The Republic*, trans. with intro. by Desmond Lee (Harmondsworth: Penguin, 2nd rev. edn 1974).

Pocock, J. G. A., *Politics, Language and Time: Essays on Political Thought and History* (London: Methuen, 1972).

——, *The Machiavellian Moment: Florentine Political Thought and the Atlantic Republican Tradition* (Princeton University Press, 1975).

——, *The Political Works of James Harrington* (Cambridge University Press, 1977).

——, 'The Political Economy of Burke's Analysis of the French Revolution', *The Historical Journal*, 25, 2 (1982) 331–50.

Porter, R. and Rousseau, G., (eds), *The Ferment of Knowledge* (Cambridge University Press, 1980).

Price, L. M., *The Reception of English Literature in Germany* (University of California Press, 1932).

Price, R., *Observations on the Nature of Civil Liberty, the Principles of Government, and the Justice and Policy of the War with America* (London, 1776).

Prickett, S., *Coleridge and Wordsworth: the Poetry of Growth* (Cambridge University Press, 1970).

——, *Romanticism and Religion: the Tradition of Coleridge and Wordsworth in the Victorian Church* (Cambridge University Press, 1976).

Preyer, R., 'Bentham, Coleridge and the Science of History' in *Leipziger Beitrage zur Englischen Philologie*, 41 (Verlag Poppinghaus, 1958) pp. 1–99.

Priestley, J., *An Essay on the First Principles of Government; and on the Nature of Political, Civil, and Religious Liberty* (London, 1768).

——, *Hartley's Theory of the Human Mind, on the Principle of the Association of Ideas (Extracted from 'Observations on Man . . .); with Essays Relating to the Subject of It* (London, 1775).

——, *Disquisitions relating to Matter and Spirit* (London, 1777).

——, (With Richard Price), *A Free Discussion of the Doctrines of Materialism and Philosophical Necessity* (London, 1778).

——, *Institutes of Natural and Revealed Religion*, 2 vols, 2nd ed. (Birmingham, 1782).

——, *An History of the Corruptions of Christianity* (1772–4), 2 vols (Birmingham, 1782).

——, *An History of Early Opinions Concerning Jesus Christ, Compiled from Original Writers; Proving that the Christian Church Was at first Unitarian*, 4 vols (Birmingham, 1786).

——, *Defences of Unitarianism, in three parts* (London, 1787–90).

——, *Experiments and Observations on different kinds of Air*, abridged edn, 3 vols (Birmingham, 1790).

——, *Letters to the Rt. Hon. Edmund Burke, Occasioned by His Reflections on the Revolution in France* (Birmingham and London, 1791).

——, *Discourses on the Evidence of Revealed Religion* (London, 1794).

——, *The Present State of Europe Compared with Antient Prophecies; a Sermon, Preached at the Gravel Pit Meeting in Hackney, Feb. 28th, 1974 . . . With a Preface, Containing the Reasons for the Author's Leaving England* (London, 1794).

Read, H., *The True Voice of Feeling: Studies in English Romantic Poetry* (London: Faber & Faber, 1953).

Richards, I. A., *Coleridge on Imagination* (London: Kegan Paul, 1934).

Ricouer, P., *The Rule of Metaphor: Multi-disciplinary Studies of the Creation of Meaning in Language*, trans. R. Czerny with K. Maclaughlin and J. Costello (London: Routledge & Kegan Paul, 1978).

Robbins, C., *The Eighteenth Century Commonwealthmen: Studies in the Transmission, Development and Circumstance of English Liberal Thought from the Restoration of Charles II until the war with the Thirteen Colonies* (Cambridge, Mass.: Harvard University Press, 1959).

Robinson, H. C., *The Diary, Reminiscences and Correspondence of Henry Crabb Robinson*, ed. T. Sadler. 3 vols (London: Macmillan, 1869).

Rossi, P., *Philosophy, Technology, and the Arts in the Early Modern Era*, trans. S. Attanasio. ed. B. Nelson (New York: Harper & Row, 1970).

Rousseau, J. J., 'Discours sur l'origine de l'inégalité parmi les hommes', *Oeuvres complètes*, 13 vols (Paris: Librairie Hachette, 1909) I, 71–152.

——, 'Essai sur l'origine des langues', *Ouevres completes*, I, 370–408, trans. in *On the Origin of Language: J. J. Rousseau, "Essay on the Origin of Languages," J. G. Herder, "Essay on the Origin of Language"*, trans. J. H. Moran and A. Gode (New York: Frederick Unger, 1966).

Ruoff, G. W., 'Wordsworth on Language: Towards a Radical Poetics for English Romanticism', *Wordsworth Circle*, 3, 4 (1972) 204–11.

Sanders, C. R., *Coleridge and the Broad Church Movement* (Durham: Duke University Press, 1942; London: Cambridge University Press, 1943).

Sandford, M. E., *Thomas Poole and his Friends*, 2 vols (London: 1888).

Said, E., *The World, the Text, and the Critic* (Cambridge, Mass.: Harvard University Press, 1983).

Schelling, F. W., *Das älteste Systemprogramm des deutschen Idealismus* (1796), trans. in University Studies, pp. xi–xiv.

——, *Abhandlung zur Erläuterung des Idealismus der Wissenschaftslehre* (1796–97).

——, *Erster Entwurf eines Systems der Naturphilosophie* (Jena, 1799).

——, *System des transcendentalen Idealismus* (Tübingen, 1800).

——, *System of Transcendental Idealism*. Trans. Peter Heath with intro. Michael Vater (Charlottesville: University Press of Virginia, 1978).

——, *Bruno; oder über das göttliche und natürliche Princip der Dinge: ein Gesprach* (Berlin, 1802).

——, *Philosophie der Kunst* (Jena, 1802–3).

——, *Vorlesungen über die Methode des akademischen Studiums* (1803), *On University Studies*, trans. E. S. Morgan, ed. N. Guterman (Ohio University Press, 1966).

——, *Über Dante in philosophischer Beziehung* (1803), *On Dante in Relation to Philosophy*, trans. E. Rubenstein in *German Aesthetic and Literary Criticism*, ed. D. Simpson, pp. 140–8.

——, *Über das Verhältnis der bildenden Künste zu der Natur*, (1807), 'The Plastic Arts in Relation to Nature', trans. M. Bullock in *German Aesthetic and Literary Criticism* pp. 149–58.

——, *Über das Wesen der menschlichen Freiheit* (1809), *Of Human Freedom*, trans. J. Gutmann (Chicago: Open Court, 1936).

——, *Uber die Gottheiten von Samothrace* (1815), *Treatise on "The Deities of Samothrace"*, trans. with intro. Robert Brown (Montana: Scholars Press, University of Montana, 1974, 1977).

——, *Die Weltalter, Ages of the World* trans. with intro. and notes F. de Wolfe Bolman Jr (New York: AMS Press 1967).

Schiller, F., *Works: Essays Aesthetical and Philosophical* (London: George Bell, 1884).

——, *On the Aesthetic Education of Man, in a Series of Letters*, ed. and trans. E. M. Wilkinson and L. A. Willoughby (Oxford: Clarendon Press, 1967).

Schlegel, A. W., *Lectures on Dramatic Art and Literature*, trans. John Black, 2 vols (London, 1815; 2nd edn, 1840).

Schlegel, F., *The Aesthetic and Miscellaneous Works of F. von Schlegel*, trans. E. J. Millington (London: Bohn, 1849).

Shaffer, E. S., 'Coleridge's Theory of Aesthetic Interest', *Journal of Aesthetics*, 27 (1968–69), 399–408.

——, 'Metaphysics of Culture: Kant and Coleridge's "Aids to Reflection"', *JHI*, 31 (1970) 199–218.

——, *'Kubla Khan' and the Fall of Jerusalem: the Mythological School in Biblical Criticism and Secular Literature, 1770–1880* (Cambridge University Press, 1975).

Shaftesbury, see Cooper, A. A.

Sharrock, R., 'The Chemist and the Poet', *Notes and Records of the Royal Society of London*, 17 (1962) 57–76.

——, 'Coleridge's Revolt against Literature', *Essays in Criticism*, 3 (1953) 396–412.

Shelley, P. B., *Poetical Works*, ed. Thomas Hutchinson (London: Oxford University Press, 1934).

——, *Shelley's Prose or The Trumpet of a Prophecy*, ed. David Lee Clark, with intro. and notes (Albuquerque: University of New Mexico Press, 1954).

Simpson, D., *Irony and Authority in Romantic Poetry* (London: Macmillan, 1979).

——, *Wordsworth and the Figurings of the Real* (London: Macmillan, 1982).

——, ed. with intro. *German Aesthetic and Literary Criticism: Kant, Fichte, Schelling, Schopenhauer, Hegel* (Cambridge University Press, 1984).

Snelder, H. A. M., 'Romanticism and Naturphilosophie, and the Inorganic Natural Sciences, 1790–1840', *Studies in Romanticism*, 9 (1970) 135–215.

Snyder, A. D., 'Coleridge on Giordano Bruno', *MLN*, xlii, 7 (Nov. 1927) 427–36.

——, *Coleridge on Logic and Learning* (New Haven, Conn.: Yale University Press, 1929).

Southey, R., *New Letters of Robert Southey*, ed. Kenneth Curry, 2 vols (New York and London: Columbia University Press, 1965).

——, *Poetical Works, collected by himself*, 10 vols (London, 1837–38).

——, *Sir Thomas More: or, Colloquies on the Progress and Prospects of Society*, 2 vols (London, 1829).

Spivak, Gayatri, 'The Letter as Cutting Edge', *Yale French Studies*, 55/56 (1977).

Staël-Holstein, Baroness, *Germany*, 3 vols (London: John Murray, 1813).

Stephen, L., *History of English Thought in the 18th Century*, 2 vols (1876; 3rd edn 1902; rpt. with new preface by Crane Brinton, London: Harbinger, 1962).

Stokoe, F. W., *German Influence in the English Romantic Period 1788–1818, with Special Reference to Scott, Coleridge, Shelley and Byron* (Cambridge University Press, 1926).

Storch, R. F., 'The Politics of Imagination', *Studies in Romanticism*, 21 (Autumn 1982) 448–56.

Taylor, T., *Thomas Taylor the Platonist: Selected Writings*, ed. with intro. by K. Raine and G. M. Harper (London: Routledge & Kegan Paul, 1969).

Tennemann, W. G., *Manual of the History of Philosophy*, trans. A. Johnson, rev., enlarged and contd by J. R. Morell (London: Bohn, 1852).

Teich, N., 'Coleridge's "Biographia" and the Contemporary Controversy about Style', *Wordsworth Circle*, 3, 2 (1972) 61–70.

Thelwall, J., *Poems, chiefly written in Retirement* (Hereford, 1801).

——, (ed.), Walter Moyle's *The Constitution and Government of the Roman State* (1699).

Thompson, E. P., *The Making of the English Working Class* (London: Victor Gollancz, 1964; rpt. Pelican Books, 1968).

——, *The Poverty of Theory and other Essays* (London: Merlin Press, 1978).

——, 'Disenchantment or Default?: a Lay Sermon', *Power and Consciousness*, eds. C. C. O'Brien and W. D. Vanech (New York University Press; London: London University Press, 1969).

——, 'Patrician Society, Plebeian Culture', *Journal of Social History*, 7, 4 (Summer 1974) 382–405.

Todorov, T., *Theories of the Symbol*, trans. Catherine Porter (Oxford: Basil Blackwell, 1982).

Toland, J., *Christianity not Mysterious* (1966; Faksimile, London, 1796), mit einer Einleitung von G. Gawlick und einem textkritischen Anhang (Stuttgart-Bad Cannstatt, 1964).

——, *Letters to Serena* (1704; Faksimile, Frommen Verlag, Stuttgart-Bad Cannstatt, 1964).

—— (ed.), *The Collected Historical, Political and Miscellaneous Works of John Milton* (Amsterdam, 1698).

—— (ed.), *The Oceana of James Harrington and his other Works* (London, 1700).

Venturi, F., *Utopia and Reform in the Enlightenment* (Cambridge University Press, 1971).

Vico, G. B., *The New Science* (1725. rev. trans. of the 3rd edn 1744, by T. G. Bergin and M. H. Fisch, Ithaca: Cornell University Press 1968).

Volney, C. F. C., *The Ruins: or a Survey of the Revolutions of Empires*, trans. from the French (London, 1792).

Warburton, W., *Alliance between Church and State, or, the Necessity and Equity of an Established Religion and a Test-Law Demonstrated* (London, 1736).

——, *The Divine Legation of Moses Demonstrated on the Principles of a Religious Deist*, 2 vols (London, 1738–41; Revised and extended edn, in 5 volumes, London, 1765).

Watson, G., *Coleridge the Poet* (London: Routledge & Kegan Paul, 1966).

——, 'The Revolutionary Youth of Wordsworth and Coleridge', *Criticial Quarterly*, xviii (1976) 49–65.

Weiskel, T., *The Romantic Sublime: Studies in the Structure and Psychology of Transcendence* (Baltimore and London: Johns Hopkins University Press, 1976).

Wellek, R., *Immanuel Kant in England 1793–1838* (Princeton University Press, 1931).

——, *A History of Modern Criticism 1750–1955*, 6 vols (New Haven, Conn.: Yale University Press, 1955–86).

——, *Confrontations: Studies in the Intellectual and Literary Relations between Germany, England, and the United States during the 19th Century* (Princeton University Press, 1965).

Whalley, G., 'The Bristol Library borrowings of Southey and Coleridge, 1793–8', *The Library*, IV (1949) 114–32.

——, 'Coleridge and Southey in Bristol, 1795', *Review of English Studies* (Oct. 1950) 324–40.

——, 'The Integrity of the Biographia Literaria', *Essays and Studies*, 6 (1953) 87–101.

——, 'Coleridge's Lecture on the Prometheus of Aeschylus', *Proceedings and Transactions of the Royal Society of Canada*, 54, ser. 3 (June 1960) 13–24.

Wheeler, K. M., *Sources, Processes and Methods in Coleridge's Biographia Literaria* (Cambridge University Press, 1980).

——, 'Coleridge's Friendship with Ludwig Tieck', *New Approaches to Coleridge: Biographical and Critical Essays*, ed. Donald Sultana (London; Vision, Barnes and Noble, 1981) pp. 96–112.

White, R. J., *From Waterloo to Peterloo* (London: Heinemann, 1957).

Wilbur, E. M., *A History of Unitarianism in Transylvania, England and America* (Cambridge, Mass: Harvard University Press, 1952).

Willey, B., *The Eighteenth Century Background: Studies in the Idea of Nature in the Thought of the Period* (London: Chatto & Windus, 1940).

——, *Nineteenth Century Studies* (London: Chatto & Windus, 1949).

Williams, R., *Culture and Society 1780–1950* (London: Chatto & Windus, 1958).

——, *The Long Revolution* (London: Chatto & Windus, 1961).

——, *The Country and the City* (London: Chatto & Windus, 1973).

——, *Keywords: a Vocabulary of Culture and Society* (Glasgow: Fontana, 1976).

——, *Marxism and Literature* (Oxford University Press, 1977).

——, *Problems in Materialism and Culture: Selected Essays* (London: Verso, 1980).

Wimsatt, W. K., 'The Structure of Romantic Nature Imagery', *The Verbal Icon* (University Press of Kentucky, 1954).

Wordsworth, W., *Wordsworth's Poetical Works*, ed. with intro. and notes Thomas Hutchinson, new edn rev. E. De Selincourt (Oxford University Press, 1936).

——, *The Prelude, or Growth of a Poet's Mind*, text of 1805, ed. with intro. and notes by E. De Selincourt, corr. by Stephen Gill (Oxford University Press, 1970).

——, *The Prose Works of William Wordsworth*, eds W. J. B. Owen and J. Worthington Smyser, 3 vols (Oxford: Clarendon Press, 1974).

——, *The Letters of William and Dorothy Wordsworth: the Early Years 1787–1805*, ed. E. De Selincourt, 2nd edn, rev. Chester L. Shaver (Oxford: Clarendon Press, 1967).

Wright-St. Clair, R. E., *Doctors Monro: a Medical Saga* (London: Wellcome Historical Medical Library, 1964).

Woodring, C. R., *Politics in the Poetry of Coleridge* (Madison: University of Wisconsin Press, 1961).

Yates, F., *Giordano Bruno and the Hermetic Tradition* (London: Routledge & Kegan Paul, 1964).

Yolton, J., *Thinking Matter: Materialism in 18th Century Britain* (Oxford: Basil Blackwell, 1984).

Young, R. M., 'The Human Limits of Nature', in *The Limits of Human Nature*, ed. with intro. by Jonathan Benthall (London: Allen Lane, 1973) pp. 235–74.

Index